American Politics and Public Policy

SEVEN CASE STUDIES

American Politics and Public Policy

SEVEN CASE STUDIES

edited by
Allan P. Sindler

Contributors

Bruce I. Oppenheimer, University of Houston
Gerald M. Pomper, **Rodney Forth**, and **Maureen W. Moakley**,
  Rutgers University
Robert Reinhold, *New York Times*
Austin Sarat, Amherst College
Allan P. Sindler, University of California, Berkeley
Steven S. Smith, George Washington University
Paul N. Stockton, Harvard University

CQ Press

a division of

CONGRESSIONAL QUARTERLY INC.
1414 22nd Street N.W., Washington, D.C. 20037

Politics and Public Policy Series

Advisory Editor

Robert L. Peabody

Johns Hopkins University

Printed in the United States of America

Library of Congress Cataloging in Publication Data

Sindler, Allan P.
   American politics and public policy.

   Bibliography: p.
   1. United States — Politics and government — Case studies. 2. Policy sciences — Case studies.
JK421.A63   320.973   82-12524
ISBN 0-87187-237-4

Preface

American Politics and Public Policy consists of seven case studies written specifically for this volume and designed to complement the topics generally covered in American government and public policy courses. Our studies focus on the major institutions of American national government—president, Congress, bureaucracy, courts, and political parties—as they deal with important and sometimes controversial issues:

—the effort by reformers to replace the electoral college system of presidential election with direct national election;

—the response by Congress, and especially by the House Democratic leadership, to President Reagan's redirection of federal spending and policy as embodied in his budget initiatives in 1981;

—the politics of regulation by the bureaucracy, illustrated by the effort to require druggists to provide leaflets giving information to patients on the proper use and side effects of certain prescription drugs;

—public policy on abortion as fought out in the courts, Congress, and state legislatures;

—the decline of political parties and strong party organizations and the concomitant development of policy parties and candidate-centered politics;

—the difficulty in developing a coherent policy on oil pricing and energy conservation during the 1970s; and

—the continuing controversy over the development of the MX missile.

The accounts demonstrate the American political system's strengths and weaknesses and capacity to formulate and carry out public policy. Each study is self-sufficient, enabling readers to understand the topic without consulting additional sources. The authors have blended direct observation, scholarly research, and news accounts so that the material is unencumbered by extensive footnoting.

Students are encouraged to use these studies to raise larger questions about policy and politics in the United States. In the closing section of each chapter ("Some Questions to Explore"), the authors pose specific questions designed to stimulate further inquiry. Commentary is also provided to channel and guide discussion, but there is ample opportunity for instructors and students to formulate other questions and weigh competing judgments. A selective list of readings is included at the end of each study.

A final note on who is responsible for what in this book: the editor conceived the volume and recruited the contributors' studies. Each contributor chose his topic and developed his own study with an eye toward the book's purpose, its overall coverage, and consideration of the editor's suggestions on successive drafts. While each author's responsibility is limited to his own study, collective cooperation is reflected in the book's coherence and timely completion. As editor, I would like to express my pleasure and gratitude for working with such congenial colleagues in this collaborative venture. I am also appreciative of the unfailing cooperation and professional skills of Susan Sullivan, developmental editor at CQ Press; her suggestions strengthened the studies and her firm shepherding of the manuscript ensured its timely publication.

Allan P. Sindler

Contents

The Courts

Political Parties

Domestic Policy

Defense Policy

American Politics and Public Policy

SEVEN CASE STUDIES

1

The President

Should Direct National Election Replace the Electoral College System?

Allan P. Sindler

*. . . the electoral college is a loaded pistol pointed at our
system of government.*

— Senator Estes Kefauver

*. . . we should hesitate a long time before replacing a humpty-
dumpty system that works with a neat one that may blow up
in our faces.*

— Professor Clinton Rossiter, *The American Presidency*

Bitingly referring to the 1980 presidential contest between Democratic incumbent Jimmy Carter and Republican challenger Ronald
Reagan as offering voters "not a choice but a dilemma," John Anderson
launched an independent candidacy aimed at making the election a
genuine three-way race. For a while it looked as if he might succeed. He
gained a place on the ballot in every state, a feat no third-party
candidate had accomplished since 1916, and pollsters reported that he
was attracting 20-25 percent scores for national support. Once the
seriousness of his candidacy was demonstrated, speculation began on
how Anderson's race could produce an unwanted election outcome
leading to controversy and perhaps to crisis.

The speculation was grounded on solid fact: under our electoral
college system a presidential election can be deadlocked and result in no

winner, or it can produce what to many Americans would be the "wrong" winner. Basically, the system works as follows: each state is awarded a number of electoral votes equal to its congressional delegation, the combined number of its U.S. representatives and senators. Citizens vote within their respective states for state electors who are expected to vote for designated presidential candidates. The electors of the candidate who has the most popular votes in the state cast all the electoral votes of the state for that candidate. The candidate who wins an absolute majority of the total electoral votes is declared the president. (Currently the total is 538, including 3 electors for the District of Columbia.) If none so qualify, contingency procedures require the U.S. House of Representatives to select the president and the U.S. Senate to select the vice president.

The 1980 election would be deadlocked if Anderson gained some electoral votes and if Carter and Reagan divided the balance about evenly, with neither receiving the majority of 270 electoral votes needed to win. Were this to happen, the House, under the Constitution, would have to choose the president by majority vote, with each state delegation having one vote, from among the three candidates with the most electoral votes. (As it turned out, Reagan won 489 electoral votes, Carter 49, and Anderson none.) The Senate is authorized to select the vice president from the two leading candidates. In the event the House fails to designate the president, the vice president would become acting president. Should neither post be filled, the provisions of the most recent presidential succession act (1948) would take effect. Its order of succession is, first, the Speaker of the House; next, the president pro tempore of the Senate; and next, the cabinet officers of the preelection administration, starting with the secretary of state, treasury, and defense.

At no point in this postdeadlock process is the popular vote principle assigned an explicit role, let alone a decisive role. Electoral votes—not popular votes—define deadlock and identify the three candidates for House selection. And "one state, one vote" expresses pure federalism unconnected to the population principle. In sum, when no presidential contender secures an electoral vote majority, the candidate who leads in the national popular vote is given no preference in the contingency procedures that must then be used to choose the president.

Another speculative concern fostered by the apparent strength of Anderson's candidacy was that even if he captured no electoral votes himself he might deprive the major-party candidate who had the most popular votes of an electoral vote majority, that is, the "wrong" presidential winner would result. The Carter camp was especially troubled by this possibility, believing that Anderson would draw disproportionately from those who otherwise would have opted for their candidate. Even if Carter gained a national popular vote plurality, a narrow loss to Reagan in several states because of the Anderson vote might result in his receiving only a minority of the electoral vote. Reagan would then be president despite his lesser total of popular votes.

Anderson's "wild card" candidacy (as the media often called it) thus provoked fears that either of two distasteful election results might occur: deadlock or a runner-up president.* Who or what was to blame for this situation? While there was some finger-pointing at Anderson himself, many commentators held the election system responsible. An old and durable American debate on a central institutional and policy question was thus rekindled: by what method should we elect the president?

A clear public preference on this issue has emerged in the last two decades. The present election system has come increasingly under fire: "A game of Russian roulette" was Senator Estes Kefauver's character- ization of it, and other critics have likened it to a "political time bomb waiting to explode." An influential study commission of the American Bar Association branded our election method as "archaic, undemo- cratic, complex, ambiguous, indirect and dangerous." In the past critics of the existing system disagreed on a suitable replacement, but that no longer holds. Direct national election is an idea whose time, it appears, has now come. In 1967, the national Gallup Poll found clear majority support for direct national election, and ten years later 75 percent of those asked and 84 percent of those with an opinion favored it. Diverse interest groups have backed its adoption, including the American Civil Liberties Union, League of Women Voters, American Bar Association, Chamber of Commerce, and the AFL-CIO. And at the close of both the 1960s and 1970s, Congress attempted (unsuccessfully) to enact a consti- tutional amendment mandating direct national election of the president and vice president.

At the present time, then, our effective choice is the question posed in the title of this study: should direct national election replace the electoral college system? By offering a balanced appraisal of the two election methods, including consideration of how each might be strengthened, this study seeks to provide a suitable basis for your own informed judgment of which is better for the country's needs.

---

* A third speculative theme merits brief mention. By attracting a sizable popular vote himself, Anderson could deprive Carter of both a popular and an electoral vote majority and could confine Reagan's popular vote to a plurality instead of a majority. Such possibilities are inherent, however, in any three-way race, whether conducted under the existing system or direct election. Under the electoral college system, the outcome would be the "right" winner, but with a plurality rather than a majority of popular votes. This has occurred often in our presidential elections and has occasioned little upset or concern with the existing method.

PERSPECTIVES ON THE PROBLEM

Setting Boundaries for Our Analysis

Rejection of the District and Proportional Plans. In the past, two variations of the existing system, the district plan and the proportional plan, have been offered as principal reforms. Under the district plan, each state would establish as many electoral districts as it had U.S. House districts. Each district would cast one electoral vote for the presidential candidate who led in popular votes in the district. In addition, each state would be assigned two electoral votes to be awarded to the statewide popular vote leader. Under the proportional plan, each presidential candidate would receive the same share of the state's electoral vote as he or she had of the state's popular vote. For each plan, the proportion of the total electoral vote required to win has varied in different versions from 40 percent to a majority.

Conservative interests have favored these plans because they eliminate a feature of the electoral college system believed to advantage liberals, the winner-take-all practice whereby the candidate with the most popular votes in the state receives all the state's electoral votes. Under either plan, the political power of "safe" voting areas (those easily won by the dominant party by a large margin) would be heightened at the expense of that of closely divided areas. With the proportional plan, those states regularly providing relatively large net electoral vote margins for a party would increase their influence over the election outcome and, therefore, within that party as well; the same effect would hold for safe electoral districts under the district plan. In addition, the district plan poses a special problem of its own because the boundaries of the electoral districts would be set by state legislatures. The rich history of partisanship and gerrymandering in the determination of state legislative and congressional district lines provides little ground for confidence that electoral districts would be laid out fairly. Although in the two most recent congressional attempts at electoral revision (1969-1970 and 1977-1979) some conservatives continued to push for these plans, their broader appeal peaked in the 1950s and has receded since then.

"Housekeeping" Reforms of the Existing System. Two "housekeeping amendments" that clean up problems of the existing system but otherwise leave it intact are widely endorsed.

The first stems from the recognized incompatibility between the Constitution's grant of full voting discretion to electors and our expectation that they should function as agents, not as principals. We expect electors simply to register the popular vote verdict in their state. But if they do only that, why continue the office? And if they choose not to do that, how can the office be tolerated? Never a serious problem historically, it became salient to Congress in the 1960s when southern party dissidence and third-party activity led to unpledged electors and an occasional "faithless" elector, one who disregarded the obligation to vote for the state's popular vote winner. The obvious remedy is to eliminate the post, or if it is retained (to provide ceremonial party rewards or to complicate access to the ballot by third parties), to require electors to vote for their party's presidential candidate.

The second noncontroversial correction would end the provision for state voting equality in the House of Representatives when selecting the president. The contingency procedure most commonly offered in its place is a joint session of Congress, with each member having one vote. (The inclusion of the Senate is intended, presumably, to appease less-populated states whose power would be greatly reduced by the change.) By shifting to a mix of the population and federal principles, with greater emphasis on the former, this change would square better with contemporary values.

Ironically, these two revisions (which have been packaged as the "automatic plan") have not come close to being adopted by Congress in spite of their widespread backing. A shrewd political maxim provides the explanation: lesser change is the enemy of greater change. The maxim has special force when—as in the present situation—it must be assumed that no more than one constitutional amendment on the subject will be enacted and that its terms will fix the method of presidential election for the indefinite future. In such circumstances, enactment of the automatic plan involves an implicit rejection of more major change. These amendments will be ripe for congressional adoption, then, only when two-thirds of each chamber is satisfied that more extensive revision of the ongoing electoral college system is unwarranted.

Applying Multiple Criteria and Examining a Range of Effects

Deciding whether direct presidential election is preferable to the present electoral college system is *not* a narrow technical question of how votes should be counted. The presidency is our preeminent national political institution, and the way the president is elected helps determine his legitimacy, leadership, power, policy goals, and relations with other governmental officers. Moreover, the election method has significant consequences for the separation of powers principle and institutional checks and balances, federalism, the party system, and voter behavior. It follows that only a wide-ranging inquiry, involving multiple criteria and considering broad effects, can analyze the problem effectively.

Distortion of Popular Vote. It comes as a shock to some to learn that our current electoral system distorts the counting of the popular vote in presidential elections. Their assumption, apparently, is that the electoral vote distribution among the candidates should reproduce faithfully their underlying popular vote division. A moment's reflection, however, shows the error of that assumption. What would be the point of restating the popular vote by another measure which exactly mirrors the initial figures? Take a two-candidate race, for example, in which the popular vote split 40 million to 20 million. Why set up a system in which, say, two million votes equaled one "critical vote block" (CVB) and then go on to report the election results as 20 CVB to 10 CVB? Once the mistaken assumption is cast aside, it will be realized that *any* indirect election method (of which our electoral college system is but one example) must distort its translation of the popular vote division.

Two inferences follow from the fact that electoral vote and popular vote distributions will differ. First, it becomes possible for the presidential candidate who wins the office by the electoral vote not to have gained the highest popular vote. Second, some popular votes must, in effect, count differently from others—that is, some degree of vote and voter inequality must exist. How you react to these inferences decisively shapes your approach to the problem.

No Single Absolutist Criterion. If you hold that the candidate with the most popular votes *must* win, you will reject automatically any type of indirect election (including our current system) and insist on direct national election. Likewise, if you maintain that the election method *must* reflect federalism, you will dismiss direct election and require some form of state-based indirect election. In either case, you would be applying a single absolutist criterion: any election method that satisfied that criterion would be judged better than any that did not, regardless of their other good and bad effects.

Suppose, however, that you broaden your examination to include multiple criteria related to the wide range of effects of a presidential election method. You would consider some criteria more important than others, of course, but none would be elevated to an absolutist standard. Your ultimate judgment would turn, then, on your net assessment of the benefits and deficiencies of each method.

A Preferred But Not Absolutist Criterion. The belief that the winning presidential candidate should have the most popular votes is a core democratic standard. It expresses the values of majority/plurality rule (as contrasted to minority rule) and of equality of votes and voters, and it provides the winner with legitimacy and a political mandate to govern. Both the dissatisfaction with the existing system and the preference for direct election are rooted in the appeal of this standard. In recognition of its special importance, we give this core standard a distinctively heavy weighting without, however, transforming it into an absolute requirement.

Applying this approach, we first acknowledge that the electoral college system is a "faulty adding machine," just as some of its critics have mockingly asserted. While we do not view this defect lightly, we do not repudiate the existing system simply because the electoral vote count distorts the popular vote division. The critical test relates, rather, to the direction and magnitude of the distortion, that is, how often and seriously does it threaten to result in a violation of the core standard? Any indirect election method that runs a realistic risk of not regularly meeting the core standard may properly be rejected at once, without need to examine its other effects. By the same token, an indirect method that promises a perfect or near perfect record in satisfying the core standard merits the fullest review of its other effects before final judgment of its worth is made. As it happens, the existing system has exactly that kind of record. In sum, in appraising the two election methods we grant direct election a significant edge because of its greater certainty in satisfying the core standard. Even so, the electoral college system retains a reasonable chance of being judged the better of the two if it can overcome that handicap by demonstrating its superiority in other important criteria.

The Burden of Proof: Who Has It and What Is It?

We generally assign the burden of proof to those who advocate doing things differently from what presently obtains, and this standard presumption holds as well for governmental processes. The more far-reaching or long-lasting the proposed change—such as a constitutional amendment revising how we elect our president—the greater the burden of proof properly placed on its proponents. As Viscount Falkland put it in a well-turned phrase: "When it is not necessary to change, it is necessary not to change." The American version, less elegant but no less clear, is: "If it ain't broke, don't fix it."

As the promoters of basic change, direct election partisans must demonstrate that the existing system is gravely flawed. Next, they must show that direct election better satisfies the nation's needs. Since direct presidential election has no track record, the quarrel over its merits turns on differing speculative estimates of its likely consequences. The resulting ambiguities should be resolved on the basis of probabilities grounded in political reality, not of remote logical possibilities. The following guidelines reflect this perspective and should help you in appraising the various claims and arguments.

(1) Since our present method of electing the president has a lengthy record of performance, the evidence it supplies should be given heavy (although not necessarily controlling) weight in its appraisal.

(2) Any election method, if subjected to do-it-yourself manipulations on paper, can be shown to have a theoretical capacity to produce perverse results. Under our current system, for example, an electoral majority could be based on a slim minority of the national popular vote if the presidential winner carried a dozen or so large states by narrow popular margins and gained very few popular votes elsewhere. And direct election might allow an intensely sectional candidate to win by attracting 90 percent of the popular vote in his or her heartland of support and getting virtually no votes elsewhere. Such hypothetical constructions ignore the critical difference between arithmetical possibilities considered in a vacuum and probabilities grounded in genuine politics. They are unrealistic not only because the election outcomes they construct are unlikely to occur but also because no election method would long be tolerated if it actually produced such outcomes with any frequency.

(3) The impact of various election methods cannot be demonstrated accurately by simply refiguring past elections in terms of a different voting formula. At the risk of overstating the obvious, there are several variables that determine election outcomes; while the structure of electoral machinery is only one of them, a significantly altered method would likely have changed who was nominated, how he or she campaigned, and what policies were adopted—and, therefore, how voters responded. The findings from such "reruns" of previous elections are suggestive and obviously better than nothing, but they are necessarily inconclusive.

(4) Because different election methods distribute power and advantage differently, a realistic analysis must take into account the play of political interests and the political feasibility of proposed changes. The support of two-thirds of each chamber of Congress and of three-quarters of the states is needed to adopt a constitutional amendment. "What is best," therefore, may have to concede to "what can be passed." Senator Birch Bayh of Indiana, as chairman of the Senate Judiciary Committee's Subcommittee on Constitutional Amendments and the chief sponsor of direct election, addressed a subcommittee about this problem of feasibility:

> Our responsibility in this committee, and particularly mine as chairman, is really twofold. One is to try to determine, after sorting out all the evidence, which plan we believe would do the best job of electing our president, and two, to try to see if we can pass this. If we cannot pass the best, then what is our fallback position, our second best. Hopefully we will be able to get the best.

EVALUATING THE ELECTORAL COLLEGE SYSTEM

Popular Vote Distortion

We choose our president by means of 51 separate election units, one for each state and the District of Columbia. Each state casts its electoral votes for the candidate who leads in popular vote within the state; the electoral vote outcome in each state is then summed, and the candidate who receives a majority of the total electoral votes (270 of 538) is declared the winner. Of the several distinct features of this process that give rise to significant distortion of the popular vote, two merit closest attention:

(1) *Allocation of electoral votes to the states.* Because each state (and the District of Columbia) is automatically given two electoral votes to reflect equal Senate representation, 19 percent of the electoral votes (102 of 538) are allocated without regard to the population principle. In addition, each state is guaranteed at least one U.S. representative (and hence the electoral vote reflecting that representation), regardless of its population size. These distortions favor low-population states; relatively fewer citizens control an electoral vote in such states as compared with residents of high-population states.

(2) *Casting of electoral votes by the states.* Under the winner-take-all procedure (also known as the "state-unit" or "general ticket" rule), the candidate who has a plurality of popular votes in the state—whether that plurality is 42, 51, or 85 percent—is awarded the state's entire electoral vote.* By reporting a state's divided popular vote as a unanimous electoral vote, two categories of popular votes are "wasted": the losing candidate's popular votes earn no electoral votes and the winning candidate's popular votes in excess of what was needed to carry the state are given no additional electoral vote credit. In every state, then, the electoral vote value of a popular vote cast for the winner is higher when the winner's margin of victory is narrow rather than lopsided. The political significance of this bias is greatest for states which have a large number of electoral votes up for grabs by either major party. In sum, this distortion favors those high-population states that are not dominated by one party and whose presidential election outcomes are relatively close.

---

* The Constitution allows each state to determine how it casts its electoral votes. Since the mid-nineteenth century, every state has operated by the state-unit rule. Recently, however, Maine (with four electoral votes) chose to replace it by the district method; as of this writing, no other state appears interested in abandoning the winner-take-all procedure. In terms of relative influence over the election outcome, states casting a divided electoral vote would be competitively disadvantaged compared with those casting a unified vote.

Relative Advantage to Populous and Low-Population States

The first distortion favors low-population states and the second favors populous states with competitive elections. Which bias is dominant?

At first blush, the first distortion seems paramount because the Framers' design so obviously enhances the relative power of small-population states. Small states generally cast a greater percentage of the total electoral vote than of the total popular vote. In the 1976 presidential election, for example, when the national average of the number of popular votes per electoral vote was 151,825, the ten most advantaged states ranged from 84,756 to 40,794 (56 to 27 percent of the national average)—and all had only three or four electoral votes apiece. These ten states cast a combined total of 34 electoral votes and about 2,400,000 popular votes; Michigan (21) and Indiana (13) together had the same total of electoral votes but cast about two-and-a-half times as many popular votes (5,900,000).

Notwithstanding the special protection for small-population states built into the electoral college system, the prevailing practices of presidential campaigns underscore the preeminence of the second source of major distortion, the state-unit system. Presidential contestants typically give disproportionate attention to voters and interests in "pivotal" states such as New York, Illinois, California, Pennsylvania and Ohio, that is, to states characterized by large populations, a large number of electoral votes, and uncertain election outcomes. For instance, *Newsweek*'s October 1980 article on "The Electoral Numbers Game" ran this headline: "Both Carter and Reagan are concentrating on six key states in the nation's industrial crescent." Within these pivotal states, well-organized interest groups whose campaign efforts might determine which candidate carries the state often gain political "clout" beyond their numbers. The policy preferences of most such cohesive groups are liberal rather than conservative.*

Clearly, our presidential election system primarily advantages populous, industrialized states and their constituent minority groups. For critics, the existence of such bias provides additional reason to oppose retention of the system. For some defenders of the electoral college scheme, however, the bias is welcomed as a positive contribution to strengthen checks and balances among diverse and often divergent interests and constituencies. John F. Kennedy, then a young senator

---

* This explains why conservatives oppose retention of the state-unit practice and push instead for either the proportional or district plan. Recall that the proportional plan would distribute a state's electoral vote exactly as the popular vote divides, and that the district plan substitutes, in effect, a district-unit rule for the state-unit rule for the casting of 436 of the 538 electoral votes.

from Massachusetts, made just such an argument in 1956 as part of a successful effort to defeat the proportional plan, the leading reform proposal at the time. Called by some a "doctrine of countervailing inequity," the argument asserted that maintaining two wrongs that tended to cancel each other out provided for more effective checks and balances than just remedying one of them. The state-unit rule's bias, Kennedy argued, was a justifiable counterweight to the inflation of nonurban and conservative influence resulting from state equality in the Senate, the seniority rule for assignment of committee memberships and chairs in Congress, and malapportionment of representation in state legislatures.

Although Kennedy's position was arguably sound, liberals in recent years have been disinclined to emphasize it. One reason is that some of the "other wrongs" have been remedied fully (state legislative apportionment) or partially (seniority procedures in Congress). Most importantly, however, both the climate of liberal opinion and the choice before Congress underwent great change. Since 1956, the civil rights movement and the pursuit of political equality and fair political representation took center stage, and direct election emerged as the leading replacement for our present system. In these changed circumstances, many liberals felt it awkward to oppose direct election at all, let alone on grounds that left them open to charges of inconstancy and opportunism for preferring to keep a system that promoted voter inequality simply because they benefited from its bias.

Implications for Political Strategy

The political strategies employed during congressional consideration of direct presidential election reflected the divergent sets of beneficiaries from the two major distortions of the popular vote and the reluctance of many liberals to reject direct election. The state-unit rule was lambasted by conservatives because it favored liberal interests and by some spokesmen for small states because it advantaged populous states. Among liberals—who in the mid-1950s comprised the core support for the present system—there was considerable defection to the direct election camp. As a consequence, defense of the existing system was muted. Clearly, then, had the question before Congress been whether to adopt the electoral college scheme as a new method, it would have been defeated decisively.

The actual question before Congress, however, was quite different: whether to substitute direct election for the electoral college procedure. On that issue, the reform's backers found that the coalition of diverse interests dissatisfied with the current arrangement did not hold together in common support of direct election. For one thing, conservatives opposed direct election above all else; if they could not gain adoption of the district or proportional scheme, they were prepared to stick with the present method. For another, the resentment of small-state interests against the winner-take-all rule provided an uncertain basis for recruiting them to support direct election—how influential would low-population states be, after all, under direct election? Finally, some liberal interests (including many black and Jewish organizations) remained faithful to the "countervailing inequity" argument and reaffirmed their preference for the electoral college system.

The sponsors of direct election responded to this complex of political forces by pursuing a strategy of playing the biases of the present system against each other. One basic theme, stressed repeatedly, was that fundamental election reform should derive from democratic norms free from considerations of relative advantage. The mere fact that the electoral college scheme produced voter bias—in whichever direction—made it inferior to direct election which, they asserted, was bias-free. By insisting on the moral superiority of direct election, its advocates succeeded in shaming some liberals and others into approval of the reform and keeping their opponents on the defensive. The strategy additionally made specific appeals to both populous and low-population states. Large states were reminded of the small-state bias caused by the allocation of electoral votes to the states and were assured that their concentrations of population guaranteed their high political influence under direct election. Small states were reminded of their disadvantage caused by the state-unit rule and were assured that direct election would lead presidential candidates to give greater attention to more diverse populations.

Despite appearances to the contrary, the backers of direct election were not talking out of both sides of their mouths. Rather, they were adjusting to a difficult situation which required a subtle shading of themes that were neither fully consistent nor clearly inconsistent. Just as the existing election scheme was the common target for attack by different interests and criteria, so direct election was promoted by linking clusters of different arguments to sets of different interests. And just as that strategy had succeeded in sharply eroding support for the current system, so it was hoped it also would succeed in amassing the necessary two-thirds vote in Congress endorsing direct election.

The Record on Presidential Winners:
Majority, Plurality, and Nonplurality Presidents

What has been the record of election outcomes, how have electoral and popular votes been related, and have candidates lacking a popular plurality won the presidency? The 27 elections held over the past 108 years (1872-1980, excluding the disputed election of 1876) provide the data for the examination that follows. (In the 1876 election there was fraud on both sides that probably involved more votes than the close victory margins. Democrat Samuel J. Tilden initially won narrowly in both the electoral and popular vote, but a partisanly rigged commission settled the dispute by awarding the election to Republican Rutherford B. Hayes.)

In 18 of the 27 elections, a candidate received a popular majority. In every case that candidate won, but with a substantially larger proportion of the electoral vote, on the average (79 percent), than of the popular vote (56 percent).

In the remaining nine elections, no candidate got a popular majority. In eight of those nine instances, the candidate who led in popular votes won, averaging 47 percent of the popular vote and receiving from 52 to 62 percent of the electoral vote in seven elections and 82 percent in the other (Woodrow Wilson in 1912).

In only one of the 27 elections was there a "wrong" winner in terms of the core standard; in 1888 the victor (Benjamin Harrison) had a smaller share of the national popular vote—47.8 percent—than the loser (Grover Cleveland), who received 48.7 percent.

Table 1-1 presents more detailed data on the popular vote/electoral vote relationship for the major-party presidential candidates in the 27 elections under review. The electoral vote distribution is typically more lopsided than the popular vote division. Of the 54 candidate races covered, 42 of them (78 percent) fell *within* 40.0—59.9 percent of the total popular vote; on the electoral vote split, however, 40 of them (74 percent) fell *outside* the same percentage range. Virtually the identical pattern holds for just the 27 presidential winners: the counterpart data are 23 (85 percent) within the range on popular votes and 19 (70 percent) outside the range on electoral votes. On the average, the presidential winner received 52 percent of the popular vote and 72 percent of the electoral vote.

The 1888 election—the sole exception to the pattern of the "right" winner—deserves brief discussion. In that election, Grover Cleveland received only 42 percent of the electoral vote while leading Benjamin Harrison by less than one percent of the total popular vote (a margin of under 100,000 votes). The "inefficient" distribution of Cleveland's popular votes accounted for that outcome, which, in turn, reflected regional response to Cleveland's proposal for tariff reform. He carried the South by oversized majorities and lost many key nonsouthern states narrowly, thereby "wasting" many of his popular votes in those states where he had a decisive majority. In contrast, a much larger share of Harrison's electoral votes came from states won by slim rather than huge popular vote margins. It is also instructive to note that

Table 1-1 Relationship of Popular Vote and Electoral Vote Proportion, Democratic and Republican Presidential Candidates, 1872-1980 (Except 1876).

Proportion of Total Popular Vote	Proportion of Total Electoral Vote						Total
	Losers				Winners		
	39.9% or less	40.0-44.9%	45.0-49.9%	50.0-54.9%	55.0-59.9%	60% or more	
39.9% or less	8	—	—	—	—	—	8
40.0-44.9%	8	—	—	—	1	1	10
45.0-49.9%	5	3	3	2	4	1	18
50.0-54.9%	—	—	—	—	1	7	8
55.0-59.9%	—	—	—	—	—	6	6
60% or more	—	—	—	—	—	4	4
Total	21	3	3	2	6	19	54

Source: Compiled by author.

Cleveland did not protest the election outcome, and Harrison's mandate to govern was widely accepted by the nation.

Judged by the historical record, then, the bias of the state-unit rule has been instrumental in ensuring that the election itself will produce a presidential winner (no deadlock), that a runner-up candidate will ordinarily lose, and that the "right" winner will be given the appearance of even greater public backing because his or her electoral vote share far exceeds the corresponding popular vote share. Conceding the strength of this record, the promoters of direct election nevertheless downgrade it by stressing what could have happened in the past and what might readily occur in the future.

The current method's potential for yielding nonplurality presidents is dangerously high, they insist, especially when the leading candidate has only a popular plurality or a relatively small popular vote margin or both. They note that candidates with 45 to 49.9 percent of the popular vote (18 of the 54 major-party candidates covered in Table 1-1) divided almost equally between winners and losers and received widely varying proportions of the electoral vote. And they stress that the outcome of many elections would have been reversed had there been relatively small shifts in popular vote in a few close states. In 1976, for example, a shift of less than 10,000 votes in Ohio and Hawaii would have given Gerald Ford an electoral vote majority, and a shift in fewer than 15,000 votes in Ohio and Delaware would have produced electoral deadlock—and in both instances Jimmy Carter would have had a 1.7 million lead in popular vote over Ford.*

The nub of the direct election supporters' indictment of the existing system, in short, is that the practice of awarding all the state's electoral votes to its plurality leader, no matter how thin his or her vote margin, cannot help but produce nonplurality presidents at times. The reason this unwanted outcome has not occurred more frequently in past elections is simply because of luck, they assert, not because the design of the present system is foolproof.

Supporters of the current method reject this indictment as grossly overdrawn and off the mark. The historical record provides solid evidence of the unlikelihood that the system will produce a runner-up president, they claim. Only under specific conditions—not luck—is there a real risk of the "wrong" winner. The 1888 election suggests what these conditions are: where there is a close division of the total popular vote between the two major candidates (and note that in 1888 neither candidate had a popular majority), and where the popular vote leader's

---

* The reader is reminded that selective modifications of past election results should be skeptically received. In the real world, vote shifts would seldom be confined to one or a few states but would be part of a larger regional or national trend, and hence the national popular vote division between the major candidates would be changed as well.

strength is sectionally overconcentrated. Since pronounced sectional imbalance in a candidate's backing is often associated with one-party states, there is even less chance than in the past that the electoral system will "backfire" because one-party states are fewer in number and cast a smaller proportion of both the popular and electoral vote.

Some defenders of the existing system go beyond arguing the improbability of a runner-up candidate winning the election to raise a fundamental disagreement about the core democratic standard itself. Why, they ask, should a nonplurality president automatically be considered the "wrong" winner? The design of American government, in their view, stresses qualitative rather than simple quantitative majoritarianism, a scheme sensitive to the character as well as the numerical size of popular support. To win office, a presidential candidate should have to attract not just sheer numbers of votes but also a geographic spread of support that reflects considerable backing by varied interests. The conclusion follows that the electoral college system has no reason to plead guilty or to apologize for producing a nonplurality president in elections like that of 1888. In such circumstances the "right" winner may well be the runner-up candidate who has the greater breadth of geographic support, and awarding the office to him rather than to the popular vote leader may better satisfy certain democratic values.

Judged from this perspective, then, the current method is superior to direct election because the state-unit rule provides greater incentive to appeal to a wider range of interests and states and more severely penalizes overly sectional patterns of voting support in close national contests. More broadly, this argument rejects an exclusively arithmetical definition of the core standard and majority rule as mistaken, dogmatic, and an oversimplification of the subtleties of American democracy.

Promoting Moderate Two-Partyism

How an election method affects the maintenance and strength of our moderate two-party system is, for many, a criterion rivaling the core standard in importance. Advocates of direct election share that outlook, as illustrated by the comments of Republican Senator Howard Baker of Tennessee: ". . . if I thought for one moment that [direct election] would disrupt the basic tenets of the two-party system, I would not propose it, because I believe the two-party system in the American format is one of the things that has made our great experiment in democracy what it amounts to today." The kind of two-party system considered important to sustain is one that is open to occasional serious third-party movements but resistant to persistent multipartyism. In addition, a moderate rather than polarized party system is sought by most, one in which candidates and policies reflect broadly based support cutting across regions and classes rather than consolidating them into separate and opposed blocs.

In examining the record on third parties in presidential elections, we will focus on power-seeking parties that attempt to influence election outcomes, to alter the policy positions of the major parties, or to compete directly with the Democratic and Republican parties. Some examples are parties of economic protest (Populists); "spoiler," "splinter," or "blackmail" parties of defection from a major party (various southern dissident movements from 1948 on); and balance-of-power state parties (Liberal and Conservative parties in New York). The following scoreboard provides a rough measure of the impact of such third parties on presidential elections from 1872 to 1980.

No third party has come close to winning a presidential election. The largest proportion of popular votes (27 percent) and electoral votes (17 percent) was garnered in 1912 by Teddy Roosevelt's Progressives in their factional split with the Republican party. Third parties have won electoral votes in five of the 28 elections (1892, 1912, 1924, 1948, and 1968), and in all but one of them the third party got a larger share of the popular than the electoral vote. (The exception was the States' Rights party in 1948.) No electoral deadlock has occurred during this period. The most explicit attempt to produce deadlock was undertaken by George Wallace's American Independent party in 1968; Wallace then intended to have his electors vote for Richard Nixon in exchange for policy concessions. Wallace got 46 electoral votes (five Deep South states and one "faithless elector" from North Carolina) and 13.5 percent of the popular vote, but Nixon still received 301 electoral votes and won the presidency.

Support for a third party may change outcomes between the major parties in one or more states and may thereby affect the national result, although this is difficult to measure. (Note that such a possibility exists just as strongly under direct election.) In the 1880, 1884, 1912, and 1916 elections, the third-party candidacy influenced the major-party winner. Only in 1912 did the third party win any electoral votes.

This record of third parties in presidential elections documents the strong association of the electoral college system with the maintenance of two-partyism. Serious third-party activity in presidential elections has occurred, but at a level and frequency well short of any reasonable definition of persistent multipartyism or of any sustained threat to the two-party system. Moreover, the composition of that system has been stable; Democrats and Republicans have consistently monopolized presidential victories in the 1872-1980 period. (A third party displaced a major party only once, with the emergence of the Republican party in the immediate pre-Civil War period.)

How much credit should go to the current presidential election method for the maintenance of moderate two-partyism? On this question there is considerable disagreement which reflects, at bottom, divergent explanations of the causes of persistent two-partyism in America. Some insist that noninstitutional factors are responsible, such as our history, culture, and tendencies toward centrist and nonideological politics. Others stress the consequences of institutional forms, including the contribution of the electoral college system and the election of national senators and representatives by the single-member-district and plurality vote procedure, which makes it impossible for a third party to gain representation by pooling its losing votes across district or state lines.

The state-unit rule discourages third parties, the institutional explanation asserts, by giving one major party a comfortable electoral vote majority and awarding the remainder to the other major party. Faced with an inhospitable election structure, disgruntled rivals of the major party presidential nominees seldom choose to mount a full-scale general election challenge. And when such a challenge is made, as that by John Anderson in 1980, its popular support is depressed because most Americans equate voting for a third party with a wasted vote—Anderson got under 7 percent of the vote, less than a third of his polled support during the summer.

Similarly, the election system encourages policy accommodation and compromise because a geographic spread of backing and the support of diverse interests are required to gain an electoral majority. True, the winner-take-all rule can be exploited by dissidents who may try either to win a state directly or to affect which major party carries a state. Such episodic and transient third-party eruptions are better understood, however, as efforts to bring about policy changes *within* the major parties than as threats to topple the two-party system and install multipartyism in its place.

Summary

When tested by the core standard, the current system passes comfortably. Its record in awarding the presidency to popular vote leaders is near perfect; the one exception (1888) involved a close national vote and an excessive reliance on sectional support by the candidate with the most popular votes. It is appropriate for the election method to penalize such a sectional pattern, say the defenders of the present system, because it then sustains the qualitative majoritarianism built into the design of American government. They point to equal state representation in the Senate, the presidential veto, judicial review, and other devices of checks and balances as similar examples. The same justification is offered for the voter inequality caused by the state-unit rule: the extra influence gained by pivotal populous states is a commendable inequity because it helps counter biases elsewhere in the system that favor opposing interests.

The current method protects and invigorates federalism by incorporating the states as integral building blocks in the entire presidential selection process, including the nominating contests, party conventions, general election campaigns, and the conversion of popular votes to electoral votes. Finally, the electoral college system is credited with greatly helping to maintain a moderate two-party system and discouraging durable third parties, serious multipartyism, or polarized politics along ideological or class lines.

EVALUATING DIRECT NATIONAL ELECTION

Relative Advantage and Federalism

Direct election provides for literal vote equality: all votes, wherever cast, have equal weight. This feature would end the special advantages enjoyed under the present election scheme by politically competitive populous states and by low-population states. The strategy of the promoters of direct election is, as we have seen, to convince these interests that their loss would be more apparent than real. Walking a very fine line, they assure populous states of continued high influence under direct election despite the end of the state-unit rule, and they assure small states of increased influence under direct election because of the elimination of that rule.

Although this strategy, complemented by an emphasis on the intrinsic desirability of direct election, met with considerable success, not all the interests affected are persuaded by it. Black organizations, for example, reject the argument that the reduced power of black voters in states like New York and Illinois would be compensated for by a national pooling of black votes in the South and in northern industrial states. National Urban League President Vernon E. Jordan observed, "Take away the electoral college and the importance of the black vote melts away. Blacks, instead of being crucial to victory in major states, simply become 10 percent of the total electorate, with reduced impact." Similarly, some small-state spokesmen, doubtful about how much influence such states would have under direct election, cling to the view that they would fare better under the present method—small states, after all, have a much larger share of the electoral vote than of the popular vote.

Some critics are concerned about the potential effects of direct election on the federal system itself, regardless of its impact on *specific* states. Since direct election would deprive the states of any formal role in presidential elections, would it weaken federalism? Not at all, assert such advocates of direct election as columnist Neal Peirce: "The vitality of federalism rests chiefly on the constitutionally mandated system of congressional representation and the will and capacity of state and local governments to address compelling problems, not on the hocus-pocus of an eighteenth-century vote count system." Federalism would indeed be diluted, rejoin the opponents of direct election, who consider the current method to be an important energizer of political federalism.

No longer needing a state-structured campaign strategy, presidential candidates might concentrate on appealing to mass national constituencies at the expense of important but less numerous local groups presently concentrated in pivotal and other states. Some developments already well under way would be accelerated further, such as the displacement of state party organizations by a reliance on the news media and a greater emphasis on a plebiscitary type of presidential campaign rather than on coalition-building among diverse interests. As a final concern, those who prefer the present system predict that direct election would soon be followed by a shift to national presidential primaries as the mode of nomination, which would additionally sap the vitality of federalism and the political place of the states.

Modifying the Core Standard: The 40 Percent Rule

Simple plurality vote is the common form of direct election in America: in contests for Congress, state legislatures and most governorships and other statewide posts, we award the office to the popular vote leader no matter how slim the share of the total vote he or she received. This procedure guarantees that the candidate with the most popular votes will win (the core standard) and that only a single election will be needed. We are not willing, however, to extend this standard practice to the election of the president because of concerns shared by all sides in the dispute over electoral reform.

The electoral college scheme, by heavily discounting popular votes cast for candidates unable to win states, discourages multiple third parties. Under a system of direct election, in contrast, every vote counts equally wherever and for whomever cast, and the sum of each candidate's votes is duly compiled and credited on a national basis. There is general agreement, therefore, that of the two methods direct election is more open to the presence of a larger number of serious candidates—indeed it may strongly encourage them. Given this expectation, simple plurality vote is deemed unacceptable for at least the following two reasons:

— With a crowded field of entrants, the winner's vote can be well below a majority, calling into question presidential legitimacy and the president's capacity to lead and govern effectively.

— In response to the temptation to increase the number of presidential competitors, persistent multipartyism might develop at the presidential level and subsequently spill over to congressional and state politics, undercutting the two-party system and stimulating multipartyism.

Acknowledging the force of this argument, advocates of direct election concede the need to amend the core standard to ensure a minimum level of vote support for the presidential winner. Once such a requirement is imposed, however, a contingency procedure must then also be added to cover election situations not meeting the requirement. As a result, direct election takes on greater complexity and invites disagreement on each successive stage of its procedure.

In deciding how best to modify the core standard, the backers of direct election have settled on "the 40 percent rule," which requires the plurality leader to receive at least 40 percent of the total popular vote. In their judgment, this minimum percentage is high enough to satisfy the criteria of presidential legitimacy and governance capability and low enough to be met regularly by the plurality leader, thus providing for a single election and little or no use of a contingency procedure. They grant that more candidates and parties would enter the presidential contest, but argue that the 40 percent rule would confine their effects to manageable proportions.

Conservative critics of direct election deride the 40 percent rule as contradicting the claim that direct election is "the only system that guarantees the election of the people's choice." Is that a fair description, they ask, of a winner opposed by as many as three out of every five voters? How politically effective could such a president be? (True, the same thing can happen under the present system, but the winner then at least has an electoral majority.) These critics would require a majority vote, which would give even greater encouragement to third parties and lead to more frequent use of the contingency procedure. So stringent a standard, as they are well aware, would cause Congress to reject direct presidential election altogether.

Hard proof or disproof of the validity of the specific figure of 40 percent is not possible. The figure is justified in part by its intuitive plausibility and in part by the fact that in all but one election since 1860 the winner has comfortably met that support level. (The single exception was Abraham Lincoln's sectional victory in 1860; he had only 39.8 percent of the popular vote, but his name was not on the ballot in several southern states.) But intuitions differ, and the record of elections under the present system scarcely provides a reliable guide to the impact of third parties on major-party candidates under direct election. In effect then, there is a standoff on whether the 40 percent rule adequately satisfies its several purposes—neither the optimism of one side nor the anxiety of the other seems conclusive. (Recall, however, that the proponents of change are properly assigned the burden of proof.)

This unresolved dispute carries over to the question of what post-election contingency procedure to adopt. The salience of this question is obviously high for those who doubt the 40 percent rule adequately checks third parties and who believe, therefore, that the contingency procedure will have to be used relatively frequently. However, because the contingency procedure itself independently affects the capacity of the 40 percent rule to contain third parties, it becomes a matter of concern to all sides.

Contingency Procedure I: A Runoff Election

The contingency procedure that best expresses the spirit of direct election is one that calls for a second round of popular choice between the top two contenders; the winner of the runoff election has, by definition, a popular majority. However, political science analysis indicates that the runoff device, when combined with direct election, additionally encourages multiple candidacies. Voters under the existing system are generally reluctant to "waste" their votes on presidential candidates other than the major-party nominees. In contrast, once voters are assured of a possible second voting chance in the runoff, they are more willing in the initial election to support nonmajor-party candidates and to back protesters, dissenters, or extremists. Responding to this new incentive, numerous challengers may then enter the race and, in the process, transform the first election into something like a wide-open national primary. When many small streams of third-party votes are nationally summed, they can account for 10, 15, 20 percent or more of the total vote and perhaps prevent the leading candidate from getting as much as 40 percent of the vote.

The fear that numerous candidates and parties may emerge is not fanciful. The availability of a runoff tempts those losing the presidential nomination to continue as rival candidates in the general election. Moreover, geographically concentrated parties have at least as much incentive under direct-election-with-runoff as under the current method, while nonsectional parties have greater incentive. Many groups, such as factional dissidents or those intensely concerned with a single issue (such as abortion, gun control, school busing), are willing and able, given the appropriate election structure and circumstances, to enter candidates and fragment the presidential vote. And for all groups there is the appeal of gaining enough votes in the initial election to become a bargaining force in the runoff.

Serious problems exist, then, if the runoff remains the contingency procedure for direct election. The chances of deadlock in the initial election, which are inherently greater under direct election than under the electoral college system, are increased further when the second-stage procedure is a runoff election. The runoff's incentives raise a genuine risk of promoting the durable presence of multiple candidates and parties, failing to give the plurality leader the minimum 40 percent support necessary to elect, and requiring frequent use of the runoff as part of a two-election sequence needed to determine who will be president.

Contingency Procedure II: Selection by Congress

Congressional selection of the president is the existing contingency procedure for direct election and also has been proposed with the district and proportional plans. The sponsors of direct election also are willing to accept it, albeit grudgingly, if that should prove necessary for legislative endorsement of their reform. Although different modes of congressional selection have been suggested, all sharply modify the exclusively federalistic cast of the present process by injection of the population principle. Some proposals involve the House alone, others the Senate as well; for the latter, some suggest separate sessions and others joint sessions. Whichever, the choice of Congress is confined to the top two contenders, each legislator is given one vote, and majority vote is required to win.

As a contingency procedure for direct election, congressional selection and the runoff present an arresting contrast of opposites: the strength and weakness of one are mirror images of the weakness and strength of the other. The major virtue of congressional selection is that, unlike the runoff, it gives no further encouragement to multiple candidates and parties to enter the presidential race; hence it promises fewer deadlocked elections. Some deadlocked elections should nevertheless occur because of the basic stimulus to third parties supplied by direct election itself. As the way to resolve an inconclusive popular election, however, congressional selection of the president is markedly inferior to popular determination by a second election.

One fundamental difficulty is that congressional selection must violate either the core standard or the 40 percent rule. The core standard requires that the candidate with the most votes wins, and the crux of the case for direct election is that it guarantees the core standard will be met, whereas the electoral college system does not. But if Congress is free to choose between the two leading candidates, it may award the presidency to the runner-up in popular vote. On the other hand, if Congress is obligated to select the plurality leader, then the 40 percent rule is in effect abrogated and the contingency procedure is reduced to a mere formality, that is, the winner is always the candidate with the most popular votes, period.

Another basic flaw is that the active involvement of Congress in the designation of presidents risks abuse of the separation of powers principle and loss of legitimacy for the outcome. Suppose, for the moment, that you were a member of Congress. Consider the variety of plausible responses you might make to the key question of what guidelines to follow in choosing between the top two presidential rivals:

(1) Vote for the national plurality leader? As just discussed, this standard in effect replaces the 40 percent rule by simple plurality vote.

(2) Vote for the candidate with the larger vote in your state? This is the equivalent of the current system's state-unit rule whereby the entire vote of the state's congressional delegation, rather than of the state's electors, goes to the plurality leader.

(3) Vote for the candidate with the larger vote in your district? This guideline converts what starts out as one national election and electorate into 435 separate district elections. It closely resembles the district plan and shares its central failing that partisan considerations too often determine district boundaries. Most House districts, for example, are safe for one or the other major party; only a minority of them regularly have a high degree of party competition.

(4) Vote for your party's candidate? Under this rule, the party that enjoys a majority in Congress would automatically win the presidency as well, if the election is deadlocked. This seriously breaches the separation of powers by fusing together what the Constitution seeks to keep apart. The independence of the executive and legislative branches rests in good part on the separateness of their electorates and their election bases, which would be greatly weakened by a practice that enabled a party to "pyramid" its control of Congress into control of the White House.

(5) Vote in terms of your own judgment and concerns? Rather than deciding which candidate to select on the basis of party label or some attribute of the candidate's record, this rule emphasizes the legislator's discretion to satisfy a wide variety of personal objectives and needs. These can range from an estimate of who will make a better president for the country to policy preferences and patronage or power objectives.

The contradictory guidance provided by five voting rules constitutes a serious indictment of the congressional selection method. Moreover, each of these voting guidelines is open to substantive objection. Nevertheless, it would be better for Congress to operate by a single decision rule, even one somewhat unsatisfactory, than to have legislators free to decide on whatever basis they please. In the absence of such a rule, empowering Congress to choose the president is too chancy and unreliable to be an acceptable contingency procedure.

The direct election reform thus turns out, upon close examination, to be far more complicated, wide-ranging in its effects, and problematical than it initially seemed. You should now be in a good position to assess its strengths and defects and those of the electoral college system. Treat the overall judgment you reach at this time as tentative, however, because several new proposals will be introduced in the final section. Before turning to them, you should be aware of how Congress responded to the question of replacing the current system by direct election. Toward that end, what follows is an account of Congress's rejection of direct election two different times in the recent past.

DIRECT ELECTION: CONGRESS SAYS NO

The 1969-1970 Defeat

Congress acted on serious proposals to change the method of presidential election in 1950 and 1956. At those times direct election was not considered a politically feasible reform and the focus, therefore, was on other indirect election schemes. In 1950, the proportional plan passed the Senate with better than two-thirds support but was then bottled up by the House Rules Committee. In 1956, a Senate majority of less than two-thirds supported a constitutional amendment permitting each state to choose either the district or proportional method in advance of each presidential election.

Various events in the 1960s served to rekindle interest in electoral reform:

— Concern about a runner-up president was provoked by the unusually close elections of 1960 and 1968, and by George Wallace's deliberate attempt to deadlock the latter election.

— Five southern states changed their laws to permit the election of unpledged or independent electors, a failing effort was made in 1960 to deny the presidency to John Kennedy by having some electors defect from him, and in 1968 a Republican elector chose to vote for Wallace.

— In 1966, President Lyndon Johnson, who opposed direct election on its merits and because he believed it could not get through Congress, passively proposed the "automatic plan," which would do away with the position of elector and revise the contingency procedure. Birch Bayh, a freshman Democratic senator who became chairman of the Constitutional Amendments Subcommittee of the Judiciary Committee when Estes Kefauver died in 1963, agreed to sponsor the President's proposal. When the automatic plan attracted little support, however, Bayh shifted to the direct election plan, with the contingency procedure of a joint session of Congress.

— In 1966, the U.S. Chamber of Commerce announced that a policy referendum of its member organizations showed two-thirds support for direct election, one-third for the district plan. The following year, the American Bar Association strongly attacked the current system and called for direct election, the 40 percent rule, and the runoff as the contingency procedure. Bayh accepted that package, and it was in that form that Congress considered the direct election proposal.

Congress thus was prepared to take on election reform when President Richard Nixon recommended it in February 1969. Citing his personal belief that the plurality leader should be president, Nixon nevertheless did not propose direct election because he shared his predecessor's estimate that small-state opposition precluded its adoption by Congress. Instead, he promised to support any plan that Congress could pass that abolished the electors, made the electoral vote division more closely approximate the popular vote division, and allowed a 40 percent electoral vote plurality to win. Nixon also indicated his preference for the runoff as the most appropriate contingency procedure.

Although the legislative backers of direct election were pleased to have the President put electoral revision on the congressional agenda, they greatly resented his dismissal of their reform as politically unpassable—a "retreat to expedience," Bayh called it. They were no less angered by Nixon's unwillingness to involve himself further in congressional resolution of the issue. The *New York Times* scolded Nixon for an "abdication of leadership" and a congressional supporter of direct election tartly told the President: "You will help us if we get [direct election] through Congress but you won't help us get it through Congress." Taking Nixon's stance as a challenge, Representative Emanuel Celler, a New York Democrat and veteran of 47 years' service in the House and chair of its Judiciary Committee for the previous 20 years, assumed personal responsibility for securing House adoption of direct election.

Celler achieved his objective with votes to spare. On September 18, 1969, after beating back with ease 15 proposed changes, the House passed the direct election package intact by a resounding 338-70 vote, 66 votes more than two-thirds support. Two of the 15 changes proposed adoption of the district plan and drew about 160 votes in favor. This was well over one-third of the total vote, hence more than enough to block direct election unless considerable vote shifting occurred—which is exactly what happened. Once the district plan was defeated, about 90 of the 160 chose direct election to no reform; the remaining 70 did the reverse.

Impressed by the House action, President Nixon shifted his position by endorsing direct election and urging the Senate to do likewise; however, the reform was not given a high priority on his political agenda. In the course of the Senate's consideration of electoral change, uneasiness grew about the likelihood of direct election's promotion of multipartyism. In response, Senator Bayh was prepared to revise the contingency procedure and perhaps other parts of the direct election package by means of floor amendments during Senate debate on the measure. Conservative opponents, recognizing that an amended plan had a greater chance of being approved than the original and knowing that their own preference, the district plan, had inadequate support, decided to prevent any vote on electoral reform by launching a filibuster in September of 1970.

The proponents of direct election thus had to try to end debate and fix a time to vote through adoption of a cloture motion, which required two-thirds approval. Two cloture votes were taken in September, about two weeks apart, and both failed: 54-36 and 53-34. Even if the full Senate (100) had been present and voting, the anticloture vote was just large enough to prevail. Technically, the direct election proposal remained pending business that could be called at any time; in fact, however, electoral reform was dead for the session and for the better part of the upcoming decade.

What was the composition of the congressional lineup for and against direct election in 1969 and 1970? Contrary to the conventional wisdom, the small states provided no solid phalanx of opposition. Outside the South, those from relatively low-population states (the 23 states with eight or fewer electoral votes) did vote against direct election at a higher rate than the rest of the nonsouthern legislators, but not nearly as strongly as Presidents Johnson and Nixon had anticipated or as conservatives had hoped. In the House, the district plan attracted the support of less than half of the small-state legislators, and 85 percent of them approved direct election in the final vote. In the Senate, only one-third of those from small states voted against cloture, and nearly all of them were Republicans.

The South was the major center of resistance to direct election. In the House, three-quarters of the representatives from the 11 former Confederate states at first voted for the district plan and less than half subsequently endorsed passage of direct election. Southerners accounted for almost half of the House vote for the district proposal and for three-quarters of the 70 votes cast against adoption of direct election. In the Senate, 86 percent of the southerners opposed cloture, comprising over half that vote. Some nonsouthern Republicans allied themselves with the South, most from a shared conservatism but a few because of small-state concerns.

These regional and ideological bases of division precluded either major party, considered as a whole, from responding to direct election in unified fashion. Within the Democratic camp, for example, nearly all nonsoutherners voted for direct election in the House and for cloture in the Senate, whereas most southerners went in the opposite direction. In the House, proportionately more Republicans than Democrats supported the district plan and later voted for final passage of direct election. In the Senate, two-thirds of the Democrats favored cloture while the Republicans split almost evenly.

The 1977-1979 Defeat

The narrowness of Jimmy Carter's victory over Gerald Ford in the 1976 election set the stage for another congressional pass at the issue of electoral reform. (With 50.1 percent of the popular vote, Carter got only 27 electoral votes more than the required 270.) The impetus for action was provided in March 1977, when the President urged Congress to adopt direct election, and Senator Bayh once again assumed the leadership role on its behalf. On balance, however, the political context was less favorable than seven years earlier.

On the plus side for direct election, Carter's support marked the first time a Democratic president had endorsed that reform. Moreover, as a Georgian, Carter's backing might be of special value in reducing southern opposition. In addition, through a change in its rules the Senate now permitted cloture to be imposed more easily to prevent or end filibusters.

On the negative side, Celler had been defeated for reelection and the new chair of the House Judiciary Committee, Democrat Peter Rodino of New Jersey, was lukewarm to direct election and insisted that the House would not take up the issue until the Senate had acted on it. The burden of carrying the reform thus fell squarely on Bayh and the Senate; the momentum and pressure generated in 1969 and 1970 by prior House passage of the measure were not available this time. Carter's endorsement did not offset that loss because, like Nixon before him, he invested little political energy in electoral reform. Perhaps the most damaging change in the political environment was the absence of a sense of urgency or of an aroused public interest. An impressive coalition of diverse interests testified for direct election in the late 1970s, but the issue was not a high priority for any of them. The same was true of the general public, as Bayh ruefully observed during Senate debate on direct election in mid-1979: "I must say that if anybody while I was back home on July 4 had come up and talked to me about direct election instead of inflation, gas rationing or SALT, I would have thought he was out of his mind."

As Bayh began his battle in early 1979, he had 44 cosponsors of the measure. Most were liberal northern Democrats, but there were also several southern Democrats and over a dozen Republicans among them, including Minority Leader Howard Baker of Tennessee. Most conservative opponents now pushed for the proportional or automatic plan rather than the district scheme, while some liberal Democrats (like Daniel Patrick Moynihan of New York) preferred retention of the present system to any of the proposed changes.

Bayh's accomplishment in 1977 was to prevent opponents from killing the proposal at the committee stage. The following year, however, he was unable to arrange for floor consideration of the measure because of the press of other Senate business and because the Senate's managers feared its foes might launch a filibuster. By mid-1979 Bayh found it necessary to negotiate an agreement with the opposition in which they promised not to filibuster in exchange for scheduling a straight up-or-down vote on direct election. The ensuing vote on July 10 made clear whose interests the agreement favored: direct election was defeated handily, 51-48.

The reasons for this defeat resembled those for the 1969-1970 outcome, even though nearly two-thirds of the senators present in 1979 had been elected since 1970. Small-state senators, taken as a group, split evenly on the vote for direct election. Direct election was supported by more than twice the proportion of Democrats as Republicans (67 to 30 percent) and, within the Democratic party, by exactly twice the proportion of nonsoutherners as southerners (78 to 39 percent).

One modest difference deserves comment. Nine liberal northern Democrats opposed direct election in 1979, whereas only two did so in 1970. The continued resistance of black and Jewish organizations to elimination of the electoral college system provides, at most, only a small part of the explanation. A more fundamental concern was involved, one that by now should be thoroughly familiar to you: the worry that direct election might undercut the two-party system, expand the media's influence over presidential election campaigns and outcomes, and fractionalize politics in the manner of multipartyism.

POSSIBLE SOLUTIONS I:
STRENGTHENING THE DIRECT ELECTION PLAN

Can the central problems of direct election—its risks of multipartyism, inconclusive elections, and too frequent use of the contingency procedure—be effectively corrected? Several different kinds of solutions are presented in this section for your consideration.

Repressing Third Parties

The most direct way to ensure that the candidate who leads in popular votes secures at least 40 percent of the total popular vote is to rig the election structure so thoroughly in favor of the two major parties as to enable them to monopolize presidential elections. Under this scheme, the popular vote leader would typically receive a majority of the total vote cast. One way to accomplish this is to make it more difficult for third parties to enter the competition in the first place. The states could stiffen their requirements for access to a place on the ballot, or public campaign funds could be allocated to disadvantage any but the established parties. Another way is to minimize the election impact of third parties that have entered candidates by using a vote counting formula that discriminates against candidates whose vote falls below, say, 10 percent of the total vote.

In thinking about this proposal, note that while many parts of the American political process consciously operate to disadvantage third parties (for example, the state-unit rule of the electoral college system), its aggressive repression of third parties goes well beyond the present level of discrimination. Because of its extreme character, this solution inescapably raises basic questions of law, policy, and feasibility. Key democratic values and constitutional rights are necessarily involved in view of the solution's consequences for political expression and representation. Would state legislatures or Congress be willing to adopt such a solution? Would the courts find it constitutional? And, independent of its political and legal feasibility, would this method of remedying direct election's chief vulnerability be worth its high cost?

Relaxing the 40 Percent Rule

If the repression of third parties is an unacceptable way to ensure that the plurality leader passes the 40 percent test and that no election deadlock occurs, then what about reducing the likelihood of deadlock by *relaxing* the 40 percent rule? Specifically, for those elections in which no candidate gets as much as 40 percent of the vote, can new conditions be set which, if met by the plurality leader, would entitle that front-runner to the presidency without turning to a contingency procedure? This approach proposes, in effect, a new "under-40 percent rule."

What qualitative dimensions of the plurality leader's vote might be an acceptable alternative to the 40 percent rule in providing a minimally adequate basis for winning the presidency through an election? The basic answer relates to the characteristics that distinguish the voting pattern for major-party candidates from that of third-party contestants. One basic difference is that major-party presidential nominees tend to lead in the balloting in most areas of the nation, while third-party candidates tend either to spread their support thinly across many areas or to concentrate their strength in relatively few areas. In a word, major parties have the stronger backing across the larger geographical spread—and the under-40 percent rule should reflect and capitalize on this distinction.

During the Senate's consideration of electoral reform in 1970, friends of direct election who were concerned about its threat to two-partyism introduced three versions of an under-40 percent rule that emphasized the factor of a geographically distributed vote. Republican Robert Griffin of Michigan and Maryland Democrat Joseph Tydings proposed that an under-40 percent plurality leader would win if he had a majority of electoral votes. Conservatives ridiculed the proposal as an instance of "intellectual schizophrenia": "It spurns what it embraces," jibed Nebraska Republican Roman Hruska during debate, "and embraces what it spurns." That criticism was superficial, however, and spoke to the plan's appearance rather than to its consistency with the objective of providing less encouragement to third parties.

Another kind of under-40 percent rule was offered by Republican Edward Brooke of Massachusetts. His version awarded victory to a plurality candidate lacking 40 percent of the vote if the candidate carried a majority of House districts. If that condition was not met, each district carried by the weakest national candidates would be credited to the candidate with the next highest vote in the district. As this process worked itself out, it would result in the automatic production of a winner without recourse to a contingency procedure because eventually one candidate would be allocated a majority of House districts.

The third proposal, introduced by Thomas Eagleton, D-Mo., and Robert Dole, R-Kan., and dubbed the "federal plan," provided the largest array of alternate conditions, including the ones offered in the preceding two versions. In the federal plan, an under-40 percent plurality leader would be declared the presidential winner if any *one* of the following conditions was met:

— If the candidate carried, by a plurality vote, a *majority* of House districts;
— If he or she carried, by a plurality vote, a *majority* of states;
— If the total votes of the states he or she carried by plurality vote constituted a *majority* of the national vote;
— If he or she gained a *majority* of electoral votes.

Although the proposal's elaboration of numerous alternatives makes it appear cumbersome, it also virtually guarantees that a plurality leader would pass one of these tests and become president without use of a second-stage procedure. Moreover, the diversity of conditions probably enhances the proposal's political appeal by reflecting both the federal and population principles.

Basic to your review of these proposals is your position on their common premise. Do you agree that when no candidate attracts as much as 40 percent of the popular vote, the leading candidate nevertheless deserves to be president if his or her voting pattern exhibits geographical diversity rather than sectional concentration? If so, you must decide how best to implement an under-40 percent rule, including what contingency procedure to adopt. If, on the other hand, you believe that an under-40 percent rule is inherently unwise and would threaten the legitimacy of the presidential election process, you would reject this approach and search for another remedy.

Requiring Wide Geographic Backing If No Popular Majority

For strong believers in majority rule, the automatic award of the presidency to the plurality leader who has more than 40 but less than 50 percent of the vote is a troubling aspect of direct election. These critics urge that such a leader's vote pattern must demonstrate wide geographic backing; otherwise the president should be chosen through a contingency procedure.

In an early version of their 1970 federal plan, Senators Eagleton and Dole required under-50 percent plurality leaders to meet at least one of the four conditions set forth in that plan. In 1979, some moderate opponents of direct election sought to require the under-50 percent leader to carry at least one-third of the states in order to win.

Imposing these conditions on an under-50 percent leader would not have much effect on election outcomes or on the rate of use of the contingency procedure. After all, if plurality leaders with less than 40 percent of the vote are expected to be able to pass with ease one or more of the tests required by the Eagleton-Dole federal plan, then plurality leaders with between 40 and 50 percent of the vote are virtually guaranteed to do so. What it would accomplish would be to give to presidential winners who lack a popular majority the appearance of greater support and a more justified claim to victory, both of which should theoretically strengthen their capacity to govern. (Under our present system, the state-unit rule performs the same function by giving the winning candidate a larger share of the electoral than the popular vote.)

Although proposals to promote geographic breadth for winning presidential candidates are primarily intended to reduce the risk that severe multipartyism might develop under direct election, they also reflect an enduring normative concern about the nature of American democracy and the presidential selection process. As a participant in the Senate debate in 1970 on direct election expressed that concern, ". . . I had rather see a president who has received a good vote from a lot of the States than to see a president who received a large vote in a few States elected as president of the United States." For choosing the president, should the core standard—which defines the winner as the candidate with the most votes—control the process without qualification and to the exclusion of other values?

Considered in this context, the emphasis in these proposals on the geographic spread of the plurality leader's vote testifies to the desire to add qualitative criteria to the simple quantitative measure derived from the core standard. The continued preeminence of the core standard remains clearly evident, however. The new conditions introduced by the proposals apply only to candidates with less than 50 percent of the vote (not to those with majority support) and to plurality leaders (not to any candidate with more than a specified minimum proportion of the vote). Their objective, in other words, is to strengthen direct election, not to repudiate or subvert it.

POSSIBLE SOLUTIONS II: STRENGTHENING THE ELECTORAL COLLEGE SYSTEM

Can the chief vulnerability of the electoral college system—the risk of a runner-up president—be effectively eliminated? Two proposals that merit further review are considered in this section.

Requiring a Popular Vote Plurality

In 1970, after the second failing cloture attempt to end the filibuster against direct election, Senator Bayh desperately explored whether revisions of the plan might produce the two-thirds support he needed. Senator William Spong, D-Va., proposed a significant change: a winning presidential candidate would be required to have *both* a popular plurality and an electoral vote majority; otherwise, a joint session of Congress would decide. When Bayh sounded out the opponents of direct election for their reaction to this proposal, they were so sure of their ability to block Senate adoption of direct election that they refused even to consider it. We examine the proposal on its merits, then, without evidence one way or the other on its political feasibility.

The Spong plan would revise both direct election and the current system by combining the key attribute of each into a dual requirement for election victory. However, the plan does not assign equal weight to each attribute. Like the existing system, and unlike the previously discussed proposals to strengthen direct election, Spong's formula would make a candidate who has a *popular majority* pass another test as a condition of winning the presidency. The plan thus gives greater emphasis to the requirement of an electoral vote majority; the companion requirement for a popular plurality, although important, has secondary status. This consideration alone would probably offend enough direct election supporters to preclude the plan from serving as an acceptable compromise.

Hence, even though Spong's scheme was introduced to revise Bayh's direct election plan, it is better understood as an effort to strengthen the electoral college system. It plainly ends the current method's major vulnerability by eliminating the possibility of a runner-up president; that outcome would be transformed into an instance of election deadlock. The plan would change little beyond that, however, because it fully retains the existing election structure and provides no new incentives to alter the behavior of candidates, parties or voters.

In reviewing this hybrid plan, you should weigh the seriousness of any problems it may cause against its effectiveness in preventing the occurrence of a "wrong" winner. Although the scheme requires the winner to be ahead in popular votes, it is indifferent to the size of the leader's share of the total popular vote. At the one extreme, then, an under-40 percent plurality leader may win the election while, at the other, a majority leader may not, depending on whether the leader also has gained a majority of electoral votes. Are you willing to insist on a geographically wide vote (for which an electoral vote majority serves as a rough measure) as an added requirement for a candidate who has attained a majority of popular votes? (The Spong proposal could be amended, of course, to exclude majority leaders from its coverage. It then would become just a variant of the under-40 percent and under-50 percent rules proposed to modify direct election that were discussed in the preceding section.)

The "National Bonus" Plan

In 1977, the Twentieth Century Fund, a nonprofit research foundation, set up a Task Force on Reform of the Presidential Election Process. Its 12 members were a bipartisan mix of campaign strategists, journalists, and political scientists. Although some members strongly favored the direct election reform while others supported the current election method, the task force was able to achieve near-unanimity in recommending a novel election arrangement. The group's plan was introduced by Senator Bayh in 1978 as a proposed constitutional amendment. No hearings were held on it, however, and it played no role in the Senate's subsequent defeat of direct election.

The proposal, called the "national bonus" plan, retains the existing state-based structure of 538 electoral votes, but would add to it a national pool of 102 electoral votes (two votes for each state and the

District of Columbia). The new total of electoral votes would thus be 640. The 102 votes constitute a "bonus" to be awarded on a winner-take-all basis to the candidate with the most popular votes. The candidate who gains a majority of electoral votes (321 of 640) would win the presidency. In the event of deadlock, the two rivals receiving the most popular votes would enter a runoff election. The victor of this second election, however, would be the candidate who secured an electoral vote majority (321 of 640), not a popular majority. Advocates of this plan claim that the particular mix of elements it draws from direct election and the current system provides an innovative hybrid process superior to both.

Compared with the Electoral College System: The bonus plan gives greater assurance (as compared with the present system) that the popular vote and electoral vote outcomes would not diverge, that is, the plurality leader would win and runner-up presidents would not be elected. The chances of a deadlocked election would also be reduced: to thwart a third party's attempt to deadlock the election, a major-party candidate must now carry enough states to get 270 electoral votes, whereas only 219 state-based electoral votes would be needed under the bonus plan. In the absence of a deadlocked election, no contingency procedure would have to be used.

Compared with Direct Election and the 40 Percent Rule: By preserving the state-based electoral vote system (which comprises 84 percent of the 640 electoral votes), the bonus plan retains in large degree the current system's advantages over direct election: maintenance of a federal base for presidential elections, promotion of moderate two-partyism, discouragement of multipartyism, and penalization of excessively sectional voting support. Consequently, the bonus scheme is a better bet than direct election to produce decisive elections that result in a presidential winner without reliance on a contingency procedure. At the same time, the bonus plan can reasonably be expected to match the performance of direct election (with the 40 percent rule) in ensuring victory for the candidate who has a popular plurality.

Believing, then, that the bonus plan has something for each side and provides a better election method, its proponents offer it as a compromise to end the congressional stalemate on electoral reform. Notwithstanding their claims, however, the bonus plan constitutes no golden mean between the present electoral college system and direct election. Like the Spong proposal, it assigns unequal weight to what it takes from each method but its emphasis goes in the opposite direction: it is centrally concerned with popular pluralities no matter what share of the national vote they represent, and only secondarily with electoral votes.

Thus, under the bonus plan the plurality leader is given an electoral vote reward just for being the plurality leader. It is so large a reward—16 percent of the total electoral vote (102 of 640), 19 percent of the state-based electoral vote (102 of 538)—that the plurality leader is ordinarily assured of winning the presidency. As a consequence, the relative significance of the requirement for an electoral vote majority is sharply reduced: the plurality leader need get only 41 percent of the state-based electoral vote (219 of 538) to gain a bare majority of the total electoral vote (321 of 640). The same arithmetic and conclusion apply to the contingency procedure of the runoff election in which, unlike the initial election, no more than two candidates can compete.

The bonus plan may fairly be characterized, then, as an attempt to achieve direct election's key benefit—the award of the presidency to the candidate with the most popular votes—by a method that conforms closely to the existing election process in appearance but deviates markedly from it in operation. The plan's rationale is perhaps as much strategic as substantive; a disguised direct election plan, especially one dressed in the familiar garb of the electoral college system, might have better prospects for congressional adoption. Once its true character as a variant of direct election becomes clear, however, opposition to the bonus plan can be expected not only from defenders of the existing system but from those in the reform camp who are put off by its backdoor, convoluted approach to direct election.

SOME QUESTIONS TO EXPLORE

Both sides on the issue of electoral reform largely agree on which concerns are paramount, such as the core democratic standard, moderate two-partyism and anti-multi-partyism, federalism, decisiveness of the initial election in producing a president, legitimacy of the election process and of the presidential winner, and nonreliance on a contingency procedure. Most of their differences arise from how they evaluate the effect of alternative election methods on those concerns. Thus both camps attach high value to two-partyism and federalism; they disagree on the extent to which direct election would adversely affect them. Again, both sides believe in the core standard; they disagree on the likelihood of its violation in the future under the electoral college system.

The opposing sides do differ on at least one central value question: Should the vote-equality principle embodied in the quantitative definition of the core standard (the most votes win) be complemented or modified by the federal/diversity principle? As we have seen, the latter is customarily implemented by emphasizing an electoral vote requirement to encourage the geographic spread of the winner's vote. If you favor a combination of the two principles, what should their exchange ratio be, or roughly how much of one should offset or substitute for how much of the other? Remember that the higher the minimum support levels required to win, whether for popular or electoral votes, the greater the likelihood of broader geographic backing for the candidate meeting that level—but the greater also the incentives to third parties, the chances for deadlock, and the importance of contingency procedures.

In thinking through your position, you may find it helpful to work out the implications of the following hypothetical mixes of the two criteria:

Suppose the existing election method were altered to award the presidency

— to the candidate with an electoral vote majority; if none, then to the candidate with the highest popular vote.

— to the candidate with a popular vote majority; if none, then to the candidate with the highest electoral vote.

— to the candidate with either a popular vote plurality or an electoral vote plurality; if two candidates qualified, then use of a contingency procedure to decide between them.

— to the candidate with a popular vote majority (or plurality?) and an electoral vote majority (or plurality?); if none, then use of a contingency procedure to decide between the two candidates with the most popular (or electoral?) votes.

Note that any plurality requirement in the above schemes can be modified to set a minimum support level as well.

We are presently in a quiet period with respect to the issue of changing our presidential election method. This reflects the natural rhythm of public attention to problems of this sort, because electoral reform has no large, continuing, and intense body of supporters. As an officer of the League of Women Voters aptly observed in 1979, "It's one of those issues that is sexless except after close elections. It's an issue that people can afford not to care about. It doesn't arouse high emotions unless we've gone through a squeaker." Just as major attempts to replace the existing election method took place after the "squeaker" elections of 1968 and 1976, we may expect renewed attention to the issue whenever a presidential election, in prospect or retrospect, comes close to "misfiring" or involves a third-party effort to deadlock the outcome.

At that time, Congress will resume consideration of direct election and alternatives to it, including retention of the existing electoral college system with modifications. The choice before Congress will be the same choice this case study has posed for you. Hence those who accept this study's invitation to puzzle through the electoral reform problem can be confident the issue remains alive and will return again—

and perhaps again and again—until a congressional resolution is ratified by the states and another amendment to the Constitution has been added.

SOURCES AND READINGS

The hearings on electoral reform held by the House Judiciary Committee in 1969 and by the Senate Judiciary Committee in 1969 and 1970 and in 1977 are invaluable sources. Comprising several thousand pages, they include formal statements of interest groups, legislators, and experts; the text of resolutions and bills on the subject; reprints of newspaper editorials and journal articles; considerable data and analysis on presidential elections; and the record of the testimony of witnesses and their exchange of views with committee members.

The *Congressional Record* for the relevant time periods covers the floor debates, amendments, and votes in the House and Senate respectively on the proposed constitutional amendments on electoral reform. The *New York Times*'s coverage of the same subject can be followed easily by use of that newspaper's index. The *Weekly Report* published by Congressional Quarterly (CQ) also should be consulted; see especially the March 10, 1979, issue.

For a vigorous argument in favor of direct elections that blends scholarship and journalism, see Neal R. Peirce, *The People's President: The Electoral College in American History and the Direct Vote Alternative* (New York: Simon & Schuster, 1968). A revised edition (1981), coauthored by Lawrence D. Longley, updates the coverage through 1980. Also in support of direct election is Lawrence D. Longley and Alan G. Braun, *The Politics of Electoral College Reform* (New Haven: Yale University Press, 1972). The influential ABA report that stimulated interest in the direct election reform in the late 1960s should be read: American Bar Association, *Electing the President: A Report of the Commission on Electoral College Reform* (Chicago, 1967).

For a defense of the existing system, together with a critique of direct election, the following readings cover the ground effectively: Alexander Bickel, *The New Age of Political Reform* (New York: Harper & Row, 1968), Chapter 2; Wallace S. Sayre and Judith H. Parris, *Voting for President: The Electoral College and the American Political System* (Washington, D.C.: The Brookings Institution, 1970); Judith Best, *The Case Against Direct Election of the President: A Defense of the Electoral College* (Ithaca, N.Y.: Cornell University Press, 1975); and Martin Diamond, *The Electoral College and the American Idea of Democracy* (Washington, D.C.: American Enterprise Institute, 1977).

Several of the author's writings analyze important aspects of the electoral reform problem. "Presidential Election Methods and Urban-

Ethnic Interests," *Law and Contemporary Problems* (Spring 1962): 213-233, examines the "countervailing inequity" thesis and also treats the political consequences of the district and proportional plans and of the existing system. "Basic Change Aborted: The Failure to Secure Direct Popular Election of the President, 1969-70," in *Policy and Politics in America*, ed. A. P. Sindler (Boston: Little, Brown & Co., 1973) covers congressional events, together with considerable analysis of the various plans of electoral revision. *Political Parties in the United States*, (New York: St. Martin's Press, 1966), pp. 49-71, reviews and discusses the diverse arguments on what causes and sustains American two-partyism.

The Congress

Budget Battles of 1981:
The Role of the Majority Party Leadership

Steven S. Smith

"I'm feeling a little shell-shocked," confessed a senior aide to House Speaker Thomas P. "Tip" O'Neill as the outcomes of the November 1980 elections became evident. The aide's reaction was understandable because the Democrats suffered their most devastating defeat in three decades. Ronald Reagan not only beat incumbent Jimmy Carter more decisively than anticipated (50.7 percent to 41.0 percent in popular votes and 489 to 49 in electoral votes), but the Republicans also displayed unexpectedly great strength in the congressional races. In the Senate, the Republicans gained 12 seats and assumed control of the Senate, converting the 58-41 Democratic edge in the 96th Congress (1979-1981) to a 53-46 Republican advantage for the 97th Congress. The only remaining Democratic bastion was the House of Representatives. Even there, while retaining majority control, the Democrats suffered a significant loss of seats: their margin of 114 seats in the 96th Congress was cut to only 51 seats in the 97th Congress (243-192).

Given the character of the congressional parties, the closer party division in the House would make actual working control of the House difficult for the Democrats. In Speaker O'Neill's estimate, House Democrats in the 97th Congress would be composed of 33 percent conservatives, 40 percent moderates, and just 27 percent liberals. What, then, should or could be the role of House Democrats in responding to the policy initiatives proposed by the new administration and supported by the Republican-controlled Senate? And what should or could be the role of the majority party leadership in the House in promoting and shaping that response?

This study focuses on the House's response to the Reagan administration's 1981 budget proposals. All sides agreed that these proposals represented a policy change so fundamental as to warrant the term "revolution" frequently used to describe them. Labeled "Reaganomics" by the media, the new administration proposals were a combination of traditional Republican economic thinking, emphasizing reduced federal domestic spending and smaller deficits, and the more recently popularized "supply-side economics," advocating deep personal and business tax cuts to stimulate economic growth.

On the spending side, Reagan proposed to reduce projected domestic spending by over $150 billion by 1984. This was to be done by slashing funding for dozens of domestic programs, including mass transit, education and student aid, housing, food stamps, health care, Social Security, school lunch subsidies, and job training. Many of the cuts came in the form of eliminating categorical grant programs in which federal aid for very specific purposes was given to state or local agencies. The Reagan administration proposed to combine many of these categorical programs into broad block grants and to permit state or local governments to expend the grant funds as they chose, without extensive federal restrictions. The new block grants would be funded at levels far below the projected aggregate levels of the categorical programs. In contrast to the social program cutbacks, the administration proposed the largest peacetime increases in defense spending ever.

On the tax side, the administration proposed the largest personal and business income tax reductions in history. The personal income tax reductions involved 10 percent cuts in marginal income tax rates in three successive years, for a total of 30 percent by 1984. These across-the-board cuts would benefit, in terms of absolute tax savings, the highest-income persons the most. The projected business income tax cut involved major accelerations in the rate at which businesses could depreciate equipment, machinery, and buildings for tax purposes. The projected loss of revenue to the federal treasury from the personal and business tax cuts, according to the original administration estimates, was well over $300 billion by 1984. The "supply-side" aspect of these cuts was the expectation that they would stimulate personal savings and reinvestment in plant and equipment and eventually create greater long-term economic growth. The economic growth, in turn, would yield higher tax revenues for the federal treasury, which, along with the spending cuts, would produce a balanced budget in fiscal 1984 and thereafter.

Reagan's strategy from the beginning of 1981 was to focus his political resources and public and congressional attention on his budget and tax proposals. The administration put off—and tried fairly successfully to keep conservative members of Congress from pursuing—controversial proposals to change the direction of several federal social policies in order to prevent any distraction from the budget issues. Social issues such as abortion, affirmative action, busing, and school prayer were deliberately set aside so as not to clog the congressional schedule or draw media attention to nonbudget issues.

The political, economic, and social stakes in the Reagan budget proposals were monumental. In the minds of many members of Congress, the budget battle involved nothing less than fundamental principles of government and the future shape of society. For O'Neill and other senior Democrats, the administration proposals were a direct attack on a lifetime's work.

THE 1974 BUDGET REFORM

The events of 1981 were played out in the context of budgetary procedures that had undergone major reform in 1974, through the Congressional Budget and Impoundment Act. President Nixon provoked the reform by refusing to spend funds appropriated by the Congress for selected environmental and social programs, on the grounds that Congress was fiscally irresponsible in authorizing excessive levels of expenditure. Known as "impoundments," these presidential actions challenged the power of the purse granted the Congress by the Constitution. An unusual coalition—conservatives seeking to strengthen Congress's ability to act in a fiscally responsible manner and others seeking to curb presidential incursion into Congress's budgetmaking jurisdiction—created a new congressional budget process.

The 1974 reform sought to treat several major problems in how Congress handled fiscal matters:

— Many critics inside and outside of Congress had long complained about its lack of coordination in its spending and revenue decisions. Appropriations and taxes were determined by separate committees and considered separately on the House and Senate floors, with no procedure available for considering how each of these parts fit into the whole.

— Spending decisions were made each year in at least 13 different appropriation bills and, even though a single committee in each chamber handled all of these bills, there was no mechanism which ensured consideration of their aggregate effect on budget deficits and economic policy.

— The authorizing committees, with jurisdiction over program structure and policy but not program appropriations, were often able to ensure certain spending levels of programs, thus circumventing the appropriations committees. One strategy was to put individual benefit entitlements into the statute authorizing the program, which then obligated the government to provide the benefits even if funding for the program ran short. Due to its mandatory character, such spending was uncontrollable unless Congress revised the authorization and entitlements standards, which were within the jurisdiction of the authorization committees, not the appropriations committees.

In short, because Congress was not able to adopt an identifiable budget or to set overall priorities, coordination of budgetary and economic policies was not possible.

The budgetary system introduced in the 1974 act was added to the existing committee structure, providing new mechanisms for integrating the work of the appropriations, revenue, and authorization committees and producing a congressional budget for each fiscal year. House and Senate budget committees were created, an analytical staff (the Congressional Budget Office) was established, and a timetable for constructing a budget for the next fiscal year was fixed (see Table 2-1).

The budget resolutions required by the act fixed targets for spending in broad programmatic categories, set total revenues, and stipulated the deficit or surplus and the total federal debt. The first resolution was intended to provide guidelines for the work of the money committees during the summer months and the second resolution would be binding. A "reconciliation" process was created to reconcile the fiscal decisions of the summer months with the second budget resolution figures. Congress was allowed to pass additional budget resolutions to change the figures of the second budget resolution any time during the course of the fiscal year. In addition, the reform included a procedure for congressional review and veto of presidential decisions to delay (deferrals) or to cancel (rescissions) the use of appropriated funds, making presidential impoundment of funds more difficult.

The new budget process provided a major integrating or centralizing mechanism in congressional decisionmaking. In an article published in 1981 in a collection entitled *The New Congress*, Allen Schick put it succinctly:

> [While] legislative norms have propelled Congress toward the fragmentation of power, budgeting calls for the concentration of power. Budgeting's essential purpose is the coordination of many decisions and many decision makers to achieve a reasonably comprehensive and consistent outcome. Budgeting requires attention to how the parts relate to the whole and to the relationship between tax and spending policies.

Table 2-1 Congressional Budget Timetable

Deadline	Action to be Completed
15th day after Congress convenes	President submits his budget, along with *current services estimates*.[1]
March 15	Committees submit views and estimates to Budget committees.
April 1	Congressional Budget Office (CBO) submits report to Budget committees.[2]
April 15	Budget committees report first concurrent resolution on the budget to their Houses.
May 15	Committees report bills authorizing new budget authority.
May 15	Congress adopts first concurrent resolution on the budget.
7th day after Labor Day	Congress completes action on bills providing budget authority and spending authority.
September 15	Congress completes action on second required concurrent resolution on the budget.
September 25	Congress completes action on reconciliation process implementing second concurrent resolution.
October 1	Fiscal year begins.

[1] *Current service estimates* are estimates of the dollar levels that would be required next year to support the same level of services in each program as this year's budget. The Budget Act originally required submission of the current services estimates by November 10 of the previous year. Since the president was still in the midst of developing his budget proposals for the next year, Congress later agreed to permit simultaneous submission of the current services and executive budgets in January.

[2] The Budget committees and CBO have found April 1 too late in the budget process to be useful; hence, CBO submits its report(s) in February, although April 1 remains the date required by law.

SOURCE: Allen Schick, *Budget Handbook, Congressional Quarterly's Seminar: The Congressional Budget Process* (Washington, D.C.: Congressional Quarterly, 1981), p. 4.

NOTE: Congress has not always adhered to these deadlines. In recent years, Congress has fallen increasingly behind schedule.

THE LEADERSHIP ROLE IN THE HOUSE

The majority party leadership in the House has also been viewed as a major centralizing force. For several decades, a strengthened majority party leadership has been the goal of many reformers seeking to overcome the fragmentation of congressional decisionmaking. Through a strong majority party leadership, it has been hoped that the activities of majority party members, especially their committee activities, could be coordinated to fashion well-integrated policy. To that end, the House Democrats adopted reforms in the mid-1970s to strengthen the political resources of their leadership, several of which bear directly on the budget process:

— Democrats transferred the responsibility for committee assignment nominations from the Ways and Means Committee Democrats to a revitalized Steering and Policy Committee. The Speaker chairs the committee and 16 of its present 29 members are either his appointees or other party leaders. As a result, the leadership can play a decisive role in the appointment of Democrats to the Budget Committee.

— The Speaker was given the authority to nominate the Democratic members of the Rules Committee, which writes the special orders ("rules") under which important legislation is considered on the floor. Hence, the Speaker can shape the proposed rules under which the budget resolutions and reconciliation legislation are considered on the floor.

— In addition to these changes in Democratic caucus rules, the Budget Act provided that the two major parties of the House may place one of their party leaders on the Budget Committee, giving the leaders ready access to and a vote in all Budget Committee deliberations. House Democrats have always assigned that seat to the Majority Leader; since 1977, this has been Jim Wright of Texas.

The leadership has been involved with the budget process in a wide variety of informal ways as well. In 1979, for example, the party leadership endorsed Democrat Robert Giaimo of Connecticut to chair the Budget Committee. In 1980, the Democratic leadership of both houses of Congress, along with key members of the budget committees, participated in discussions at the White House to work out a balanced budget with the Carter administration. And in each of his first four years as Speaker (1977-1981), O'Neill created task forces of some two dozen members, each of whose job was to promote the budget resolutions reported by the Democratically controlled House Budget Committee. The leadership has always played a central role in the effort to pass the budget resolutions on the floor of the House.

Despite the leadership's active involvement in the budget process and its acquisition of new political resources, the House became more difficult to manage during the 1970s. New members seemed to be less deferential to their elder colleagues and insisted on a significant role in all party and House decisions. Special interest caucuses multiplied and placed greater demands on the leadership. Most importantly, a series of reforms gave subcommittees and their chairs greater independence from their parent full committee chairs. It was no longer possible for the party leaders to consult just the major committee chairs to set party strategy; a top aide to the Speaker ruefully observed in mid-1981, "It's impossible to tell who we should be consulting around here."* The House is now a more fluid, more fragmented, less hierarchically operated body than it was in the 1960s.

Not surprisingly, the high partisan stakes involved in the 1981 budget fight put both the Democratic leadership's role and the reformed budget process to a severe test. We now turn to an account of that conflict and its outcome.

THE PRELIMINARIES TO THE BUDGET BATTLE: NOVEMBER 1980 - JANUARY 1981

The 1980 election made conservative Democrats pivotal to the new balance of power in the House. Assuming that members of the President's party remained unified, the defection of only 27 Democrats would be enough to enable the Republicans to carry the House. Acting upon their strengthened bargaining position, some 40 conservative Democrats, mostly from the South, formed the Conservative Democratic Forum (CDF) within a month after the election. Dubbed the "Boll Weevils"—a term long applied to southern Democrats in Congress—the CDF members quickly made several demands of their leadership to enhance their influence within the party.

Partly in response to CDF threats to join with Republicans to organize the House and write its rules, the Speaker appointed three southern conservatives to the Steering and Policy Committee for the new 97th Congress. Three more CDF members were given seats on the Budget Committee while, in contrast, the Black Caucus failed for the first time to have one of its members on that critical committee. The appointment to the Budget Committee of one conservative Democrat, Phil Gramm of Texas, was especially controversial because he vehemently opposed liberal Democratic economic and budget policy. Despite warnings that Gramm's appointment would be a mistake, O'Neill deferred to Majority Leader Wright who pushed for his fellow Texan's appointment after receiving Gramm's promise that he would support the party's budget position on the floor. As reported in the *Washington Post*, Wright wrote in his diary,

> [Gramm is,] after all, one of 'our own'. . . . He is energetic, indefatigable, resourceful. He is genuinely interested in the budget process and deserves a chance to work at it. . . . There's one other possible consola-

---

* Quotations and references not attributed in the text come from material supplied to the author on a confidential basis through interviews and personal observations.

tion in Phil's being on the committee; as a party to its deliberations, he'll be less likely to undermine the final product of those deliberations on the House floor.

The factional division within the party made its clearest appearance in this early period during the contest for the chair of the Budget Committee. The two leading contenders were liberal David R. Obey of Wisconsin and moderately conservative James R. Jones of Oklahoma. The policy differences between them encapsulated a critical choice for House Democrats: a Jones-sponsored budget proposal would be more likely to gather the support of conservative Democrats and many Republicans, whereas one developed by Obey would probably be endorsed more enthusiastically by Democratic moderates and liberals, but by few others. It took the party caucus three ballots to unlock the tie between the two candidates; Jones finally won by a 121-116 vote.

How did Speaker O'Neill react to the rising pressures within the party? Although personally a liberal in the New Deal/Great Society mold, O'Neill in the past often had not made aggressive use of his powers as Speaker on behalf of the leadership's goals. He preferred to operate informally through warm personal relationships with members of all factions of his party and avoid alienating members or polarizing the party into warring camps. To some, the Speaker's style was a source of valuable strength, especially in view of the party's vulnerability after the 1980 election. Thomas S. Foley of Washington, the new majority whip, expressed that viewpoint: "O'Neill has extraordinary skills and is a bridge to many people. The Democratic party needs that." To others, particularly many liberals, the Speaker was seen as an ineffective leader, a poor articulator of Democratic policy positions, and too prone to accede to the demands of the conservative wing of the party.

O'Neill's posture toward rising CDF influence conformed to his customary style of party leadership. In general, he accommodated the CDF. Thus, in the contest over the Budget Committee chair, the Speaker conspicuously neither gave a personal endorsement nor sought a Steering and Policy Committee endorsement for any candidate, as had been done on behalf of Robert Giaimo in the previous Congress. His careful neutrality reflected the top priority he assigned to reducing factional friction within the party.

THE FIRST BUDGET RESOLUTION FIGHT: FEBRUARY - MAY 1981

Reagan Sets the Agenda

President Reagan set the agenda for the next session of Congress in his inaugural address on January 20. He devoted most of his speech on the west front of the Capitol to the economy and the federal budget.

Reagan's strategy was to keep Congress focused on his budget and tax proposals by not sending other major proposals to Capitol Hill until action on the budget was completed. This strategy contrasted sharply with that adopted by President Carter who, in his first year in office, sent many major pieces of legislation to Congress. As events turned out, Reagan's effort to set the agenda proved highly successful.

The administration attempted to create an early stampede of support for its budget plans immediately after assuming office. On February 5, President Reagan appeared on prime time television and claimed that an "economic calamity of tremendous proportions" awaited the nation if his budget, not yet formally disclosed, was not adopted promptly by Congress. Soon thereafter newspaper editors were invited to the White House for briefings on the budget. Cabinet members made over a dozen appearances on interview programs in the following three weeks, all stressing budget issues. The effort was capstoned by Reagan's February 18 speech before a joint session of Congress in which he outlined his "Program of Economic Recovery." On the following day, over 450 supporters of the administration met at the White House to plan and gain publicity for a "grass-roots" effort to encourage congressional support for Reagan's program. This well-orchestrated administration effort served to stimulate positive public response and mute negative reactions, especially because the budget issue was cast in terms of reducing the size and waste of government rather than in terms of the funding cuts in specific programs. In fact, many Democrats complained that even constituents slated to lose benefits from federal programs were supporting the President's programs.

The Democratic Response

Speaker O'Neill provided no hard-hitting response to the administration's proposals because he feared, in light of Reagan's great popularity, that such actions would only create a backlash against Democrats. Following his dicta that "all politics is local" and "all politics is timing," O'Neill hoped that the public would soon realize the implications of the budget cuts and that the public's support for the program would dwindle. Democrats would then have a "crack in the president's armor" to exploit. Additionally, some felt that the administration had placed the burden on Congress to move on the budget proposals, making sharp criticism from the Speaker look like partisan nit-picking or even obstructionism, the "politics as usual" the President had warned about in his speeches. As a result, O'Neill's public response during February and most of March was limited to low-profile, untelevised press conferences prior to the opening of each session of the House, at which his most frequent complaint was simply that Reagan's budget proposals were too ambiguous to respond to in detail.

Nevertheless, Speaker O'Neill did attempt to draw attention to the negative impact of the budget proposals by indirect means. First, with the help of Budget Committee Democrats, he frequently encouraged the press to study and report the substance of the administration's individual proposals. Second, he repeatedly but quietly urged committee and subcommittee chairs to hold hearings on the budget proposals. Hearings would force administration officials to outline and defend their proposals publicly and also would provide interest groups a forum from which to protest the budget cuts.

In contrast to O'Neill's approach, Majority Leader Wright, one of the most articulate members of the House, frequently lashed out at statements made by administration officials. He also took it upon himself to prepare and distribute to Democrats a set of questions and answers criticizing the administration's budget and economic claims. Wright's aggressive role was not the result of a collective leadership decision. Indeed, the Speaker's staff was disturbed by Wright's "hit and miss approach to the budget cuts" and his failure to "project a coherent stance." O'Neill gave other leaders a great deal of freedom—he could not really do otherwise—and the other leaders, including Wright, usually but not always followed the cues from O'Neill's actions.

The major responsibility for crafting a Democratic response was assumed by Budget Committee Chairman Jim Jones, who regularly discussed budget strategy with O'Neill and other party leaders. By the end of February, Jones was committed to devising budget cuts nearly as extensive as those proposed by the administration, although the cuts would be made where and how the Democrats saw fit to make them. The Speaker made it clear that the Democratic alternative to be supported by the leadership would be drafted by Jones and the Budget Committee Democrats. What Jones and O'Neill were seeking to construct was a first budget resolution which might attract the support of enough conservative Democrats, and perhaps a few Republicans, to win on the floor of the House. For Jones, at least, this approach was more than mere political expedience; he later argued that his plan was a good "transitional program" for the party as it moved to a position of greater fiscal responsibility while continuing its commitment to meeting the social needs of the nation. O'Neill also believed that the public was demanding a new direction in federal spending, although he personally dreaded the actions he felt that demand dictated.

Democratic Frustration Increases

In March, just as Jones began organized discussions with House Democrats and with dozens of interest groups seeking to devise the

Democratic budget alternative, 40 members of the CDF met with President Reagan over breakfast at the White House. Many of them informed the President of their support for even deeper cuts in federal spending than he had proposed. Phil Gramm and other conservatives had prepared a list which tallied to about $11 billion worth of additional cuts. This event led party leaders and Budget Committee Democrats to conclude privately that the only chance of beating Reagan would be to follow Jones's approach of matching Reagan's aggregate level of cuts but redirecting the cuts in ways that would leave intact many programs Reagan would radically alter or eliminate.

At about the same time, some Democrats, including a couple of committee chairs, voiced angry complaints about a "timid leadership and a runaway Budget Committee chairman determined to sell us out in the false hope of gaining conservative votes." One committee chair claimed that the party was developing such a "weak-kneed" image as to undercut the ability of all Democrats to make credible criticisms of the administration. Important lobbyists, such as one from the AFL-CIO, expressed dismay that the Democratic leadership was not more vigorously resisting cuts in programs vital to the people they represented. The absence of a more aggressive opposition by Democratic leaders made it more difficult to stimulate their rank-and-file members and other lobbyists to work for the Democratic cause on the budget.

Further irritating liberals, Majority Leader Wright made the headlines in mid-March by cosponsoring a bill with CDF stalwart Phil Gramm and Republican Whip Trent Lott that mandated a balanced budget in fiscal 1984. While Wright had authored similar legislation in the past, partly out of personal conviction and partly for "home consumption," his action gave the impression of disarray among Democratic party leaders. A Michigan Democrat commented that the episode confirmed his fear that he was "aboard a rudderless ship," and the *Washington Post* headline read "Wright, O'Neill Split on Balanced Budget." O'Neill's only public observation about Wright's move—which was somewhat of a surprise to him—was a curt comment to reporters that he had not seen the bill.

The frustration felt by many Democrats was apparent in the efforts of the committees in mid-March to prepare for the Budget Committee their "views and estimates" on spending in programs within their jurisdiction. Most committee Democrats felt that their efforts were futile because Jones intended, contrary to the wishes of the Democratic majorities on most of the committees, to include deep cuts in the first budget resolution. The committees eventually reported, but the Education and Labor Committee made a symbolic protest by recommending substantial increases in spending for the social service and education programs within its purview.

Toward the end of March, Speaker O'Neill prepared "to take off the gloves" and attack Reagan's program more vigorously, partly in reaction to the pressures within his own party but also because political conditions had begun to shift in a favorable direction. The media were now reporting the impact of the cuts, often in the form of case studies of persons who would be adversely affected by them. Committee hearings had publicized the details of the budget and several studies had challenged Reagan's argument that the reductions were evenhanded in their effects. O'Neill reported that his mail had finally begun to turn against Reagan's budget plans and noted that Reagan's performance ratings in public opinion polls had begun to slip.

O'Neill's plan to press the attack in a speech before the AFL-CIO Building and Construction Trades conference during the week of March 30 had to be aborted after Reagan was wounded in an assassination attempt after a speech before the same group. Public and media attention to the shooting, together with the outpouring of sympathy for the President, halted what little momentum the critics of Reagan's budget plans had managed to build. Columnist David Broder declared that "the honeymoon has ended and a new legend has been born." In fact, Reagan's job approval rating showed an increase of 11 percentage points by the end of the week. O'Neill had to cancel his speech and thus relinquish the opportunity to seize the reins of his party's counteroffensive, just a week before Jones planned to unveil the Democratic budget alternative.

The Democratic Alternative

By the first week of April, Jones had completed his version of the first budget resolution. Called the chair's "mark," Jones's proposal was the starting point for the Budget Committee's deliberations. Although the proposal was initially developed by Jones alone, to the dismay of other Budget Committee Democrats, he achieved a consensus among all but one of the Budget Committee Democrats by the time he announced his plan publicly. His plan was reported by the Budget Committee with few major changes during the first full week of April. Phil Gramm was the only Democrat on the committee who voted with the Republicans against reporting the resolution to the floor of the House.

The resolution reported by the Budget Committee, which was endorsed by the Democratic leadership of the House, reflected Jones's effort to gain the support of all elements of the party. It assumed that:

— none of the block grant proposals of the administration would be adopted;

— nearly all federal programs would continue to exist, although many would suffer funding reductions—sometimes severe ones—but provided for about $20 billion more spending than the administration proposed for fiscal 1982;

— Congress would enact a smaller tax cut, resulting in higher revenues and a smaller deficit; and

— defense spending would increase nearly as much as the administration proposed.

The protection of domestic programs would attract moderates and liberals, it was hoped, while the deficit and defense features would attract conservatives. The defense spending increase, however, did not quite match the administration's plan. In order to attract conservatives, Jones and O'Neill left open the possibility of a leadership-endorsed floor amendment to the committee's resolution to bring the defense increase up to administration-requested levels. Finally, the committee's proposal included reconciliation instructions to 14 House authorizing committees to report legislation saving nearly $16 billion in spending (outlays) for fiscal 1982 and larger savings for the following fiscal years.

During the markup (line-by-line consideration) of the first budget resolution, the Budget Committee rejected a substitute budget plan offered by Phil Gramm by a vote of 17-13. The 12 Republicans on the committee and Gramm voted in support of his substitute against all other Democrats. The Gramm substitute accepted nearly all of the Reagan budget and added over $5 billion in additional spending reductions. The administration openly backed Gramm's effort and within two weeks President Reagan publicly endorsed what became known as the "Gramm-Latta" substitute, named after Gramm and the ranking Republican on the Budget Committee, Delbert L. Latta of Ohio. The Gramm-Latta substitute included a tax cut of the size the administration had proposed and reconciliation instructions to 17 House committees to produce over $36 billion in savings for fiscal 1982, over $20 billion more savings than the Jones resolution. The large Gramm-Latta reconciliation package also set a scale of projected savings for future years which, taken together with the 1982 savings, would necessitate dozens of permanent changes in authorizing statutes not required by the version reported by the Budget Committee.

The Campaign for the First Budget Resolution

A fatalistic atmosphere pervaded most Democratic leadership offices during the Easter recess that followed the Budget Committee markup. O'Neill left for Australia and New Zealand to attend official ceremonies, raising the ire of many Democrats who believed that he should have remained in Washington to help organize the Democratic campaign for Jones's resolution. Members also complained that O'Neill had not created a leadership task force on the budget resolution, as had been standard operating procedure since he became Speaker.

Nevertheless, Wright assumed the personal responsibility of telephoning all of his southern brethren in a desperate effort to gain their support. Some senior Democrats also met informally with interest group representatives. While some groups were already actively lobbying and attempting to arouse constituent pressure on members, many groups were hesitant to devote their resources to a legislative fight to which the Democratic leadership did not appear fully committed. Some groups were not willing to support any resolution, Democratic or otherwise, that drastically reduced the funding for programs important to them.

In contrast to the feeble Democratic efforts, the Reagan administration executed a "southern blitz" to enlist the support of Boll Weevils for the Gramm-Latta substitute. The White House arranged speeches and local television appearances in southern states for Vice President George Bush, former President Gerald Ford, several cabinet members, and well-known Republican members of Congress. President Reagan made phone calls to many House Democrats to ask for their vote. He received national media attention for speaking to a conservative Pennsylvania Democrat, Eugene Atkinson (who later switched parties), on a live local radio talk show when the representative, while still on the air, pledged his support for the Gramm-Latta substitute. Once again, newspaper editors, state and local politicians, and corporate executives were brought to the White House to receive publicized briefings on the budget. The Republicans also began to contact major contributors to the campaigns of southern Democrats to encourage them to ask their beneficiaries to support the President's program. Finally, the President appeared before a joint session of Congress on Tuesday, April 28, just after the Congress returned from its recess, making his first public appearance since the assassination attempt. He received a hero's welcome and proceeded to argue for the "bipartisan" Gramm-Latta substitute.

With the vote on the first budget resolution little more than a week away, informal head-counts showed that the outlook was bleak for the Democrats. O'Neill made pessimistic public statements that were interpreted as "throwing in the towel." However, the Speaker, working with Jones and other party leaders, continued to explore ways to attract conservatives. One result was a proposal by Jones, presented at a meeting of the Democratic whips, to support floor amendments to the Budget Committee resolution which would (1) match the administration's higher defense spending figures and (2) provide for a delay in the personal income tax cut until fiscal 1983 (and proceeding with the 1982 business tax cut), permitting a balanced budget in fiscal 1982. There was a hostile reaction to Jones's proposal, especially to the tax cut delay.

After learning about the strong opposition of Dan Rostenkowski of Illinois, the chair of the Ways and Means Committee who had been working hard to devise a Democratic tax cut alternative, O'Neill vetoed the tax cut delay idea. The leadership decided to proceed with an amendment to bring the defense figure up to the level provided in the Gramm-Latta substitute.

The disappointing results of a whip poll were reported by Majority Whip Tom Foley six days before the expected vote on the Gramm-Latta substitute: 155 Democrats were committed to the Budget Committee resolution developed by Jones, but at least 26 were committed to vote for the Gramm-Latta substitute and most of the remainder reported that they were undecided. The conclusion was inescapable. If the Republicans held ranks, as they were expected to do, the Gramm-Latta substitute would be adopted. Moreover, it was clear that many of the members reporting indecision intended to vote for the Gramm-Latta substitute but were unwilling to say so when asked by their whips. Further erosion could be expected, therefore, when it became obvious to members that the substitute version would win.

In the view of many Democrats, the only chance for defeating or emasculating the Gramm-Latta proposal was to structure the rule for floor consideration of the first budget resolution in a favorable manner. They urged the Speaker to have the Rules Committee report an open rule, or at least a "modified closed" rule, which would permit floor amendments to the Gramm-Latta substitute. Amendments, they argued, would strip away the political protection afforded Gramm-Latta supporters in being able to vote for the consolidated package of budget cuts by a simple up-or-down vote on the substitute plan. By forcing Republicans to go on record on the drastic spending reductions in specific programs, they hoped that some Republicans—particularly those from the Midwest and Northeast—would find it too risky to vote against funds for programs vital to their districts.

O'Neill and Wright felt that if the Gramm-Latta substitute already had majority support, any rule providing for amendments to it could not gain a majority on the floor. In their view, Democrats would only suffer unnecessary criticism for employing parliamentary tricks, obstructing a straightforward vote on Reagan's plan. As the Speaker explained, the House would have opportunities to vote on spending for specific programs when the reconciliation legislation came to the floor in June. As a result, O'Neill planned to request that the Rules Committee report a "modified closed" rule permitting, in order, votes on a leadership-backed amendment to increase defense spending, a substitute drafted by the Black Caucus, a liberal substitute drafted by Representative Obey, the Gramm-Latta substitute, and finally the Budget Committee version. No further amendments would be allowed.

As Reagan offered members the use of his box at the Kennedy Center and wined and dined Democrats and wavering Republicans at the White House, passing out presidential cufflinks as they left, Democratic leaders found themselves in an increasingly helpless position. The leadership and Budget Committee Democrats continued to talk to uncommitted Democrats and encouraged interest groups and same-state Democrats to approach northern Republicans, but the results were disheartening. The 25 Republicans who were contacted on a daily basis remained unconverted. Meanwhile, two Boll Weevils on the Budget Committee who had supported the Jones version announced that they now intended to vote for the Gramm-Latta substitute because of political pressure from home. In addition, Senator Robert Byrd, the Democratic leader in the Senate, declared that he would vote for the administration's plan because "the people want to give the President a chance." O'Neill told a *Boston Globe* reporter that he was rereading *The Battle of Bunker Hill.* By the day of the vote on the Gramm-Latta substitute, O'Neill had concluded that about 70 Democrats would defect from the party.

The Vote on the First Budget Resolution

The long debate on the budget resolution was highlighted by the satiric comment of John Dingell, a Michigan Democrat, on the "bipartisan" nature of the Gramm-Latta substitute.

> You know, this comment about how the proposal is bipartisan reminds me of a little story.
>
> This fellow went into a restaurant and said, "I would like some rabbit stew."
>
> The fellow said, "Well, we don't have any rabbit stew, but we got some horse and rabbit stew."
>
> So he got his bowl of it, and it tasted awful. He said, "My God, this is awful. What kind of stew is this?"
>
> The fellow said, "It is horse and rabbit stew."
>
> He said, "What is the recipe?"
>
> The fellow said, "Well, it is one to one."
>
> He said, "What do you mean?"
>
> He said, "Well, you take one horse and one rabbit," and that is about how bipartisan this thing is. You got one horse and one rabbit.

The defense increase amendment endorsed by the Democratic leadership was adopted by a voice vote on Tuesday, while the Black Caucus and Obey substitutes were defeated on Wednesday by votes of 69-356 and 119-303, respectively. On Thursday, the debate on the Gramm-Latta substitute ended with dramatic speeches by Jack F. Kemp of New York and Minority Leader Robert H. Michel on the Republican side and Jim Wright and Tip O'Neill for the Democrats.

O'Neill's speech, which was not delivered well, concluded with a pointed plea to certain Democrats:

> I have been in public life for 46 years and the day I have to look at the next election, instead of looking at America, then I do not want to be in public life. I hate to think that in the members of this body there would be such shallowness.

The 15-minute roll-call vote was anticlimactic. After about 35 Democrats had voted for the Gramm-Latta substitute and all Republicans appeared to be falling into line, the expected wave of additional Democratic votes for the substitute came. In the end, 63 Democrats voted for the substitute and, with no Republican desertions, the final tally was 253-176. Of those who voted against the leadership, five were members of the Steering and Policy Committee, two were committee chairs, and 28 were subcommittee chairs. Thirteen members of the CDF stayed with the leadership, but it was still a decisive victory for Reagan. Within a week, the Senate passed its version of the first budget resolution, a conference committee resolved the differences between the House and Senate versions with little difficulty, and both chambers ratified the conference report.

A *Washington Post* headline on the day following the key House vote read "Shattered: Democratic Coalition Falls to Pieces in First Test With Republican Reagan." While it appeared that there were only 30 to 35 Democrats genuinely committed to the Gramm-Latta substitute—no more than had voted for Republican budget-cutting amendments in the previous year—the avalanche of criticism about the Democratic leadership testified to the accuracy of the headline. Several Democrats went public with their criticisms. As reported in the *Washington Post*, Parren J. Mitchell, chair of the Small Business Committee, asserted:

> We who are liberals are not going to pull the Democrats' chestnuts out of the fire. You'll see liberals pulling away from the Democratic leadership. I don't know what our alternatives are, but it's not enough for us to play conscience of the party and always lose.

In stark constrast, the same May 8, 1981, article quoted these scathing remarks of an unidentified party leader:

> the liberals have been asking for this. Reagan is the product of a decade of growing concern about the cost and efficiency of a lot of programs and regulations and about the neglect of the military balance in the world. The Democratic party has given greater weight to the liberal wing than its numbers deserved, and groups that held the party's conscience—women and minorities—have vetoed rational moves to adjust our policy. Well, that veto is over.

Liberals and Boll Weevils alike thus came away from the vote pointing fingers and saying "I told you so."

THE RECONCILIATION PROCESS: MAY - JULY 1981

The Process

The adopted budget resolution and the Budget Act together outlined the mechanics of the reconciliation process. Each committee identified in the budget resolution was instructed to devise legislative language which would reduce federal spending (outlays) by a specified amount. For example, the House Education and Labor Committee was instructed to make changes in programs under its jurisdiction which would save $11.2 billion from projected spending for fiscal 1982. These entitlement and authorization changes would be sent to the Budget Committee which would report them to the floor without making any changes.

The decision had been made earlier to package the committees' reports in a single reconciliation bill. If committees failed to achieve the specified levels of savings according to guidelines issued by the Congressional Budget Office, or otherwise took actions opposed by members of the House, the Budget Committee or other members could attempt to amend the reconciliation bill on the floor. Alternatively, the Budget Committee could simply accept the savings reported by the committees, even though they were less than the required level, and then seek to prevent House members from challenging the bill by securing a special order from the Rules Committee waiving points of order for violations of the reconciliation instructions. The committees were instructed to report their language to the Budget Committee by June 12, with floor action set to follow soon thereafter.

Debate Over the Rule Begins

Speaker O'Neill took a more aggressive approach after the vote on the first budget resolution. He appeared to be reacting, at least in part, to the critics of his leadership; he declared at a caucus meeting, for example, that "this old dog wants to learn new tricks." O'Neill also recognized Reagan's new vulnerability on issues that began to receive media attention immediately after the budget vote, especially tax cuts and Social Security reform. For the first time in several years, the Speaker accepted invitations to appear on television and radio news interview programs, at which he gladly fielded questions about his leadership and responded with strong defenses of his actions over the previous several months. Reflecting his greater activism, O'Neill promised that when the reconciliation bill came to the floor in June there would be votes to retain the authority and funding for several domestic programs, even if such actions violated the reconciliation instructions.

As chair of the Budget Committee, Jones took the traditional chair's role of protecting the budget process when he argued that Democrats should not attempt to subvert the reconciliation instructions in any way. He insisted that Democrats could not afford to be perceived as "unraveling" the budget cuts ordered by the first budget resolution. Consequently, Jones disagreed with O'Neill that floor amendments should be permitted to restore funding for programs that committees might decide to cut. Except for a possible Budget Committee amendment to achieve savings that committees might fail to report, Jones urged that no amendments to the reconciliation bill should be allowed on the floor.

The appropriate rule for the floor consideration of the reconciliation bill was the subject of continuous discussion among House Democrats during the last two weeks of May and the first two weeks of June. While most Democrats cheered O'Neill's position at a meeting of the Democratic caucus on May 20, several counterarguments were made by various liberals and moderates:

— O'Neill's approach would allow many Republicans to "get off the hook" by giving them an opportunity to vote for the funding of popular programs;

— While O'Neill's approach would allow desirable amendments to restore funding for important domestic programs, only amendments for programs catering to the middle-class constituents of Republicans would pass and restoration amendments for programs for the poor would fail; and

— "Zero sum" amendments which made offsetting cuts in programs such as defense to compensate for restorations in social programs should be proposed, allowing the overall savings targets to be met.

The arguments for some modification of O'Neill's approach were convincing to many Democrats, even among those originally favoring O'Neill's strategy. As May ended, many Democrats were unsure about the best approach to take on the rule.

The Reconciliation Alternatives

Even though meeting the reconciliation instructions was a distasteful task for many Democratic committee members, most committees complied. (One notable divergence from the Reagan plan was the absence of block grants in the committee packages; the relevant committees proposed instead to retain the structure of most programs but at reduced funding levels.) Problems did develop on two committees, however. When Chairman John Dingell of the Energy and Commerce Committee found he could not attract enough committee support for his package of cuts because of conservative Democratic opposition, he decided not to report any reconciliation language and to ask Jones to include his package in a Budget Committee amendment or substitute. Chairman Carl Perkins and other Education and Labor Democrats initially considered refusing to recommend any cuts but finally approved over $12 billion of reductions, relying upon an "absolute guarantee" from O'Neill and Rules Chairman Bolling that amendments would be allowed on the floor. The committee Democrats met their reconciliation instructions by adopting a strategy of making deeper cuts in program funding they believed they could successfully restore on the floor, while cutting the funding for other programs less severely. O'Neill confirmed his private guarantee when he publicly identified six specific budget reductions made by the Education and Labor Committee that he intended to open up to floor amendments.

The reconciliation bill, which made detailed changes in hundreds of federal programs, was the largest bill in the history of Congress. The accompanying committee report came in three volumes totaling about 1,200 pages. (The final conference report was the product of over 250 conferees working in 58 subconferences.) Members of Congress were being asked to evaluate and vote on a single bill affecting programs which had been enacted in hundreds of separate bills over the years.

Republicans and conservative Democrats developed an alternative package, dubbed "Gramm-Latta II," which proposed deeper cuts and touched on nearly every committee involved in reconciliation. Its purported rationale was that the committees had sometimes reported changes which did not actually achieve the claimed savings or had failed to adopt many of the major administration proposals which would save money far into the future, such as the block grants. The Republican plan also included a substantial number of "sweeteners" to attract support which provided for greater spending in certain programs than was requested in the committee reports.

Faced with the possibility that Gramm-Latta II might undercut the reconciliation work of the House committees and enable passage of the administration's program to be determined by a single floor vote, House Democratic leaders became more favorable to the closed rule position advanced by Jones. Chairman Perkins was urged to persuade his Education and Labor Committee Democrats to revise their reconciliation report so that no floor amendments would be necessary, and the committee did so quickly. Chairman Dingell also tried, but without success, to have his Energy and Commerce Committee report a package of cuts. Responding to the growing consensus within the party for a closed rule, Speaker O'Neill changed his position. "Our boys want it closed," O'Neill observed at a meeting of the Democratic caucus, "... this is a democracy. We go by the will of the group." For the same reason, Rules Chairman Bolling, who personally opposed the strategy of closing off liberal amendments, agreed to follow the lead of the Speaker and the party and told the caucus:

> I have spent a couple of decades trying to change the committee I chair from a tyrannical committee which killed more good legislation and probably caused ... virtually every problem that society has had. . . . Every program that mitigated the pains of the weak was held up in that committee forever. Too late—everything we did in the social field was too late. It was the ability of the reactionary coalition of Democrats and Republicans, from 1937 on, to bottle up any good legislation, until we broke that tyranny in 1961. And my dilemma is that I don't propose as an individual to reimpose that tyranny no matter how bad I consider your judgment.

The Rules Committee actually reported, as the leadership and Budget Committee requested, a rule governing the floor debate on the reconciliation bill which permitted a Budget Committee substitute to include the Dingell package from the Energy and Commerce Committee and other technical changes. The Republicans would also be allowed, as a matter of fairness, an amendment on the Energy and Commerce portion since they did not get a vote in committee.

Down to the Wire

Many conservative Democrats who voted with the President on the first budget resolution made it clear that they would not support Gramm-Latta II because they believed it represented a challenge to the institutional role of House committees in evaluating and writing legislation. Representative Bo Ginn of Georgia, for example, reported on the results of a meeting of the Conservative Democratic Forum: "Many of us are senior members of these committees and had a major voice in making those cuts. We told Mr. Gramm that we were tired of being manipulated by the White House." Informal head-counts showed that 25 or 30 of the 63 Democrats who voted for the original Gramm-Latta substitute would now support their party leadership on the closed rule and on the bill itself.

Noting the declining support among conservative Democrats and the signs of potential defections of midwestern and northeastern Republicans who were afraid that Gramm-Latta II cuts would cause them political trouble at home, Republican and Boll Weevil strategists decided on June 11 to pursue a more limited substitute. They chose to focus on the reconciliation recommendations of a handful of committees rather than all of them, but still to include certain sweeteners for the more liberal Republicans. The Republicans claimed that about $20 billion of additional cuts would be made by their limited substitute beyond those in the Democratic package by including block grants and deeper cuts in food stamps, student aid, school lunch, low-income housing, and other programs.

The greater reductions made by the Republican substitute immediately stimulated Democratic leaders to consider giving the Republicans the chance to propose a series of amendments, rather than closing out or permitting them one broad substitute, on the theory that the separate amendments could be defeated and that such an approach would eliminate the developing Republican criticism of the Democratic "gag rule." Some Democrats guessed that Republicans would not even bring up separate amendments in order to avoid having to go on the record for specific cuts.

This shift in leadership thinking on the rule was not well received by many Democrats—after all, the leadership had just rejected the idea of liberal amendments, contrary to O'Neill's original promise. But a whip poll showed that the Democrats could not overcome the Republican opposition to a closed rule even with the support of the vast majority of Democrats. Consequently, the leadership proceeded with their newest strategy and had the Rules Committee report a rule providing for six separate Republican amendments and a motion to recommit the reconciliation bill to committee with instructions to add block grants to the bill. With this rule, all of the major components of the Republican plan, with the exception of the sweeteners, would reach the floor. The Democrats were then in a position to claim that they had accommodated the Republican demands in the most democratic way by allowing the House to exercise its will on each of the separate amendments and that they had taken the fiscally responsible action of not allowing amendments to increase spending.

Reacting to this shift in Democratic strategy, Republicans sought the defeat or amendment of the Democratic rule so that the Gramm-Latta II substitute could be voted on as a whole. Republicans made dozens of changes in their substitute in the last few days before the vote on the rule in order to make their alternative more attractive to wavering Democrats and Republicans. This June 24th scene (described by a *Washington Post* writer) was typical:

> At 4:15 p.m. Wednesday, panic reigned in Room 2174 of the Rayburn House Office Building. Everyone was in a state of near exhaustion. For the fourth time in a week, the minority staff of the House Education and Labor Committee had been asked to rework its portion of Gramm-Latta II. . . .
>
> Sandra Glover, [minority staff director Charles] Radcliffe's administrative assistant, was cutting and pasting at her desk. Beth Berman, another staffer, punched at a pocket calculator in one corner, revising budget figures. Four other aides frantically paged through huge stacks of paper.
>
> Radcliffe sank into the couch, pencilling changes in the bill. To meet complaints from Rep. Shirley Chisholm (D-N.Y.), he changed the words "educationally deprived" on page 69 to "children from low-income families"—to make sure the extra bucks don't head toward rich

kids who happen to be doing poorly in school. Rep. Margaret M. Heckler (R-Mass.) was worried about programs for women, so Radcliffe added some words making it clear that provisions of the Women's Equity Act of 1978 would not be affected by the bill.

President Reagan, reacting to the Democratic rule, accused Democrats of "parliamentary shenanigans," "sabotage," and "backroom politics," and helped promote a quickly organized campaign to amend the rule to allow the full Gramm-Latta II substitute to receive a single vote. On Wednesday night, Reagan phoned at least 16 Democrats, some more than once, and continued to phone members on Thursday, the day of the vote, pulling them into the cloakrooms from the floor of the House to receive the calls. Last-minute deals were made with many Democrats and Republicans by Reagan and his aides. An agreement was reached with Midwest and Northeast Republican moderates, for example, to retain higher funding for Medicaid, energy assistance for the poor, mass transit, and other programs important to their region in exchange for their support for Gramm-Latta II. Louisiana Democrats John Breaux and W. J. "Billy" Tauzin openly reported an administration commitment to accept sugar price supports in exchange for their votes. A front-page story in the *Washington Post* reported that Breaux later said he "went with the best deal," indicating that while his vote was not for sale, "it could be rented." Similarly, a *New York Times* article quoted Budget Committee Chairman Jones as saying, "They're making deals like crazy in the cloakroom. . . . It's like a tobacco auction back there."

Gramm-Latta II Wins

Thursday, June 25, was the day of the vote on the rule. The initial critical vote would be on a procedural motion, namely, the motion on the "previous question" with respect to the Democratic rule reported by the Rules Committee. (A motion on the previous question is a parliamentary tactic which, when carried, has the effect of cutting off all debate and forcing a vote on the subject originally at hand. The previous question is sometimes moved in order to prevent amendments.) If this motion was adopted, debate on the rule would be closed and amendments to it would be prohibited. The first objective of the Republicans and their allies among the Boll Weevils was, therefore, to defeat the motion on the previous question. Only after that was accomplished could they then propose an amendment to the rule permitting a vote on their reconciliation substitute as a whole. This was a better strategy than defeating the Democratic rule itself since House rejection of the rule would result simply in sending the rule back to the Democratically controlled Rules Committee. By the time debate on the rule began, Majority Whip Foley estimated the Democrats would win the vote on the previous question but would lose the subsequent vote on the rule. Phil Gramm, still leading the way for the Boll Weevils, claimed that he had commitments from 23 Democrats to vote against the motion on the previous question.

With the House floor and galleries filled to capacity, the roll-call vote on Rules Chairman Bolling's previous question motion was dramatic. Four minutes into the vote, the count was 135-143 against the motion, with 18 Democrats voting against the motion. Five minutes later, six more Democrats had joined with the Republicans and the count was 172-177. Members on both sides made last-minute pleas to colleagues to switch their votes if necessary. At the end, the motion was defeated, 210-217; 29 Democrats, all but three of them from the South, voted against their party leadership.

The House proceeded to adopt the previous question motion on the Republican amendment to the rule—which permitted their substitute but no Democratic amendments—on a 219-208 vote. The amendment and then the amended rule were adopted by similar votes. A simple up-or-down vote on Gramm-Latta II was therefore the next order of business. The Republican rule had not specified the content for the substitute it had put in order, however, so the Republicans were free to change it until they moved its adoption.

The vote on Gramm-Latta II was set for the following afternoon. Not available until 11:00 that morning, just six hours before the vote on it, the substitute came in a condition that was an embarrassment even to the Republican leadership. The document was approximately 1,000 pages in length but had no table of contents, index, or pagination. It was simply a photocopy of separately written and typed titles. On many of its pages, provisions were crossed out or new provisions were written in by hand. The miserable physical condition of the substitute enhanced the Democratic argument that the Republican approach made a travesty of the legislative process, an argument targeted at senior southern Democrats who took special pride in their legislative craftsmanship and in maintaining the institutional integrity of the House of Representatives. Nonetheless, the Democrats were again defeated on a close vote, 217-211.

Liberal Democrats left Washington for the Fourth of July recess in frustration and disappointment. Some were thinking of ways to punish the Democratic defectors, but practical considerations suggested that little could be done, at least during the 97th Congress:

— expelling defectors from the caucus would risk pushing them into the Republican party and losing control of the House;

— booting defectors from their committees would require a vote of the House, a vote which the Democrats might lose;

— stripping defectors of their seniority on committees would make many of them martyrs while providing little punishment for junior members such as Phil Gramm; and

— taking any significant disciplinary action might permanently alienate members whose votes could be needed later.

Speaker O'Neill, depressed by the action of Democratic colleagues in undercutting his role in shaping the rule for floor consideration of legislation, pointedly observed, "In decency, some of those fellows should resign from the Democratic caucus." Yet he and other party leaders worked to delay until September a caucus meeting sought by some liberals to consider disciplinary actions. Party leaders hoped that the desire for retribution would fade by September, especially if the party was victorious on the tax cut bill due to come to the floor in late July.

The Reconciliation Conference

Republicans were faced with the decision either to go ahead with the conference to work out the differences between the House and Senate versions of the reconciliation bill or to have the Senate, which passed its reconciliation bill first, simply adopt the House version. Office of Management and Budget Director David Stockman preferred that the Senate adopt the House bill which, in his view, came much closer to the administration's budget position. Moreover, a conference committee, with most of the House conferees being Democrats, might undo much of what was gained in Gramm-Latta II. Congressional Republicans preferred to have a conference in order to clean up the drafting errors in the hastily drawn Gramm-Latta II and many hoped to moderate the cuts in some areas. In the end, a conference committee was appointed; it was composed of 208 members of the House and 72 senators divided into 58 "subconferences" to deal with separate portions of the nearly 250 differences between the House and Senate bills. (Speaker O'Neill, following Chairman Jones's recommendations, failed to appoint Phil Gramm to the conference committee. Jones said that it was simply a matter of seniority on the Budget Committee.)

The House Democratic leadership considered a strategy of obstructing or delaying the conference, but rejected it because the Republican Senate might decide to adopt the House version, which was less palatable to the Democrats than the likely conference report. The only issue which threatened the reconciliation conference concerned the repeal of the Social Security minimum benefit, which both the House and Senate bills had adopted in accordance with President Reagan's recommendation. When the Democratic leadership learned that the Republicans were considering deletion of the minimum benefit repeal to avoid the likely political fallout from the repeal, they moved to beat the Republicans to the punch. Majority Leader Wright sought unanimous consent on the floor of the House for the immediate consideration of a resolution urging "that the necessary steps be taken to insure that Social Security benefits are not reduced for those currently receiving them." Phil Gramm objected, thus denying unanimous consent, but the objective of drawing media attention to the Democratic effort to protect Social Security from the budget-cutting Republicans was achieved. Although the conference eliminated the minimum benefit, the Democrats had the administration on the defensive for the first time. Polls soon showed that the Social Security issue was hurting Reagan's standing with the public.

During the last week of July, as the conference committee was completing its work, 151 members of the House, including some Republicans, cosponsored a resolution to require the House conferees to go back to conference and strike the minimum benefit repeal provision. In a separate move, Rules Committee Chairman Bolling sought to force deletion of the repeal provision by threatening to refuse to report a rule for the conference report until the conference restored the minimum benefit. Acting on word that Senate Majority Leader Howard Baker was prepared to retaliate by having the Senate take up and pass the House bill, Speaker O'Neill persuaded Bolling to accept a rule to bring the conference report to the floor, with an agreement that the rule would also provide for a separate bill to restore the minimum benefit. The House easily adopted the rule, passed the bill restoring the minimum benefit on a 404-20 vote, and accepted the conference report on a voice vote. The Senate subsequently passed a restoration bill, but with other provisions; a conference later restored the benefit only for current beneficiaries, eliminating it for future recipients, and both houses agreed.

DEMOCRATIC DEFEAT ON THE TAX BILL

The battle over Reagan's tax cut proposals ended just before the reconciliation bill was enacted—with equally disappointing results for the Democrats. During the early summer, the administration limited its proposed cut to a 25 percent cut (5 percent in fiscal 1982 and 10 percent in each of the following two years) from the original 30 percent plan, although the across-the-board nature of the cut was retained. The Democratic leadership had been optimistic about the tax cut fight and, at the staff's initiative, created a campaign with Ways and Means Committee Democrats to sell the Democratic alternative to news editors throughout the country. Speaker O'Neill played a key role in converting Ways and Means Chairman Dan Rostenkowski's bill from a simple percentage cut in personal income tax rates at all income levels to one targeted at middle- and lower-income levels. The Democratic measure provided for a total cut of 15 percent compared to the 25 percent across-the-board cut in the revised administration bill.

Nevertheless, by adding provisions to attract conservatives, Rostenkowski ended up with a bill many Democrats felt was not fundamentally different than the administration's proposal, particularly in its tax breaks for oil companies and large estates. The administration, however, again gained conservative Democratic support, again organized a massive campaign for its substitute (including a nationally televised speech by Reagan), and again struck a few deals on related and unrelated policy matters. The Republicans attracted 48 Democrats with their substitute, lost only one Republican, and carried their tax measure by a 238-195 vote on July 29. The administration had rolled over the Democratic leadership once again, achieving nearly all of the legislative goals Reagan had outlined in February.

The 1981 session ended, however, with the fortunes of the administration beginning to change. The economy entered a recession which forced drastically higher projections of federal deficits for the next few years. Rather than projecting a balanced budget in fiscal 1984, for example, even the administration conceded that the estimated 1984 deficit would be $162 billion. These revisions led the administration to seek an additional $8.4 billion cut in domestic program spending for fiscal 1982, which further delayed consideration of appropriation bills that had already been delayed because the appropriations committees were waiting for the reconciliation results. The appropriations bills were not passed by October 1, 1981, and the government operated under a continuing resolution until late November. (A continuing resolution is legislation enacted by Congress to provide budget authority for specific ongoing activities in cases where the regular appropriation has not been enacted by the beginning of the fiscal year.) Reagan vetoed the first effort to extend the continuing resolution because his $8.4 billion cut was not included, but eventually signed an extension which made over $4 billion in additional cuts for fiscal 1982. The House leadership did not offer strong opposition to the continuing resolution extension. The second budget resolution, which must be adopted before Congress can adjourn its session for the year, was nearly identical to the first resolution and was approved in December with little fanfare. By the end of 1981, the administration was forced to publicly give up the initial plan for a balanced budget by fiscal 1984. Budget officials began to consider much deeper spending cuts, even in defense and Social Security programs, and tax increases to hold down the deficits. "Reaganomics" still had to prove itself in both the economy and the polling booths.

SOME QUESTIONS TO EXPLORE

The Out-Party's Competitive Disadvantage

Unlike parliamentary systems where the majority in the "lower" house of the legislature determines control of the government, the separate election of the president, the Senate, and the House of Representatives permits divided control of government in the United States. Of the 18 congressional terms between World War II and 1980, eight were controlled by the "out-party," the party not controlling the White House. With the exception of the Congress elected in 1946, the Democrats have been the out-party with a Republican president. As the out-party in the 97th Congress, Democrats were nevertheless in an unusual position—in no Congress since the early 1930s has a party controlled one chamber of Congress but not either the White House or the other chamber. Such a position is a precarious one, placing the out-party at a great competitive disadvantage. In this section, we consider the nature of the out-party Democrats' disadvantage in 1981.

President Reagan took advantage of several political resources at his disposal:

— *Ability to set the public and congressional agenda.* The President's ready access to the media gave him a critical advantage over out-party leaders in defining the national policy agenda.

— *Use of the vast resources of the executive branch.* While Congress has acquired a large staff and support agencies during the last three decades, its decentralized structure provides the congressional leadership with only indirect access to those resources. Coordination is difficult and must be done on an ad hoc, temporary basis, inhibiting advance planning and the creation of publicity campaigns by the out-party.

— *Public appeal.* Contemporary presidents can ordinarily be counted on to be effective communicators. Congressional party leaders, on the other hand, achieve their positions because of their relationships with fellow members of Congress, not because they are "telegenic" or handle questions well on their feet. In 1981, the contrast could not have been more vivid: Ronald Reagan, former Hollywood star, versus "the old pol," Tip O'Neill.

— *Unity of policy leadership.* Congressional out-party leaders were less able than the administration to establish coherent policy positions because the primary responsibility for party policy was left in the hands of the chairs of major committees. The power that these chairs have over policy matters within their jurisdiction requires that the leadership defer to their judgment except in the most extreme circumstances. In 1981, this meant that the option of devising clearly distinct liberal alternatives to the Reagan program was never a real possibility for the House Democrats.

— *Use of the reconciliation procedure of the budget process.* As that process was employed in 1981, it allowed the President to package his budget cuts and programmatic changes in a single bill, further focusing his resources and public and congressional attention. Without the reconciliation procedure, the administration would have had to devise dozens of separate pieces of legislation. If multiple bills had been required, the Democratic leadership could have then utilized the full array of parliamentary and political resources at its disposal, varying its strategy from bill to bill, with much less public attention to individual items. The results almost certainly would have been considerably different from what actually happened in 1981.

— *Control of the Senate.* Republican control of the Senate allowed the administration to focus its resources and public attention on the House of Representatives, eliminated many points of delay and adverse publicity for the President's program, and reduced the tactical options of the out-party Democrats.

Consider the following questions:

— It could be argued that the out-party's competitive disadvantage vis-à-vis the president makes for an imbalance that undercuts the effectiveness of our two-party system. If that is so, can you suggest ways of strengthening the position of the out-party? For example, should the post of "out-party leader" be established by law, with salary and some authority? If that were done, how should that leader be selected and who would it likely be? Should the mass media be obligated to provide more time, or equal time, to the out-party as an offset to its continuing full coverage of the president's activities and positions?

— It can also be argued that the separation of powers and checks and balances system contains within it the potential for governmental stalemate. How does the evidence provided in this account of the 1981 battle over Reagan's budget proposals bear on that argument? If the Democrats had wanted to resist those proposals more fully, what could they have done about it? Why, in fact, didn't the Democrats use their control of the House to block Reagan's budget—and what does this tell you about the stalemate potential of checks and balances?

Party Leadership and Party Loyalty

The ability of the leadership to shape the behavior of rank-and-file members must be viewed in the context of members' calculations of the political costs and benefits of support for the leadership. For example, the leadership services that can be offered or withheld usually cannot outweigh potentially serious threats to a member's reelection chances.

For the Democratic leadership, therefore, conservative southern Democrats present a continuing problem of policy and voting deviance from the position of the majority of House Democrats. The congressional party leadership can only deal with the symptoms of its loose national coalition.

Budget resolutions present a special problem for House Democratic leaders. *By setting overall spending, revenue, and deficit/surplus levels for the federal government, budget resolutions encapsulate the fundamental conceptions of the role of the federal government in distributing and redistributing the resources of the American society.* As a result, they stimulate the fundamental cleavages in the House—and within the Democratic party. Republicans have sought to exploit this fact by introducing broad substitutes for all first budget resolutions in recent years. Many conservative Democrats have supported these substitutes, as they did in the 1981 budget fight. In 1978, for example, the Republican substitute attracted 58 Democratic votes while losing only one Republican vote, a result remarkably similar to the 1981 vote discussed in this study. With fewer Republicans in the House that year, the Democrats were still able to defeat the substitute by six votes.

Given this pattern of southern conservative defection, it is not surprising that the sensitive issue of party loyalty occasionally erupts within the ranks of congressional Democrats. Party loyalty became an unusually salient concern in 1981 because several southern members were openly conspiring against their own party leadership at a time when their votes were critical, the Republicans were successfully holding ranks, and the issues were of great personal importance to many Democrats. By the time House Democrats met in September 1981 to consider disciplinary action, however, party leaders had persuaded liberals not to pursue any immediate retribution. Instead, Majority Leader Jim Wright, without informing Speaker O'Neill in advance, presented the following guidelines:

(1) Democrats were to be granted amnesty for past votes and defectors were invited to "return to the fold in good standing";

(2) Democrats receiving chairs and assignments from the caucus to top committees, such as Appropriations, Budget, Rules, and Ways and Means, will be expected to act with a special sense of responsibility to the party;

(3) The Steering and Policy Committee will identify, and the Speaker will notify caucus members about, "litmus test" votes on significant issues which will be scrutinized by party leaders when members seek committee assignments and other favors from the party; and

(4) A distinction will be drawn between members conspiring with the opposition and members casting occasional votes of conscience or

constituent interest against the party, even on test votes identified by the Steering and Policy Committee.

In large part, Majority Leader Wright's move should be seen as an effort to sidetrack tougher disciplinary measures and to solidify his personal support among fellow southerners whose votes he might need in a future race for the speakership. Wright's guidelines merely put members on notice of the possible exercise of powers the leadership already had. The hard questions remain: will the leadership choose to identify key votes with some regularity, and how much latitude will members of the Steering and Policy Committee give defectors who claim electoral and personal reasons for their actions?

Consider the following questions:

— When Speaker O'Neill said that membership in the Democratic caucus should be determined by members' constituencies rather than by fellow members of Congress, was he right? On what issues or votes, if any, should the leaders of a congressional party expect support from the members of the caucus? Under what conditions should a member be excused from supporting his or her party on votes identified as vital to the party? Should a nonsupporter of the leadership be disadvantaged in competition with other party members for desirable committee assignments or other party benefits even if support for the leadership would have reduced his or her reelection chances?

— To what other points in the political process should the concerns about party loyalty apply? For example, who should be allowed to vote in party primaries for nominating presidential, congressional, or state office candidates? Who should be allowed to participate in party conventions? Who should be allowed to run for office under a party's label?

— Under what conditions could we expect congressional leaders to have more influence over the behavior of rank-and-file members of their parties than they do today? Consider the nature of the national political environment, the internal operation of Congress, and leaders' personal styles. What would be the implications for the American political system if congressional leaders could compel loyalty from the members of the legislative party?

The Effects of the Budget Process

The process established in the 1974 Budget Act was designed to bring coherence to the scattered budget decisions of various House spending and revenue committees by (1) providing nonbinding guidelines in a first budget resolution, (2) setting a binding congressional budget in a second budget resolution, and (3) forcing a "reconciliation" of the various spending and revenue decisions and the provisions of the second budget resolution. The importance of the process for aggregating the fragmented decisions of the committees led the House to include party leaders in its Budget Committee. In the end, though, whether the coherence sought by the creators of the new budget process is achieved depends upon the ability of one of the contending factions (with or without the help of party leaders) to create and maintain a majority coalition at each stage of the process. Without such a majority coalition, the procedural complexities introduced by the Budget Act actually *increase* the likelihood of stalemates and delays in the process. The logic of the budget process was undermined in 1981 by the Reagan administration strategy to force decisions on major programmatic and budget changes in a reconciliation bill ordered by the first budget resolution. (This is allowed by the letter, if not the spirit, of the Budget Act.) The administration was thus able to concentrate its effort on a single piece of legislation early in its term while President Reagan was riding the crest of his postelection popularity.

The majority party leaders of the House—who would have had difficulty fighting such a popular president under the best of circumstances—had their influence undermined by the reconciliation process. Ironically, the utility of the Democratic leadership's strongest resources depended upon the maintenance of the decentralized policy process to which they were adapted. In a decentralized setting, the leadership could use a mix of its committee assignments, scheduling authority, and other resources on a bill-by-bill, committee-by-committee, and member-by-member basis. But the first budget resolution and its reconciliation instructions, along with fortuitous political circumstances, allowed the President to seize control of the centralizing power of the budget process and overcome any influence the Democratic leadership may have had over the regular authorization, spending, and revenue mechanisms. The President and his congressional coalition used the budget process designed to give Congress more collective control over the budget to impose his preferences on the committees of the House.

Consider the following questions:

— Has the new congressional budget process permitted too centralized a policymaking process? Specifically, what are the consequences for public policy of packaging dozens of programmatic changes in a single bill, as in the reconciliation bill? What are the advantages and disadvantages of the traditional fragmented, decentralized legislative process?

— What consequences for the American political system would a highly centralized policy process have? What would be the effects on interest group strategies? Would American politics be more divisive or polarized under such a process? Would there be greater pressure for ideological purity within the parties?

— Has the new budget process reestablished the independence of Congress in that area? Is it reasonable to expect Congress to take firm control of the power of the purse? Under what conditions would Congress exert more independent control of the budget process?

POSTSCRIPT: FROM STEAMROLLER TO STALEMATE

In the first three months of 1982, the majority party leadership of the House again found itself in a position of waiting on the Republicans. But the circumstances were much different than they were a year earlier. The projections for the length and severity of the economic recession had worsened. In February 1982, President Reagan proposed a budget with an expected deficit of over $90 billion by the administration's own estimates, and of over $120 billion according to the estimates of the Congressional Budget Office. Many congressional Republicans who had campaigned for a balanced budget and who were facing a fall election were outraged that the administration would ask them to support such a budget. Republicans in both the House and the Senate spent March and April attempting to design a set of budget cuts and revenue-raising proposals to reduce the size of the deficit. For the House Democratic leadership, there seemed little point in attacking the President when his fellow Republicans were deserting him with no prodding from the Democrats.

Key conservative interest groups were also breaking away from the administration. For example, the Business Roundtable, composed of the chief executives of the nation's largest corporations, criticized the projected deficit for its effect of maintaining high interest rates. Traditional Democratic groups were better prepared to generate stiff opposition to the next round of budget cuts. Public opinion was also less favorable to the administration. One early March poll indicated that 62 percent of the public favored "substantial changes" in Reagan's fiscal 1983 proposals. Other polls showed that Democrats had the potential of gaining many additional House seats in the November elections and could maintain their strength in the Senate, contrary to 1981 expectations.

The large deficit projections were the product of the economic downturn, which increased welfare spending and reduced revenues, and of Reagan's refusal to delay or eliminate any of the tax cuts scheduled for mid-1982 and mid-1983 or to modify his plan for greatly increased defense spending. In February, March, and most of April, the President ruled out compromises on taxes and defense spending and even claimed that the projected deficits were a "necessary evil in the real world today." Office of Management and Budget Director David Stockman and other administration officials, however, intimated that some room for compromise existed on defense spending. Furthermore, Republican members of Congress indicated that they were quietly working with executive budget officials on alternatives to the original administration plan.

Congressional Republicans and the administration eventually took up an offer by Speaker O'Neill to have a group representing House and Senate Democrats and Republicans, as well as the administration, attempt to work out a budget plan on a bipartisan basis. This "gang of seventeen," however, was unable to reach any overall agreement. Reagan refused to budge on taxes, and O'Neill refused to consider any cuts in social security benefits, both of which appeared to be necessary to keep the deficit even close to $100 billion for fiscal 1983.

In an effort to break the impasse, President Reagan went to Capitol Hill during the last week of April to meet O'Neill face-to-face. Participants in the closed meeting indicated that Reagan refused to be associated with any changes in scheduled social security cost of living adjustments, calling such proposals "congressional." Without Reagan's involvement in such a proposal, O'Neill would not discuss it. When House Majority Leader Jim Wright unexpectedly proposed to repeal the third-year tax cut in exchange for deeper domestic program cuts, the President indicated he had gone as far as he could go. The domestic summit ended with nothing accomplished.

The partisan stalemate, the prospects of huge deficits, and the distaste for another round of deep cuts in social programs left most observers of the House questioning the possibility of creating a majority on the floor for any budget proposal. In a somewhat desperate effort to get some budget resolution, the Democratic leadership constructed a rule for floor debate which allowed all major proposals to receive a vote on the floor. The rule, which was adopted by voice vote on May 1, divided the proposals into two groups. The first group included a balanced budget version proposed by conservative Republicans unhappy with the deficits in all other plans, two proposals written by liberal Democrats, and a plan devised by the Black Caucus. No amendments were permitted to the first group plans, which were considered as having no chance of passage. (In addition, the last budget passed was to take precedence over all earlier versions, allowing a considerable amount of "false voting" on the part of members who were fully aware that the earlier votes would not be binding.) The second group included a plan devised by the Republican leadership of the House and supported by the administration, one written by a group of moderate Democrats and Republicans, and a resolution reported by the Budget Committee and supported by O'Neill and the Democratic leadership. The second group was open to amendment.

Despite many pleas from all factions of the House to adopt something, the House proceeded to reject all of the budget plans. The Republican leadership's plan, which cut $23 billion from projected spending over three years, came the closest to adoption, losing 192-235. The plan garnered only 21 conservative Democratic votes and failed to attract the support of 20 Republicans, most of whom were moderate "Gypsy Moths." Some conservative Democratic support was lost when Democrats and many Republicans voted to shift $4.8 billion from defense to Medicare in the Republican plan. The moderate and Budget Committee plans, both of which cut only $9.3 billion over three years, lost on 137-289 and 171-273 votes, respectively.

In hindsight, it seemed that while nearly all members were willing to support one of the seven versions available, there appeared to be many members who refused to vote for a second-best choice in order to have some version adopted.

SOURCES AND READINGS

This case study relies heavily upon the author's observations of and discussions with participants in the budget process throughout 1981 as a congressional fellow of the American Political Science Association. Regular use was made of several periodicals and newspapers as well: Congressional Quarterly *Weekly Report, National Journal, Washington Post, New York Times, Wall Street Journal,* and others.

There are several excellent general works on Congress which include discussions of changes in Congress during the last decade or so. A very good textbook is *Congress and Its Members* by Roger H. Davidson and Walter J. Oleszek (Washington, D.C.: CQ Press, 1981). Shorter essays on changes in Congress, including the budget process, can be found in *Congress Reconsidered*, 2d ed., edited by Lawrence C. Dodd and Bruce I. Oppenheimer (Washington, D.C.: CQ Press, 1981) and in Thomas E. Mann and Norman J. Ornstein, editors, *The New Congress* (Washington, D.C.: American Enterprise Institute, 1981).

An excellent study of the development and brief history of the congressional budget process is Allen Schick, *Congress and Money* (Washington, D.C.: The Urban Institute, 1981). Other useful books on Congress and the budget process are Joel Havemann, *Congress and the Budget* (Bloomington, Indiana: Indiana University Press, 1978); Dennis S. Ippolito, *Congressional Spending* (Ithaca: Cornell University Press, 1981); and Lance T. LeLoup, *The Fiscal Congress* (Westport, Conn.: Greenwood Press, 1980). On the budget process more generally, see Dennis Ippolito, *The Budget and National Politics* (San Francisco: W. H. Freeman & Co., 1978) and Aaron Wildavsky, *The Politics of the Budgetary Process*, 3rd ed. (Boston: Little, Brown & Co., 1979).

For recent discussions of congressional leadership, see *Understanding Congressional Leadership*, edited by Frank Mackaman (Washington, D.C.: CQ Press, 1981). For general treatments of leadership resources and strategies, see Randall B. Ripley, *Party Leadership in the House of Representatives* (Washington, D.C.: The Brookings Institution, 1967) and, also by Ripley, *Majority Party Leadership in Congress* (Boston: Little, Brown & Co., 1969). Useful insights into leadership, especially concerning contests for leadership posts, can also be found in Robert L. Peabody, *Leadership in Congress: Stability, Succession, and Change* (Boston: Little, Brown & Co., 1976).

③

The Bureaucracy

An Aborted Regulation:
The FDA and Patient Package Inserts

Robert Reinhold

Picture this familiar Washington scene: It is March of 1980 and the House Appropriations Subcommittee on Agriculture was gathered in a sedate hearing room to consider, as it does annually, the appropriation for the Food and Drug Administration (FDA). Seated at the witness table before the subcommittee was a gray-bearded, fatherly looking man, Dr. Jere E. Goyan, the commissioner of the FDA. The proceedings were temporarily snagged over a new regulation the agency had proposed to require druggists to hand out with prescriptions little slips of paper informing patients about the proper use of the medicine their doctors had instructed them to take. "I would not want to swallow a pill about which I knew nothing," said Dr. Goyan, a pharmacist by training.

At first glance, Dr. Goyan's remarks seem unexceptionable, hardly open to much debate. In reality, however, neither Dr. Goyan's seemingly laudable objective nor the method of achieving it is so simple or immune from objections, both political and medical. The agency was trying to resolve a genuine policy problem, and its resolution took place through the political process—a process made all the more complicated by changing administrations and changing public attitudes toward the value of government regulation as a means of solving problems and enhancing the public well-being. This study focuses on the method by which one regulatory agency sought to define a problem and its solution, and on what happened to its efforts as a consequence.

THE RATIONALE FOR REGULATIONS

Probably no function of the United States government is less understood, yet more important to the everyday lives of Americans, than the writing of regulations. They are the meat of the law, the means by which laws passed by Congress are actually carried out. They interpret and define the law, honing Congress's vague intentions into sharp detail. Congress often prefers to leave the language of its bills fuzzy. Partly this is because the members do not want to resolve the conflicting political pressures surrounding much legislation. Partly it is because Congress frequently lacks the expertise with which to spell out the nitty-gritty details needed to implement a law. Thus, for example, Congress may decide that carcinogenic (cancer-causing) agents should be banned from foods, but has neither the political stomach nor the scientific knowledge to list them, to establish thresholds of carcinogenicity, or to set penalties. Or, as happened a few years ago, Congress wanted builders to construct more energy-efficient structures but did not want to get into the political morass of imposing standards. So the Department of Housing and Urban Development was asked to devise "reasonable" standards; the result was that the agency was caught in intense political crossfire. This approach gives the agencies that write the rules—as well as the lobbyists and congressional staffers to whom they respond—enormous power. Fine differences in definitions can mean millions of dollars to an industry. It also embroils the agencies in the very thing they are theoretically immune from—power politics.

Although subject to ultimate court challenge and many pressures from within the government and without, the bureaucracy can either gut a law by writing a weak regulation, or go well beyond congressional intent by writing an aggressive one. Sometimes the bureaucracy in effect writes its own law, proposing a new regulation based on its general statutory authority rather than waiting for Congress to pass a new law. At other times it succumbs to political pressures and public mood and shies away from pushing too hard.

THE STORY OF ONE REGULATION

This is the story of how one new regulation was hammered out. If it is at all typical, it does not support the widespread notion of an overbearing federal bureaucracy, heedless of anything but its own petty interests. If anything, the process of writing this regulation was excrutiatingly slow, a process marked by vacillation and uncertainty on the part of the agency as it tried to steer its way through three administrations and several agency directors, as well as changing moods in Congress and the electorate. The final product bore litle resemblance to its original proposal. However, the story of how this regulation was shaped, pounded, twisted, and squeezed is not one of misdeeds or backroom dealing. Rather it is the sometimes dull—but highly important—story of how government really works, how different interest groups bring their power and information to bear on the process, how federal agencies respond to changing political realities.

The issue in question here concerns the efforts of the Food and Drug Administration to require that druggists hand out little flyers to buyers of prescription drugs to give patients some basic layman's information on how best to use the drug and to warn of its dangers. The notion was first pushed by consumer groups at a time when they held greater sway than they do today. As simple and desirable as the notion of providing patients with more information about their treatment might sound at first blush, the proposal raised a host of complex objections on the part of doctors, pharmacists, drugstore owners, and others. They argued—persuasively in the view of two administrations— that the priorities of "consumer" organizations were not necessarily identical with the "public interest" taken in the larger context of who is to pay for implementing the regulation.

Ultimately the agency was forced to retreat from its original proposal, which would have compelled that patient information inserts—known as "patient package inserts" or "PPIs" to the trade—be dispensed with as many as 375 drugs comprising nearly all prescriptions and refills ordered in this country. The final rule—issued in the waning days of the Carter administration in 1980—applied to only 10 drugs and drug classes covering only 16 percent of all prescriptions. Even that was too much for the incoming Reagan administration. Riding into power on a promise to reduce the regulatory burden, the administration quickly ordered a temporary delay in implementing the rule early in 1981, and then ultimately decided to drop it altogether a year later, expressing the hope that better results could be achieved through voluntary efforts by industry and doctors.

Thus nearly a decade of work went for naught. Still, the agency won a victory of sorts, in that it forced druggists, doctors, drug makers, and others to think about an issue they had long avoided and take "voluntary" steps toward achieving what the agency wanted. Despite the official "failure" of the PPI rule, this study illustrates how an active bureaucratic organization, taking its often vague instructions from Congress, affects public policy. That the rule was eventually defeated, in the long run, is not as important as the process by which it evolved.

THE INVISIBLE GOVERNMENT

The odyssey of the PPI rule reveals much about the workings of an invisible kind of government that reigns in Washington. It shuns publicity and largely operates by its own rules and to a very considerable extent moves independently of the president, his top appointees, and the elected members of Congress. It responds to them, to be sure, but with all the agility of a supertanker. This invisible government, dubbed the "iron triangle" by many political commentators, is an informal network of high-level civil servants, private lobbyists, and congressional staff members. There is considerable mobility among these three groups. Congressional staffers often leave Capitol Hill after a few years to become lawyers or lobbyists for the very industries they dealt with when drafting legislation. To survive, the three elements of the triad must somehow mesh their interests.

What gives this triad power is not so much money or votes, but information, knowledge, expertise—increasingly the currency of power in a sophisticated technological era. These invisible "subgovernments" prevail by exerting their expertise, and—perhaps more importantly— staying with an issue long after others have lost interest in it. For they know that the way a law is implemented through regulations is at least as important as what that law actually says.

Thus while the public and press are often preoccupied with presidential elections and the latest scandal sensation, the wheels of government turn silently behind the scenes with little public scrutiny. That is just the way the participants in the process like it. These decisions influence the drugs we take, the contents of the food we eat, the construction of our cars, and the safety of our workplaces. Once fully implemented, regulations have the full force of law and violations can bring civil and even criminal penalties. The public interest is not necessarily the uppermost factor in the way regulations are hammered out.

THE BACKGROUND

As any consumer who has ever purchased a prescription drug knows, the container in which it comes has almost no information on the label other than instructions on how many times a day to take it and perhaps a little sticker warning against combining it with alcohol consumption. Consumer activists have long argued that because many drugs are extremely hazardous the patient has a right to know more about what he or she is taking. Ironically, over-the-counter drugs have long included little folded-up inserts on their proper use while ostensibly more potent prescription drugs have not, the rationale being that the doctor's oral instructions to the patient when writing a prescription were sufficient. But evidence has been mounting for some years that doctors often do not supply adequate information, that they are sometimes ignorant of the latest studies about drugs, and that patients easily forget what they are told.

For these and other reasons the FDA began in 1974 to investigate the issue, with a view toward new rules requiring inserts with prescription drugs. Soon after, in 1975, a coalition of consumer groups, led by the Center for Law and Social Policy in Washington, entered the picture. The center was one of a number of the many so-called "public interest" organizations that began to spring up with the rise of consumer, women's, and other movements in the 1960s. Although generally run on a shoestring and operating with minimal staff, they have wielded considerable power by virtue of their large constituency and by a widespread feeling in many quarters that private corporations, armed with high-powered lawyers and lobbyists, have historically been able to thwart the public will. They have achieved many a major victory in areas such as automobile and food safety, product labeling, and workplace safety.

The consumer groups petitioned the FDA to require warnings on drugs that posed dangers to pregnant and nursing women, drugs such as tranquilizers that involve serious hazards, and those that have been overprescribed and have caused untoward side effects. Both the petition and the drug agency's thinking reflected an evolving medical consensus that patients should play a greater role in their own care and that doctors were prescribing too many drugs. Thus the process of writing a new regulation was begun.

FDA: POWERFUL BUT EMBATTLED AGENCY

The Food and Drug Administration is a curious animal, powerful yet vulnerable in many ways, frequently derided by both industry and consumer groups. It is charged, in general, with protecting the public against unsafe and ineffective drugs, and against hazardous foods, food additives, and cosmetics. Often its decisions have major financial effects on certain industries, and thus it is as much a political as a scientific agency. Its authority under law is strong and it is widely feared among drug and food makers. In 1982, for example, it began requiring makers of infant formula to test the nutritional quality of their products throughout the manufacturing process after one firm's product was found deficient in an essential infant nutrient; nearly three million cans were ordered recalled. And when it began to make noises about requiring makers of processed foods to list sodium content on their labels, to help people on low-salt diets, companies such as Campbell's

Soup began to market a low-sodium line and label its regular products as a means of warding off more draconian regulation. For all that, the FDA has had uneven relations with Congress and it has often been politically naive. Its scientific competence has often been questioned. Nevertheless, with every new case of botulism poisoning or a failed drug, Congress invests the agency with new authority.

The agency, in this case, was not acting to implement a new law. Rather it was moving on what it believed was its statutory authority under a series of existing laws dating back to 1906. In that year, the Pure Food and Drug Act began the government's efforts to control fraudulent and deceptive drug claims. The FDA's early regulatory actions were aimed at nostrums such as "Sporty Days Invigorator," claimed to cure "male weakness," and a headache remedy called "Curforhedake Brane-Fude." The Food, Drug and Cosmetic Act of 1938 (with subsequent amendments) significantly strengthened the FDA's hand, but the agency's regulations over the years chose to exempt prescription drugs from the usual labeling requirements as long as the manufacturer provided detailed information to physicians. Under the law, the FDA's power was limited to drug makers and druggists and it had no authority to order doctors to do anything. Thus its efforts to promote patient education had to be worked through that route.

As it began the PPI project in 1974, the FDA felt it already had the authority to order the inserts under laws that authorized it to prohibit the "misbranding" of drugs. A drug was considered misbranded, under law, if it failed to "reveal facts that are material in light of representations made in the labeling or material with respect to consequences that may result from the use of the product under customary or usual conditions of use," in the FDA's words. In fact, the FDA, using this argument, had already ordered PPIs in a few isolated instances—mainly for isoproterenol inhalators for asthma patients which had caused some deaths through misuse, for contraceptive drugs and devices, and for estrogens prescribed to treat menopausal symptoms in women. But the FDA's authority to require the estrogen PPI—widely regarded as turgid, unreadable, and of minimal value—was already under legal challenge by the Pharmaceutical Manufacturers Association, and expanding the scope of the PPI concept was clearly a major regulatory step that the FDA could expect not to go down easily.

While the stated purpose of PPIs—to enhance the safe and effective use of drugs—could hardly be disputed, the issue raised other troubling concerns. On the one hand, it seemed like a straightforward way of informing patients of the risks and benefits of the drugs they take. But some doctors said it represented an insidious indirect means of increasing government control over the practice of medicine and an unwarranted interference with the doctor-patient relationship. Indeed, former FDA Commissioner Dr. Donald Kennedy explicitly stated in approving the estrogen insert in 1978 that its purpose was to cut down the number of estrogen prescriptions. "The majority of estrogen prescriptions were being written for elective post-menopausal indications for which there is no evidence of efficacy, but a substantial known risk elevation for endometrial cancer," he wrote.

A full-scale PPI program thus raised the possibility of significantly altering the practice of medicine and pharmacy in the United States. In 1976, the Department of Health, Education and Welfare (HEW) reported that about 42 percent of all office visits to doctors ended with the patient leaving with a prescription to fill. A national prescription audit conducted in 1977 for the pharmaceutical industry found that American doctors wrote 1.4 billion new and refill prescriptions annually. Very important questions were being raised, then, about whether all these prescriptions were really needed, whether doctors were telling their patients all they needed to know about the drugs, whether doctors themselves knew all they needed to know about the drugs, and whether patients were complying with their regimens.

Beyond all these philosophical issues, money also played a role. While proponents believed the PPIs would ultimately save billions in unnecessary medical costs and consumer expenses, detractors argued that the rule would cost hundreds of millions to implement without any compelling proof that it would have any substantial beneficial effect.

It was no wonder, then, that this seemingly innocuous proposal struck some raw nerves.

EVOLUTION OF THE REGULATION

It was against this backdrop that the FDA's Patient Prescription Drug Labeling Project wrestled with the problem. The project was headed by an affable young psychologist from Brooklyn, Louis Morris, who had come to the agency after taking a Ph.D. at Tulane, where he studied the placebo effects of drugs on patients. He was soon to learn that the hardball world of Washington politics bore little resemblance to the polite academic world of science and objective facts.

On November 7, 1975, the FDA published one of those turgid gray notices in the *Federal Register* saying that it was considering requiring PPIs generally, and inviting comments. It received more than 1,000— from consumers, doctors, druggists, and professional organizations. It also commissioned studies of the issue and sponsored conferences and symposia in conjunction with the American Medical Association (AMA) and the Pharmaceutical Manufacturers Association (PMA). It reviewed all the scientific literature on the value of PPIs. All of this was necessary to meet any later challenge claiming that the agency had not given full consideration to the implications of its actions. But even before the agency made up its mind on a full-blown program, trouble began brewing when it issued an estrogen PPI rule in 1978. Morris explained in an interview:

> That started to bring out a lot of the professionals against PPIs. The estrogen insert was frightening to people—it stressed the risks, and it was very difficult to read. It was a fear-inducing document, written by doctors at the FDA. Estrogen sales were cut in half. That's what we wanted. But unfortunately the message in the insert was one of fear. We could have written it a lot clearer.

Despite this harbinger of trouble, the FDA plunged ahead. By this time, in 1978, the agency had already formed a strong opinion. The original consumer petition that had asked for the inserts three years earlier, Morris said, "was if anything understated."

> We found that people got very little information from doctors. But we also found an incredible loss of memory. People are busy thinking about the diagnosis. They forget half of what the doctor told them. That formulated an important part of the policy. We always felt the doctor was the primary source of information. It is not the doctor's fault. Even if the doctors were doing their job, we would need PPIs anyway.

Thus on Friday, July 6, 1979, a dry notice appeared in the *Federal Register* announcing a "proposed rule." The rule would have required inserts for 375 of the most widely prescribed of the 5,000 prescription drugs on the market. It proposed to phase in the plan over several years, starting with about 50 to 75 drugs and drug classes the first year. It listed the first drugs under consideration, and they ranged from Acetohexamide to Valporic Acid. The notice stated:

> This action is being taken because the FDA believes that prescription drug labeling that is directed to patients will promote the safe and effective use of prescription drug products and that patients have a right to know about the benefits, risks, and directions for use of the products.

Further, the proposal stated, "It became obvious to FDA that physicians had neither the time nor the facilities to investigate carefully each product to determine its proper uses" and that the information drug companies were already compelled to provide to doctors and pharmacists "did not affect the information required to be given to patients, which remained minimal."

Finally, brushing aside the numerous objections, the proposal declared: "FDA has now determined that new information demonstrates that for the safe and effective use of prescription drug products more information about products must also be provided to patients."

The rule would have required drug makers to prepare and distribute through pharmacies a leaflet written in nontechnical and nonpromotional language. It would list, among other things, the proper uses of the drug, circumstances under which it should not be used, and possible side effects. It would have to be given to all drug buyers, except those deemed legally incompetent, whose primary language was not English, or who were blind, whose doctors directed the insert withheld, patients in emergency treatment, and institutionalized persons.

RESPONSE AND REACTION

The response was not entirely what the FDA might have hoped for. "The response was very emotional," recalls Morris. "The industry and other opponents really got together. They say it was a major issue. I learned a lot of politics. At the time I felt paranoid, but that's the way things are done. I was very depressed—we took a lot of grief." The trade press began to be sprinkled with damaging items about the FDA. Druggist groups, doctors, drug makers, and others began to write letters to members of Congress. The proposal elicited about 1,300 written comments, not all of them unfavorable, and other reactions were expressed at hearings held in three cities.

In all these preliminaries, required before a regulation takes effect, the FDA may have been its own worst enemy. Given the antiregulatory mood of the country at the time, it did something its officials now admit was naive. The proposed rule was advanced before the agency had done an economic analysis of whether the benefits of implementing the rule were worth the costs, or had examined if there were any cheaper alternatives that would achieve the same end. "We failed to protect where we were most vulnerable—on the economic side," said Morris. "We put out the regulation and then did the cost-benefit analysis. It did not have the documentation it should have had. We found out what concerned people most was the economics. How naive of us."

Naive indeed. With its soft underbelly thus exposed, the FDA ventured bravely into battle. Daggers were drawn at almost every turn. With the battle lines thus formed the arguments for and against the inserts came into sharp focus.

Arguments For: Proponents advanced the concept as a partial solution to a number of problems surrounding the prescribing and use of prescription drugs, which had increased fourfold since 1950. They argued that, given simple and accurate written information about the drugs they were taking, patients would make safer and more effective use of those products. One main argument held that patients either did not pay attention to or forgot what their doctors told them. Numerous scientific studies have shown that "noncompliance" by patients is extremely high and causes many medical problems. Patients frequently fail to space their doses properly, skip doses, take extra doses, or fail to complete the ordered regimen. A study of compliance in acute illnesses found that noncompliance ranged from 19 to 89 percent. In long-term treatments, average compliance was 54 percent, with one-third of patients not taking any of their medicine. For example, in five separate studies appearing in a variety of professional journals, compliance rates for patients taking medicine to combat high blood pressure ranged from 24 to 83 percent.

In addition, many argued that the prescribing practices of doctors left something to be desired. Some maintained that doctors, out of ignorance or laziness, have come to rely too heavily on issuing prescriptions, particularly for antibiotics and tranquilizers. Also, critics say, they tend to get much of their information from drug company representatives with a financial interest in pushing one drug or another. One study of patients at Duke University Medical Center conducted in the early 1970s found that nearly two-thirds of all antibiotics prescriptions written there were unnecessary—that is, the wrong drug or wrong dosage was ordered. Moreover, studies also have shown that doctors frequently prescribe antibiotics for common colds and other diseases for which there is no evidence the drugs help. This practice has drawn criticism from many experts because it spurs the emergence of new strains of bacteria that are resistant to existing antibiotics. Similarly, critics have charged that there is massive overprescribing of the so-called minor tranquilizers, such as Valium and Librium, which can cause dependence.

The large number of untoward side effects of drugs was another argument made for PPIs. Some studies reported in the *Journal of the American Medical Association* and elsewhere have suggested that as many as one of every 22 hospital admissions result from adverse drug reactions, costing as much as $3.5 billion annually and causing as many as 140,000 deaths a year. These particular estimates are open to dispute, but adverse drug reaction is a significant medical problem.

Finally, there was the philosophical argument that the patient has the "right to know" about his or her treatment. The FDA advanced several opinion surveys showing that people, particularly the better educated, wanted more information about their medications and wanted to play a larger role in their own health care. However, a study of the PPI issue in 1979 by the Institute of Medicine, an arm of the National Academy of Sciences, noted the contradiction between this goal and that of achieving better compliance with doctor's orders. That is, the more the patient knew about the risks of the drug, the more likely he was to challenge doctor's orders.

Arguments Against: While most people generally agreed that the more information the patient had the better, numerous doubts cropped up. Many doctors complained that the inserts would damage their relationships with the patients, that patients would be alarmed by the information and ask a lot of unnecessary questions, wasting the doctor's valuable time. The doctors feared that patients might rely solely on the inserts, possibly altering the doctor's instructions and even discontinuing the medication.

Both pharmacists and doctors also raised the possibility that the inserts might affect patients psychologically, causing them to develop side effects and adverse reactions merely through suggestion. Or, conversely, they said accurate information might inhibit the desired placebo effect that doctors sometimes strive for. And what about the cancer patient, whose illness has been kept secret for therapeutic reasons, who reads that he or she is taking an anticancer drug?

Druggists and drug makers complained that the inserts, insofar as they constituted warnings, would subject them to more damage and liability suits. And the druggists said they would be forced to respond to many questions from worried customers. (This argument is somewhat odd, given the vigorous public relations campaign that pharmacists have been waging against the widespread notion that they do nothing more than "count and pour" pills into little bottles.)

Further, the critics argued that the FDA did not have conclusive evidence that the PPIs would do what they were supposed to do, that any substantial number of people would read and heed them. Nor, they argued, did the FDA know for sure that lack of information was the underlying reason for noncompliance and other problems the inserts were meant to correct. In reviewing the existing evidence, the Institute of Medicine study said it was unable to "predict with great confidence all of the possible impacts of expanded PPI requirements on patients, health care providers, and the health care system." However, the study said that the evidence "does not support the contention that PPIs will increase the incidence of side effects or increase the demands of patients on health practitioners."

But the most strident objections were neither philosophical nor medical, but economic. The FDA estimated that the proposal would cost about $90 million a year to implement, adding only about 6.3¢ to the cost of the average prescription. All wrong, declared the opponents. Druggists, drugstore owners, and drug makers said the FDA had grossly underestimated the costs—all of which would be passed on to the consumer, of course. The druggists said they would have to redesign their stores to build huge pigeonhole racks to hold the little flyers, hire extra help to fumble with them, and otherwise alter their operations to cope with the new rules. The American Pharmaceutical Association

(APhA), representing 55,000 pharmacists, calculated that the cost would amount to $235 million for the first year and possibly as much as $1.8 billion over five years. The National Association of Retail Druggists, representing 33,000 independent pharmacy owners who fill 70 percent of all prescriptions, came up with a figure of $250 million for the first year and $100 million to $150 million for each subsequent year. The National Association of Chain Drug Stores, to which 194 chains belong, put the price at $312 million to $532 million a year. And Eli Lilly, a leading drug maker, estimated that the cost to manufacturers alone would run about $140 million annually.

THE LOBBYING ASSAULT

Armed with this and other ammunition, the industry began a concerted lobbying effort soon after the proposed rules were issued in July of 1979. One of the leaders was the American Pharmaceutical Association. Its chief lobbyist, Dena Cain, argued in an interview:

> Our association is very much in favor of patient information. But there is no proof PPIs will cure the problems. They have not been extensively tested. Given the cost, things like this should be tested first. The question is, do patients desire PPIs and are they willing to pay the additional cost. The FDA is saying this information may be good for you and therefore you should pay for it.

Cain maintained that pharmacists were increasingly serving the intended purpose of PPIs by counseling patients directly and experimenting with cheaper alternatives. For example, a number of major drugstores, such as the Peoples chain in the Washington, D. C., area, made reference books available at drug counters for customers to consult at the time of purchase. In addition, certain drug companies, such as Hoffman-La Roche, had recently begun to experiment with voluntary inserts with some drugs, such as Valium, a tranquilizer. That company also distributed through major supermarkets 500,000 copies of "The WHAT IF Book," designed to inform consumers about the proper use of drugs. Meanwhile, the American Medical Association, representing doctors, came forward with its own proposal to enhance patient education, purely on a voluntary basis. It suggested that doctors, rather than druggists, give out the printed information and proposed to do this through what it called "patient medication instruction" sheets, or "PMIs." Doctors would have pads of these sheets for each of the most widely prescribed drugs, to be issued at their discretion.

Such "voluntary" efforts probably would not have been advanced without the pressure of a potential new government regulation. This suggests that the rulemaking process serves an important function of sensitizing industry to new ideas and needs, even if the rule ultimately does not go through.

At any rate, the PPI proposal was perceived as a formidable threat by the druggists. As any cub lobbyist knows, there are many ways to skin a cat—or in this case a rule—and the APhA and other critics mounted a broad attack. Their leaders and lobbyists met with top FDA officials, including the new commissioner, Dr. Goyan, who took over shortly after the proposal was published. They asked their members to write letters to key legislators, and had their affiliated state associations lobby local members of Congress. They consulted with other interest groups that were sympathetic, like the American Medical Association. And they knocked on the executive door, meeting with White House officials and lobbing missives into the Council on Wage and Price Stability (COWPS) and the Office of Management and Budget (OMB), where they found sympathetic ears. Patricia Roberts Harris, the secretary of Health, Education and Welfare at the time, got an earful about PPIs when she addressed the annual meeting of the APhA in Washington.

At the same time, the chain drugstore group was pressing its opposition. As frequent contributors to local members of Congress, local druggists and their organizations expected to be heard by their representatives, and they were. In addition, lobbyists for their national groups went to the FDA, to Alfred Kahn (then head of COWPS) and to OMB. "PPIs may scare patients," said Ty Kelley, chief lobbyist for the National Association of Chain Drug Stores. "They may come back for refunds. It would make more sense to have doctors give the information. Why burden the pharmacist with this responsibility when it should be done in the physician's office?"

The doctors, doing their own lobbying, agreed. Their representatives told Congress and the White House that PPIs might interfere with the doctor-patient relationship. "It might be alarming to the patient," said Al Faca, an AMA representative in Washington. "He may not take the drug because of it. It is our feeling that it is really the responsibility of the doctor to make the patient aware." Like the other opponents, he said he preferred a limited test before a full-scale test was begun. However, the doctors did not take the lead on this issue. While the AMA and other medical groups issued strong public statements against the inserts, they were not as vigorous in the lobbying effort as the druggists, possibly because the druggists were more directly affected in the economic sense. In addition, organized medicine was in some disarray at this time, preoccupied with other issues that loomed even larger.

Robert J. Bolger, president of the chain drugstore group, wrote to President Carter to complain of the "immense inflationary impact" of the proposal. He contended it might swell drug prices by 8 to 16 percent—at the very time, he underscored pointedly, when the Carter administration was trying to contain the growth in health care costs. The letter made some impression on the President's health advisers. Meanwhile other members of the administration were getting similar missives. Bolger declared to Kahn, the chairman of COWPS, that the proposal would plunge druggists into a "colossal paperwork jungle." Other letters landed on the desk of James M. McIntyre Jr., powerful head of OMB. Right or wrong, these arguments were beginning to have some effect in official Washington, partly because the other side did not have the resources to mount much of a counterattack. As Kelley of the chain druggists said with a wry smile, "With the exception of a few consumer organizations, there is not much of a national outcry for this program."

CONSUMER GROUPS WEIGH IN, LIGHTLY

The consumer or "public interest" proponents of PPIs were not inactive in all this, but they were outgunned. While such groups are frequently effective at stirring up issues and provoking general alarm, they do not always have the sticking power of industry. While an industry can marshal all of its resources in support or defense of a few major issues, public interest groups by their very nature must concentrate on several fronts at once. Marsha Greenberger is a lawyer for the Center for Law and Social Policy in Washington who worked on the original petition to the FDA in 1975. "The opponents have enormous resources available to them," she said in an interview. "They have gone to congressmen, the White House, they have filed lawsuits. They do have access. We have access too. But we've got limited staff. No one in the consumer movement can devote sustained and regular attention to this issue."

Drug industry lobbyists were "all over the Hill like locusts," said Fred Wegner, a lobbyist with the American Association of Retired Persons (AARP). With 12.5 million members, the association is not without its own clout. But it is only one voice, Wegner said, while the PMA, all of its member companies as well as the various druggist groups, each employ their own lobbyists, who reinforce each other. Given the amount of money drugs cost elderly people, Wegner said that he hoped PPIs would serve to advise patients of other less costly therapies. He argued that of the "great flood" of new drugs on the market, 95 percent represented no particular therapeutic improvement over what was already available. His implication was that old people were being compelled to pay for drug development that was unnecessary and that better information might help them save money.

THE WHITE HOUSE ROLE

But voices like Wegner's were largely drowned out in the chorus of complaints, which were beginning to be taken seriously at the Carter White House. In the words of a former FDA lawyer who now represents the drug makers, the druggists "lobbed a shell into the White House compound" with an analysis of the economic consequences of the proposed regulation. The complaints struck a responsive chord with the President's Domestic Policy Staff, his science advisers, and the Small Business Administration. The only high-level ally to come to the aid of the drug agency was the President's consumer adviser, Esther Peterson.

Then, on top of all this, the proposal got "rarged" early in 1980—a Carterism meaning that the regulation was subjected to close scrutiny by a special interagency panel called the Regulatory Analysis Review Group (RARG), an arm of the Council on Wage and Price Stability. President Carter had set up the panel to review regulations with substantial economic consequences to make agencies more sensitive to the economic effects of what they did. The panel had no direct authority to alter regulations, but agencies had to respond to its inquiries and pronouncements. The panel, made up mostly of economists, tended to be sympathetic to business needs.

The review of the PPI proposal was headed by George D. Eads, a member of the Council of Economic Advisers. In an interview at the Old Executive Office Building next door to the White House, he said:

> The FDA did not understand at first. The analysis they did was primarily a cost analysis. We said they should be laying out the alternatives and their costs. We said we are not questioning your interest in developing these rules, but we are concerned that you have not laid out a path so that you will ever know they are generating the claimed benefits.

Eads said that RARG members acted as "intelligent outsiders," asking for the rationale for regulatory decisions. "The notion that there is a 'right to know' is not in itself sufficient grounds to make a decision on regulation," he said. "If you decide there is a right to know, it is not easy to know what the cost is. Some say this leaves out the human factor, but most regulations, whether we admit it or not, involve putting things into dollars. At least you should have some notion of what you are doing and know there are alternatives you are ignoring." Eads vigorously disputed suggestions that it is possible to stop a regulation just by "getting to" a White House office like his. He argued that it is wrong to claim that regulators thwart the public will. "But it is true that government bureaucrats sometimes do stupid things," he said. "Sometimes they do not understand what they are doing. We are trying to get across that regulation is an activity of government that is important enough to do well. We have to make choices."

The final RARG report took the drug agency to task, saying it had failed to consider many potential costs of the rule. Moreover, it observed, "We are troubled that FDA has not stated how the knowledge gained in its initial implementation steps will be reflected in subsequent ones." It suggested that the agency consider a limited phased-in test of the inserts rather than starting out with a full-blown program. "We call on FDA to publicly commit itself to testing and evaluation before proceeding to mandate patient labeling for all drugs." At any rate, the FDA conceded to RARG that it did not have the staff to enforce a full PPI program; a recent survey it took found that only 39 percent of druggists spontaneously gave out the inserts they are now required to distribute with estrogen prescriptions. The implication was that if the FDA could not enforce even one insert requirement, how could the agency enforce it for 375 drugs?

THE FDA YIELDS

At first the agency was distressed over the "rarging." But Louis Morris, the psychologist who headed the insert project, said that the ultimate RARG report was a "reasonable" one. "The decision on how many drugs how fast is basically a political decision," he said. "The FDA welcomes advice on that."

By the fall of 1980, the leadership of the drug agency had changed hands. Dr. Kennedy had left to become provost (and later president) of Stanford Univerity and in his place came Dr. Jere Goyan. A man of 49 years with a gentle manner, Dr. Goyan had been dean of the pharmacy school at the University of California at San Francisco. He came to the FDA job with a reputation as a champion of consumer rights. He once described himself as a "therapeutic nihilist," and had often said that Americans were "overmedicated." He seemed to many, after some months on the job, to be somewhat out of his element in the highly charged political atmosphere surrounding the FDA.

With his reputation as a foe of overmedication, it was widely assumed that Dr. Goyan would push full-speed ahead on the PPI rule. But shortly after taking office, he surprised everybody by letting it be known that he planned to scale back the regulation to include just 10 drugs on an experimental basis. Lou Morris, head of the program, read about it in the press. This frequently happens in Washington, where changes in policy direction often are tested out in leaks to the press before they are formally announced, even to the staffs involved. This practice allows an administrator to change his mind or fine tune his decision should the initial reaction be unfavorable.

In an interview at his office in suburban Rockville, Maryland, where the FDA has its headquarters, Dr. Goyan was frank in making it clear that the political opposition to the proposal was too great to resist. He said that even though he strongly believes that doctors do not give enough information to their patients,

> We had to move in a different fashion to make it work out politically. I have not been before a friendly audience on this issue. The way we were going at it looked too much like a bludgeon. The new proposals will make doctors and pharmacists more at ease with them. We reached the conclusion that with such mass antipathy on the part of almost everyone that it would make more sense to move slowly. I believe we'll be better off 10 years from now if we do this without a complete face-off.

Goyan also conceded that the agency "did not have good data" on the effectiveness of the inserts and that, as a professor and scientist, he thought it was logical to get a better scientific footing before moving much further. "If all we do is cut down a lot of trees and have little effect, what's the point?"

THE ROLE OF CONGRESS

There was also a more practical reason to cut back on the number of drugs to be covered, according to Dr. Goyan. The industry lobbyists had been at work on Capitol Hill and had elicited a positive response from the House Appropriations Subcommittee on Agriculture, which handles the FDA budget. Dr. Goyan found himself under hostile questioning at a hearing of the subcommittee in March of 1980, particularly from Representative Bill Alexander, an Arkansas Democrat who had received a $250 contribution from the National Association of Chain Drug Stores Political Action Committee the year before. Minutes after Dr. Goyan testified that "I would not want to swallow a pill about which I knew nothing," Alexander extracted a promise from him that the PPI program would begin with no more than 10 drugs.

(This illustrates one of the new facts of political life in Washington. An inadvertent result of the Federal Election Campaign Act of 1974, which set limits on individual contributions to political candidates and provided for public funding of presidential campaigns, was to spur the formation of many new "political action committees." Such groups— called PACs—had long been used as the political arms of labor unions. Legislation passed about a decade ago gave corporations the same right to form such groups, used to support campaigns of favored politicians through direct financial contributions. In 1980, for the first time, corporate PACs outspent those created by unions. According to the Federal Election Commission, the PACs raised $136.7 million in the

1979-1980 election cycle, compared with $80 million in the 1977-1978 period.

Having limited the amount of money congressional candidates can obtain from traditional local sources, the law forced many of them to turn to the national PACs to meet the growing cost of campaigning.* In the view of many observers this has distorted the political process, inasmuch as most of the PACs are narrowly focused on single issues and do not necessarily represent the best interests of the representative's local district. For example, in 1980, 18 of the 20 members of the Senate Finance Committee received contributions from chemical industry PACs; the committee was to consider, in November, the so-called "superfund" legislation to make chemical makers liable for the cleanup costs and damages in cases of toxic chemical spills and leaks from waste dumps. Some have said that the PACs are the modern equivalent of the old precinct system, under which the local political boss raised the money and thereby controlled the candidate. This is not necessarily to say that the PACs control the representatives to whom they contribute, or that their contributions amount to the "buying" of votes. Very often PACs on both sides of an issue will contribute to the same candidate. What political action committees are usually after is "access" to the officeholder, a means of knowing their voice will be heard at a crucial moment while the legislation is being drafted or voted on. This appears to have been the case with Representative Alexander, whose questions at the FDA hearing, to judge from their wording, seemed to have been provided by the druggists.

Lest there be any doubts or later misunderstandings, the Appropriations Committee wrote into its report accompanying the FDA appropriations bill for the 1981 fiscal year that the agency should proceed with the insert effort "only in an orderly step-by-step manner," and should keep the committee advised of its actions. It also directed the agency to conduct pilot tests, to investigate the cost implications of the rule, and to avoid "unnecessary inflationary costs to the consumer." It added that it expected the FDA to comply with assurances that it would test no more than 10 package inserts over the next two years.

This brought a sharp protest from Henry A. Waxman, a powerful California Democrat who chaired the Health and Environment Subcommittee of the House Interstate and Foreign Commerce Committee, which handles FDA authorizations. He charged that the Appropriations Committee was using its report to undermine the legitimate authority of the FDA, and he denounced what he called "this intrusion" into the legislative jurisdiction of his committee.

---

* See the case study on political parties in this volume for further observations on trends in campaign finance and their implications.

Such "turf battles" are common in Congress. While they frequently seem like petty squabbling to outsiders, they often serve an important role in shaping legislation and in curbing excesses, giving voice to interests that might have been excluded from deliberations at some point. For example, in 1981 the Senate passed by a 93 to 0 vote a bill to set aside 1 percent of federal research and development funds for small businesses. The idea of the bill, called the Small Business Innovation Research Bill, was to spur technological innovation by small businesses as a means of economic stimulation. There were many objections, particularly from universities that stood to lose many of their research grants when funds would be diverted to small businesses. Once in the House of Representatives, the bill had to run a gauntlet of at least six different committees, each claiming jurisdiction because the bill would affect the budgets of such different departments and agencies as Defense, Health and Human Services, Energy, and the National Science Foundation. At this writing it was unclear what the final outcome would be, but it seemed likely that—to accommodate jealous committee chairmen, each responding to a different constituency—the bill would be substantially altered and watered down.

Dr. Goyan indicated in the interview on the PPI issue that he feared that the Appropriations Committee would pass a bill forbidding the insert program altogether and the scaled-back scheme seemed like a politic way of getting half a loaf, or at least a few slices. "Politics is not necessarily a bad word," he said.

Behind Dr. Goyan's thinking, undoubtedly, was an awareness of the rocky recent history of FDA's dealings with Congress. And this underscores another motivation governing regulatory decisions: although it has considerable authority and is widely feared by industry, an agency like the FDA has only so much clout, so much staff time and energy. It can fight only so many battles at once. In recent years the drug agency had suffered several stinging political defeats. It had been put on the defensive repeatedly over such issues as its ban on additives like saccharin, the artificial sweetener, and sodium nitrites, used as preservatives in meats.

Those two issues serve well to illustrate how the FDA steers a perilous course over shoals formed by the dictates of law, the uncertainty of the science on which it must rely, and hard political realities. Back in 1958, in what then seemed like an eminently sensible measure, Congress passed what is known as the Delaney amendment to the Food, Drug and Cosmetic Act. It required the FDA to outlaw automatically any food additive found to cause cancer in humans or animals, no matter how small the risk. Since then, however, scientific techniques have become much more precise and many a substance once thought safe has come under suspicion—so much so that the food industry contends that the Delaney amendment is unreasonable and that some consideration must be given to the benefits of the additives when weighing the risks. "It would be impossible today to survive on a diet consisting only of substances that have not been found to be carcinogenic by some type of scientific study," complained Peter Hutt, former chief counsel for the FDA and now with a Washington law firm representing industry interests. Consumer activists contend this is an exaggeration, but such industry complaints have increasingly fallen on sympathetic ears in Congress.

For example, a major uproar ensued when the FDA invoked the Delaney clause in 1977 to ban saccharin, used to sweeten diet soft drinks and other products, on the basis of several studies linking its use to bladder and other cancers. Congress passed special legislation to delay the move, the majority feeling that the health benefits for the obese and diabetics outweighed the cancer risk. A similar flap arose when the agency tried to phase out nitrites. The meatpacking industry argued that the risk of cancer was far lower to the public than the potential harm of botulism poisoning from canned meats. The argument was complicated by a follow-up study that found that the original study linking nitrites to cancer was wrong. One consequence of these FDA controversies was to make Congress more receptive to revising or repealing the Delaney clause.

At the time the PPI issue was before Dr. Goyan, Congress had already intervened to nullify temporarily the saccharin ban and was threatening to extend the moratorium. In short, the FDA already had enough trouble on its hands with two politically unpopular moves without opening up still another front.

"My sense is that Dr. Goyan genuinely believed in these inserts," said a Senate staff member closely familiar with drug policy,

> But he did not want to do something, have it backfire and then have the agency discredited. They were fighting with OMB, with the antiregulatory people, and with the Domestic Policy Staff at the White House. There might have been a bill to kill it. This was at least 30 to 40 percent a political decision. Had Dr. Goyan had a free hand he might have gone with 45 to 50 drugs to start.

At any rate, this staff member and others familiar with FDA procedures said the agency could not possibly have implemented its original plan to include 375 drugs.

THE "FINAL" RULE

And so the FDA proceeded to hammer out its final, much less ambitious, rule. Given the political stress the rule had caused, it was given the unusual—although not unheard of—treatment of a personal review by the HEW secretary, Patricia Harris. And then on September

10, at a press conference led by Secretary Harris at departmental headquarters in downtown Washington—not at the remote FDA headquarters in Rockville, which reporters always seem to have a hard time finding—the rule was announced with appropriate fanfare. It was to be a three-year pilot program involving new prescriptions for 10 drugs or drug classes. Refills were exempted from the insert requirement. Secretary Harris said the program could result in savings of $80 million in worker productivity lost to drug misuse annually. "Studies show that about 40 percent of the prescriptions given to patients each year may not be taken correctly," she declared. "Misuse may prolong illness, lead to serious adverse drug reactions, costly visits to the hospital or to the doctor's office and cause needless suffering. The intention of this project is to increase the safety of the millions of Americans who rely on prescription drugs every year."

If this was the great consumer victory the secretary proclaimed it to be, it was hard to tell from the reactions. Consumer groups denounced it as inadequate, the drug makers said they thought it was terrific, and the druggists muted their grumbles. Lewis A. Engman, president of the Pharmaceutical Manufacturers Association, said the inserts would help deliver "meaningful information to the consumer," and he pledged his organization would "do all we can to help make the project a success."

Two days later, on September 12, the full rules were spelled out in 63 pages of small type in the *Federal Register*. The FDA estimated that—based on 1979 data—the 10 drugs involved accounted for 120 million new prescriptions (refills were exempted in the final version) of the 1.4 billion total dispensed every year, or about 8 to 9 percent. According to FDA calculations, the cost of dispensing inserts with these new prescriptions would amount to about $21 million a year for the three years for printing, distribution, storage, administration, lost sales to pharmacies, and the like. If these costs were passed on in toto to the consumer, the agency said the program would add 9¢ to the price of all prescriptions, new and refills, or 18¢ if the costs were applied only to new ones.

Balanced against this, the agency listed potential health and economic benefits that, in its view, far outweighed the costs. It was "plausible" to assume that "unnecessary" prescription refills for just these 10 drugs imposed a burden on consumers of $21 million to $42 million a year. Adding the cost of additional doctor visits, workdays lost, and hospitalization thought to result from noncompliance with drug therapies, the agency calculated consumer savings of as much as $792 million. If the inserts resulted in only a 10 percent reduction in noncompliance, the FDA estimated the overall savings to the public would amount to between $40 million and $79 million annually, not to speak of the alleviated suffering and other human factors that could not be evaluated in terms of dollars.

THE INSERTS

The affected drugs and drug classes were:

1. Ampicillin: A group of penicillin antibiotics (used to treat bacterial infections) that have produced serious, sometimes fatal, allergic reactions. It is often mistakenly prescribed to treat the common cold, for which it is ineffective.

2. Benzodiazepines: A group of "minor" tranquilizers, such as Valium and Librium, that are the most widely prescribed drugs in the world. Often prescribed by doctors to treat everyday stress, they can cause dependence and sometimes fatalities.

3. Cimetidine: A drug used to treat intestinal ulcers. It requires that the patient take a highly active role in the prolonged treatment.

4. Clofibrate: Widely used to lower elevated cholesterol and triglyceride levels in the blood on the theory that that will prevent heart attacks. Recent studies have shown that its use involves some serious risks, such as increased danger of gallstones and cancer, and that it actually increases the risk of fatal heart attack.

5. Digoxin: Used to treat congestive heart failure, it can cause serious side effects if not used properly, especially in combination with other drugs. Too much can cause "Digoxin toxicity"; too little can bring return of the original symptoms.

6. Methoxsalen: Capsules used to treat vitiligo, a disease marked by loss of color on patches of skin. Treatment requires the patient be exposed to a special ultraviolet light for two or three hours after taking the drug, while wearing protective eyeglasses.

7. Phenytoin: A drug in wide use to control epilepsy and other seizure disorders. Failure to comply with the prescribed regimen can cause more seizures, but patients have been deterred from compliance because of misunderstandings about side effects.

8. Propoxyphene: Sold under the brand name "Darvon," it is used as a pain killer. But it can be dangerous if used when drinking alcoholic beverages and can cause addiction. Patients are advised to avoid driving or doing any other potentially hazardous tasks while taking the drug.

9. Thiazides: A broad group of antihypertensive drugs used to control high blood pressure and to reduce excess fluid in the body. Because high blood pressure produces few immediate symptoms, patients often fail to complete their regimens, frequently with untoward consequences.

10. Warfarin: An anticoagulant used to prevent clots in blood vessels or to stop them from enlarging. Failure to adhere closely to the therapy can destroy its effectiveness, and patients must be informed about side effects such as bleeding episodes.

Typically, the wording of the inserts as proposed by the FDA was two-edged. The inserts instructed the patient on the need to maintain the prescribed regimen, but at the same time warned the user of the drug's dangers. For example, the insert for cimetidine, used in treating ulcers, was plainly didactic in tone. The drug, it said, "helps heal intestinal ulcers by decreasing the amount of acid made by the stomach. Ulcers and the pain they cause are often relieved by decreasing the amount of acid produced." It instructed users: "Do not stop taking the cimetidine without first checking with your doctor." The insert also warned of possible side effects such as diarrhea, nausea, rash, breast enlargement among men, and mental confusion.

The proposed PPIs clearly reflected the FDA's philosophy on certain drugs. For example, the agency had recently issued a public statement that tranquilizers such as Valium should not be used—as many doctors have prescribed them—to help patients cope with every-day stress. The wording for the inserts in these drugs, the benzodiazepines, stated that "they should not be used to treat anxiety or tension due to the stress of everyday life" and that they have not been proven effective for treating anxiety that lasts longer than four months.

In other respects, the inserts seemed oddly incomplete. For exam-ple, the one for clofibrate—the cholesterol-lowering drug—mentioned that users had an increased risk of contracting cancers and gall bladder disease, but neglected to mention that their risk of suffering a fatal heart attack was greater than among nonusers. This seemed a strange omission, given the fact that the drug was prescribed to prevent heart attacks. But the insert definitely seemed intended to reduce the drug's use, declaring "relatively few patients should take clofibrate."

AN UNEXPECTED ENDING

All things being equal, this would now be the end of this account. The regulations would have gone into effect and by May 25, 1981, users of three of the drugs (cimetidine, clofibrate, and propoxyphene) would have started to receive little flyers in their drug bottles. By July 1, 1981, ampicillin and phenytoin would have been added, with the rest at later dates to be determined by the FDA.

But all things were not equal at that time. In November 1980, two months after the drug agency issued its "final" rule, Ronald Reagan was elected president on a platform that included the promise to roll back what he called costly, overly burdensome, and ineffective government regulations. The opponents of PPIs, having reached a reasonably satisfactory accommodation with the Carter administration, saw the opportunity to reopen the issue and force the FDA to back off even further. A survey taken by the Commerce Department found the PPI rule among the 20 most odious new or pending regulations left over by the outgoing administration—at least in the eyes of the industry.

Soon after the new administration took office in January 1981, it began to notify the drug makers that they would not have to comply with the deadlines for the inserts imposed by the Carter administration. On April 23, the new secretary of Health and Human Services,* Richard S. Schweiker, announced that the FDA would conduct a "complete review of ways to provide health and safety information to consumers about drugs." And to permit this review, he said, the FDA would postpone the effective dates of the PPI pilot program. The Presidential Task Force on Regulatory Reform observed:

> Important questions have been raised about the utility of PPIs since the decision to use a prescription drug is nearly always made before purchase. Costs to drug manufacturers, drug wholesalers, and pharmacists, including thousands of small businesses, could be substantial and thus lead to increased prices for prescription drugs.

By this time, Dr. Goyan had been swept out of his job as FDA commissioner along with the rest of the top Carter appointees. The new FDA commissioner was Arthur Hull Hayes, Jr., a cardiologist who had been head of the Hypertension Clinic at the Hershey Medical Center, affiliated with Pennsylvania State University. Soon after taking office, he told an interviewer: "I firmly believe that patient information about the drugs they take is terribly important. It's also important to look at any way this can be done in an effective way, [keeping] the costs commensurate with what you're doing."

The new administration called for an "in-depth" study of the PPI matter, to be headed by Dr. Hayes. He promised a decision by year's end. Thus, nearly a decade after the issue first crystallized, the FDA was back to square one, commanded to restudy an issue it had already studied, restudied, and restudied again. The consumer groups, increasingly frustrated and ineffectual, cried foul. The Public Interest Health Research Group, affiliated with Ralph Nader, filed suit on April 8, 1981, charging that the new administration was illegally subverting the new rules. In a letter to Dr. Hayes, Dr. Sidney H. Wolfe, head of the Health Research Group, declared that "The suspension of the PPI program provides further evidence that HHS (Department of Health and Human Services) is more responsive to the interests of the drug industry than to the health needs of the American public." These accusations prompted the newsletter put out by the Pharmaceutical Manufacturers Associ-

---

* During the Carter administration, the old Department of Health, Education and Welfare was broken up into two departments, the Department of Education and the Department of Health and Human Services. The FDA remained under the latter roof.

ation to observe in its August 17, 1981, issue: "PPIs, the Mt. St. Helens of Drug Regulation, Smokes Again."

Meanwhile, while the Reagan administration was reconsidering, a long-awaited study of the efficacy of PPIs by the RAND Corporation was released. The study, done under a $525,000 contract from the FDA, seemed to suggest that PPIs were neither as good as their proponents suggested nor as bad as their detractors feared. It found that 70 percent of patients would indeed read the inserts. But the study also found that they did not substantially influence the way the medicine was used, nor encourage patients to return prescriptions for refunds.

Finally, under court order to announce a decision by December 24, 1981, Dr. Hayes and Secretary Schweiker issued a joint statement in late December saying they would scrap the entire proposal. But in so doing they took pains to stress that they remained solidly devoted to the notion of providing more information to patients. The question, they said, was whether it could be done better at less cost by other means. The statement said, in part:

> This department remains committed to the need for patients to have more information about prescription drugs. Patients must actively participate with their physicians and others involved in health care in deciding on the best therapeutic approach to treating illnesses.
>
> The question is what is the best system, or systems, for providing that information. Our review of the 10-drug pilot program developed last year showed it to have significant limitations and to impose unreasonable constraints on the health care system. Moreover, we learned during our review that many physicians, pharmacists and other health professionals believe there are more effective and cost-efficient ways to bring information to consumers. This is why we will propose to rescind this pilot program.

To underscore the point, Secretary Schweiker directed Dr. Hayes to set up a special Committee on Patient Education at the FDA to coordinate government efforts in this area and to stimulate private sector initiatives. "We recognize that the government has an important and necessary role to play in consumer education about prescription drugs and other health care products and that the private sector has begun to take innovative and effective steps toward more patient information," said the Schweiker-Hayes statement. "These efforts need to be encouraged and supported by the government."

And so, after years of painful labor, the regulatory system gave birth to nothing. Nevertheless, although it produced nothing tangible in the way of enforceable rules, it could be said that the entire process probably enhanced the flow of information to patients.

SOME QUESTIONS TO EXPLORE

One of the axioms of political life in Washington is that few victories are ever complete and few defeats are ever final. The winds of political fashion and power are constantly shifting and very few underlying issues are ever permanently given up for lost; their proponents merely lie dormant until a more hospitable climate reemerges. Many a victory is really won in defeat. The PPI story is reasonably typical of a broad range of economic and professional regulations and what happens to them in changing political currents.

It is manifestly clear from this account that the FDA's efforts to compel druggists to distribute patient information failed. There was little clue that this would be the result when the effort was first mounted during the early 1970s, an era in which consumers were more inclined than now to look to Washington as their advocate. The PPI project began when the consumer movement was near the pinnacle of its influence. Numerous scandals involving defective and unsafe automobiles, toys, and lawnmowers, as well as corporate bribery, mislabeled foods, chemical spills, and hazardous drugs had galvanized public opinion against industry—widely perceived as being contemptuous of the public good and worker safety—and strengthened the hand of regulatory agencies like the FDA and the Federal Trade Commission (FTC).

Gradually, however, business began a counterattack that took root in the more conservative political soil of the latter part of the 1970s and early 1980s. Industrial leaders argued that while a certain amount of regulation was undoubtedly necessary, the pendulum had swung much too far in that direction. The result, they contended, was that business was hobbling under overly burdensome rules that not only cost the consumer in higher prices but also handicapped American industry trying to compete in a world economy. The precipitous decline of the automobile industry, in particular, sensitized many to the hidden costs of regulation. Similarly, drug makers—and more than a few physicians—argued that Americans were being denied valuable new drugs because of an overly rigorous drug approval process. Business leaders made the case, which fell on the ears of an increasingly receptive public, that industry was not irresponsible and that it was simplistic to equate profits with evil.

These arguments found a strong echo in the 1980 presidential candidacy of Ronald Reagan. One of his main campaign themes was to "get government off the backs" of the people and industry through "regulatory relief." He made considerable political hay with attacks on seemingly absurd rules imposed by Washington on local schools, factories, and business practices. By the end of Reagan's first year in office, more than 100 regulations had been rescinded, frozen, revised, or subjected to new scrutiny, and many others had been undermined by lax enforcement. Reagan ordered that all new rules be submitted to the Office of Management and Budget before being publicly proposed. According to the President's "Task Force on Regulatory Relief," headed by Vice President George Bush, these actions saved industry and consumers $2 billion in annual operating costs and $5 billion in capital expenditures.

Among the affected rules, in addition to the PPI one, were regulations requiring racial "affirmative action" in hiring for federal projects, requiring that local schools make special provisions for handicapped children, and guidelines for disposal of toxic wastes. The Bush panel said the intent was to eliminate "needless confrontation and harassment."

Against this shifting backdrop of public mood and governmental leadership some larger questions about the PPI episode can be asked:

Have the regulators really lost? The very act of proposing a new rule often has the effect of sensitizing the affected constituencies to a problem or putting an issue in a different light. Despite their deep objections to the proposed FDA rule, pharmacists and medical groups began to fall all over each other propounding their commitment to enhanced patient information. Many came up with less onerous "voluntary" alternatives to the FDA rule, like the one advanced by the American Medical Association. The theme of the 1982 annual meeting of the American Pharmaceutical Association was "Patient Education: Expanding Pharmacists' Role." At the meeting, the Schering Corporation, a drug maker, told the druggists of a survey it took showing that consumers tend to patronize drugstores that maintain a high level of communication with patients. In "losing," then, can it be argued that the FDA wrought a fundamental shift in doctor-patient and druggist-consumer relations?

Is the rule really dead? The political winds are fickle. It would not take much for them to shift. A major new scandal could significantly strengthen the hand of the FDA. (A generation ago the FDA won widespread praise for having thwarted the introduction into the United States of thalidomide, a drug given to pregnant women in Europe that later was implicated in terrible birth defects. What would be the result if a relaxed regulatory environment led to another thalidomide incident?) Even without a scandal, will the FDA eventually revive the PPI rule? Institutions like the FDA have long memories. The bureaucracy usually outlives any one administration and is ready, willing, and able to reassert itself when a more congenial one enters the White House. In the meantime the proposal gets the agency's foot in the door. Often a regulation develops slowly, evolving in zigzag fashion to accommodate short-term political forces, but ultimately moving toward a coherent goal.

How should the worth of a regulation be evaluated? Behind the Carter and Reagan administrations' objections to the PPI rule was the notion that the costs of the proposed rule might outweigh its benefits. But such evaluations require reducing costs and benefits to dollars, which is often difficult. Thus the controversial concept of "risk assessment" arises, which has been used to raise persuasive objections to many rules. For example, the meat industry argued that any human cancers that might result from nitrites in meat must be weighed against the possible deaths from botulism that might result from not preserving meats with the chemical. Is it proper for the government to accept risks, even death, for some people in order to benefit others?

Moreover, *how far should the government go in protecting people?* The Reagan administration dropped a proposed rule requiring automobile makers to install automatic seat belts or air bags that inflate in a head-on collision, cushioning occupants. The flagging auto industry argued that it would cost them billions to implement the rule and force car prices to climb at a time when sales were badly slumping. In all it was estimated to cost consumers $8 billion over five years. Yet much the same safety effect would result if people would voluntarily buckle their seat belts. Is it then the role of government to force consumers to pay for protection that is readily at hand if they would only use it? If patients can get drug information with a little effort why should some consumers be compelled to pay for others who will not help themselves by buckling up or looking up the information they need?

What is the role of Congress in the regulatory process? As noted in the PPI account, Congress very often leaves crucial decisions to the regulators. This has its virtues and its defects. On the one hand, it relieves Congress, a political body with scant scientific expertise, from making technical and medical decisions. Moreover, should scientific facts change, it is usually easier to amend a regulation than to pass new legislation. The vagueness of many laws thus invests them with a certain desirable flexibility. On the other hand, the practice of leaving important policy details to the bureaucracy sometimes allows it to subvert a law with which it collectively disagrees, or to go beyond what Congress may have meant. If the popular will is properly exerted through Congress, how can Congress be sure its will is followed without becoming hopelessly entangled in technical details?

One means Congress has of seeing its intentions through is its oversight authority. Frequently Congress holds hearings on specific issues when members believe the bureaucracy is failing to administer or enforce a law or program properly. Congress exercises legislative oversight when an agency budget comes up for consideration, as when the

Appropriations Committee forced Dr. Goyan to retreat on the PPI proposal. But this tends to be a haphazard approach. Is this kind of oversight adequate? Should Congress take a stronger role in following up on how the laws it passes are implemented? Or is it better in the long run not to impose too stringent a litmus test on every action of the bureaucracy? Could it be argued that, by virtue of being somewhat insulated from day-to-day politics, the civil servants are best equipped to administer the laws rationally and evenhandedly, without undue regard for political considerations?

What does this whole episode say about the American political system? It certainly suggests that it is porous, open to many interventions by different parties at different stages. Why did the regulatory agency seem to lose control of the process it initiated? Were there ways it could have been more effective? Is there a better way of translating law into reality, of putting policy into practice?

SOURCES AND READINGS

This case study is based mostly on personal interviews with the primary participants in Washington. Some spoke for the record, others—particularly congressional staff members—preferred anonymity in accordance with the unwritten first law of Congress: all publicity goes to the elected members.

Any study of regulation must start with the *Federal Register*. While it will seldom tell the true behind-the-scenes story, this daily compendium of official federal utterances is required first reading for the participant or student of the regulatory process. A close reading of a proposed rule, as published in the *Register*, often gives a clear and concise picture of the arguments for and against the rule, and the legal and economic background for it. *Federal Register*, Vol. 44, No. 131, July 6, 1979, pp. 40016-40041, covers the official notice of the proposed PPI rule, spells out the history of the issue, and provides the rationale for the agency's decision.

Well worth reading is an analysis of the PPI issue conducted by a panel of the Institute of Medicine entitled "Evaluating Patient Package Inserts" (August 1979). This study examines the ramifications of PPIs for the doctor-patient relationship and for patient health. An earlier article by Robert Reinhold, "Pills and the Process of Government," *New York Times Magazine,* November 9, 1980, covers the PPI issue to that date in briefer and more journalistic fashion than presented here.

Because bureaucracy and regulation both shape and are shaped by the overall process of American government and politics, they are best approached initially within that broad context. The various standard texts on American government are useful, therefore, for their treatment of the operation of our politics and for their coverage of bureaucracy and the administration of policies and programs. The regulatory activity of an agency can best be understood in terms not simply of its formal structure and authority, but of its mix of relationships with the incumbent presidential administration, other parts of the executive branch, Congress, interest groups, and public opinion. An excellent discussion of the federal regulatory process can be found in Alan Stone, *Regulation and its Alternatives* (Washington, D.C.: CQ Press, 1982).

For insight into current political and policy conflicts involving the bureaucracy, weekly reference sources such as the Congressional Quarterly *Weekly Report* and the *National Journal* should be consulted.

4

The Courts

Abortion and the Courts: Uncertain Boundaries of Law and Politics

Austin Sarat

On January 23, 1973, the United States Supreme Court, in *Roe* v. *Wade*, ruled unconstitutional antiabortion statutes in Texas and Georgia. This decision, which provided constitutional protection for abortion on demand (for at least a portion of pregnancy), is one of the most controversial of the last decade. Far from putting to rest debate about abortion, the Court's decision encouraged greater public controversy about the issue. Many people believed that the Court had overstepped its authority. Still others believed that the Court had allied itself against the sanctity of life. These disputes over the proper role of the judiciary remain central elements in arguments for reform of the federal courts—especially the Supreme Court—and have engaged major figures in American political life.

One of the most important of those arguments was made in October 1981 by the attorney general of the United States, William French Smith, in a speech to the Federal Legal Council, an organization of high-level lawyers from major government agencies. Attorney General Smith used this occasion to deliver a stern warning to the federal courts. He stated that the Justice Department would seek to stop a trend toward what he called greater "judicial policymaking." Smith suggested that the courts had, in the last decade, arbitrarily recognized new rights or given preference to some rights over others; that preference revealed "a process of subjective judicial policymaking as opposed to reasoned legal interpretation." The courts, Smith commented, had acted arbitrarily in declaring "the right to marry, the right to procreate, the right of interstate travel and the right to sexual privacy" to be fundamental rights even though none are mentioned in the Constitution. According to the attorney general, the effect of this judicial policymaking was to weaken the separation of powers and federalism and to undermine the democratic process. In recent decades the federal courts have

> engaged in and fostered judicial policy making under the guise of substantive due process. During this period the [Supreme] Court weighted the balance in favor of individual interests against the decisions of state and federal legislatures. Using the due process clauses, unelected judges substituted their own policy preferences for the determinations of the public's elected representatives. We will attempt to reverse this unhealthy flow of power from state and federal legislatures to federal courts. . . .

While the language of the attorney general's attack on the courts may seem sharp, there was little new in his words. President Ronald Reagan, after all, had run on a platform that attacked many of the so-called "social issue" decisions of the federal courts—school prayer, busing, and abortion. The Republican platform recommended that no judge be appointed to the federal courts who was not pledged to the protection of human life (that is, who was not opposed to abortion). There are, however, two points that should be noted about Smith's speech. First, it came at a time when many of President Reagan's supporters were demanding action on social issues. Smith's statement was an important move in their direction. The Justice Department is a major litigant before the federal courts and often files briefs urging particular decisions in cases in which it is not directly involved. Smith's statement, thus, placed an important institutional resource on the side of those who believe that the courts have gone too far in weakening religion, morality, and the family in American life.

The second significant aspect of the attorney general's speech was its explicitly political tone. Smith urged federal judges to take note of the changed political complexion of America. Pointing to "the groundswell of conservatism evidenced by the 1980 election," he called upon federal judges to reassess the way they had been reading the Constitution and to adopt, instead, *"more principled bases that would diminish judicial activism."* (Emphasis added)

The speech before the Federal Legal Council served as the latest among many periodic reminders that the federal courts, and particularly the Supreme Court, are seldom far removed from the play of politics. Smith's statement reminds us that law and politics are inseparable, that judicial decisionmaking is not unlike political decisionmaking, that federal judges, despite their independence and life tenure, pay attention, or should pay attention, to the election returns.

This case study will describe the evolution of abortion politics in the United States since the late 1960s. It will focus on the role of the courts, especially the Supreme Court, in the development of the abortion controversy. Proponents of reform of laws making abortion a criminal offense, as well as those who fought reform, used law and legal decisions as an important political resource and, at the same time, helped to politicize the legal and judicial process. The abortion issue typifies the sort of controversy that Attorney General Smith believes does not belong in the courts where it is subject to "judicial policymaking," but rather in the hands of the elected representatives of the people.

CONTINUING CONCERN ABOUT JUDICIAL ACTIVISM

Barely one-half century ago, it was political liberals who carried on a Reagan-like campaign against judicial activism. They complained about the tendency of the federal courts to interpret the Constitution, especially the due process clauses of the Fifth and Fourteenth Amendments, as prohibiting Congress and state legislatures from regulating economic conditions or practices. Legislation requiring minimum wages for women, restricting child labor, providing incentives to farmers to reduce the amount of land which they planted, and regulating prices and competition in the coal industry had all been declared unconstitutional.

The Court routinely struck down certain laws as impediments to the freedom of contract guaranteed by the Constitution. For example, the Court reasoned that minimum wage requirements impaired women's freedom to enter into a contract with an employer for a lower wage. The Court's intervention reflected its belief that the Constitution embodied certain principles of "laissez-faire" economics, a preference for a free market unfettered by regulation imposed by the government. According to a majority of the Court, the "liberal" legislation Congress was enacting was incompatible with the limited government envisioned by the Founders.

The Supreme Court's restrictive reading of the Constitution appeared to liberals, including President Franklin D. Roosevelt, to pose a threat to the nation's ability to recover from the economic crisis of the Depression. Shortly after being overwhelmingly reelected in 1936, Roosevelt introduced legislation designed, so he said, to help the Supreme Court keep up with its workload. This legislation, the famous Court-packing plan, provided that each justice who had served ten or more years on the Court would retire at age 70. For each justice over 70 who elected to remain on the bench the president would be authorized to make one new appointment. Naturally, Roosevelt would be expected to appoint justices who were sympathetic to his views and presumably would read the Constitution less restrictively. Roosevelt was very direct in defending his plan. "We have reached the point as a nation where we must take action to save the Constitution from the Court and the Court from itself," he declared.

While Congress was considering Roosevelt's proposal, the Supreme Court reversed itself and began to uphold legislation of the same type that it had previously found unconstitutional, for example, the National Labor Relations Act and the Social Security Act. Pithily called "the switch in time that saved nine," this turnabout removed the impetus behind Roosevelt's Court-packing plan.

During the next three decades the Court shifted its attention from economic matters to issues of social policy and political rights. It relaxed its scrutiny of economic regulations, but developed a special concern, a "more searching . . . scrutiny" for official actions affecting political and social rights. That "more searching . . . scrutiny" was applied during the 1950s and 60s to invalidate *de jure** racial segregation, to require state legislatures to reapportion themselves, to prohibit prayer in the public schools, and to restrict the grounds on which left-wing political groups could be subject to criminal prosecution. Some of the most far-reaching and activist decisions of the Court under Chief Justice Earl Warren involved the rights of criminal defendants and the right of privacy.

In a series of controversial decisions the Supreme Court applied the Fifth Amendment right against compulsory self-incrimination and the Fourth Amendment guarantee against unreasonable search and seizure to *state* criminal prosecutions as well as federal ones. The Sixth Amendment's "right to counsel" provision was interpreted as requiring that criminal suspects be guaranteed the assistance of lawyers. Each of these decisions provoked considerable public outcry from those who believed that the Court was reading its own meaning into the Constitution and bending over backwards to protect criminals against legitimate law enforcement interests. In another set of decisions, the Warren Court's activism led to its recognition of a constitutionally guaranteed right of privacy, a right some justices defended vigorously while others insisted it was nowhere to be found in the Constitution.

---

* "De jure" is a Latin phrase meaning by right or legal establishment. It is often contrasted with "de facto," which means in fact or existing, but without official recognition.

RETHINKING THE RHETORIC OF
ACTIVISM AND RESTRAINT

Attorney General Smith's attack on the federal courts can appropriately be seen, then, as part of a long tradition of debate about the role of courts and their use of power. Liberals and conservatives have both taken turns as critics of activism. Indeed, because ours is a constitutional polity, controversy about the courts is built into the fabric of our politics. Americans, perhaps more than any other people, take constitutionalism seriously. For us the Constitution is more than a symbol of political legitimacy; it is a source—or more accurately a guarantee—of our political, social, and human rights. But it is, after all, words on paper until judges give life and meaning to those words; judges define the shape and scope of our rights.

Two factors combine to make their responsibility very controversial. First, the language of the Constitution is often imprecise. Crucial words or phrases have no clear or self-evident meaning. Take the Fourth Amendment, for instance. It guarantees "the right of the people to be secure in their persons, houses, papers and effects, against unreasonable searches and seizures. . . ." Or, take the Fourteenth Amendment, which tells us that no state may "deprive any person of life, liberty, or property, without due process of law. . . ." But when is a search unreasonable or a process due? What elements must be present? What practices are prohibited? Even when the language appears to have clear meaning, "Congress shall make no law . . . abridging the freedom of speech," questions arise which quickly take us beyond the text itself. If you wear an armband to register your opposition to a government policy have you engaged in speech or action? Does "no law" mean that anyone can say anything no matter how lewd, offensive, or dangerous?

The ambiguity of constitutional language means that the rights guaranteed are always open-ended, always subject to interpretation and judgment. Furthermore, most of the persons whose job it is to interpret the law are not directly accountable to the people. Federal judges are not elected, and they have life tenure. Thus, the debate about judicial activism is a debate about how judicial responsibility should be exercised and judicial power used.

Article III of the Constitution gives little guidance. It limits the courts to the resolution of "cases and controversies" (prohibiting purely advisory opinions) but does not define what constitutes a case or a controversy. Moreover, it does not specifically recognize the power of judicial review—the power of the courts to invalidate acts of Congress, the president, or state governments that violate one or another provision of the Constitution. That power, which is without doubt the centerpiece of the courts' political significance, was recognized by the

Supreme Court itself in a landmark decision in 1803, *Marbury* v. *Madison*. Speaking through Chief Justice John Marshall, the Court derived the power of judicial review from the provision in Article VI recognizing the Constitution as the "supreme Law of the Land." As interpreters and arbiters of that supreme law, the justices claimed they were empowered to declare any law or act repugnant to the Constitution null and void. Despite the absence of explicit language in the Constitution, the legitimacy of judicial review is rarely subject to serious challenge.

While judicial review gives the courts the ability to thwart popular sovereignty (as expressed through acts of the elected branches of government), it also gives the courts an important role in generating support for the political system. When courts review and uphold a challenged statute, they explicitly "declare it to be," as Professor David Kirp has said, "consistent with constitutional principles of governance." What was a partisan or political act is given an aura of propriety that transcends partisanship or politics. Yet court decisions seldom end political conflict and occasionally prompt formerly inactive groups to mobilize. What looks like a definitive resolution may simply create a new or intensified sense of grievance and injustice; what looks like a definitive decision may simply foreclose one avenue of attack but invite—albeit unintentionally—the exploration of others.

Given the power of the courts and the ambiguity of constitutional language, it should hardly be surprising that judicial decisions themselves often become the subject of dispute, as clearly happened with abortion. When Attorney General Smith reminded the courts of the results of the 1980 elections, he was calling on them to allow the people to work their will.

The debate about activism and restraint deals, in essence, with the proper relationship between courts and the political process. As a general rule, one can expect that members of the dominant political coalition will oppose judicial activism unless or until the courts can be staffed with judges who represent its views. Indeed, given the life tenure of judges, judicial decisionmaking inevitably lags behind shifts in political power. Those who call for restraint do so in order to encourage the courts not to inhibit the rearrangement of that power. This was clearly the case with FDR and it is clearly the case today. At both times a judiciary staffed largely by one party seemed to threaten the policy agenda of the other, now dominant, party.

The rhetoric of activism and restraint is never neutral. It can never be separated from the play of political interests. That rhetoric contains three different, although closely related, arguments about the nature of the Constitution, the process of judging, and the relations of courts to the majoritarian political process.

Judicial Restraint

The thesis of judicial restraint, as advanced by FDR and Smith, treats the Constitution as fixed law. It downplays the vagueness of the language of the Constitution and looks to the process of amendment as the proper way to ensure the vitality of the Constitution. Those who believe in judicial restraint argue that when the Framers used vague language to prohibit or require some action by the government, their meaning was limited to those actions which they had in mind at the time they wrote. The job of the judge is not to provide his own idea of what should be prohibited or required. Instead, it is to look for evidence of the meaning intended by the Framers. Supreme Court Justice Owen J. Roberts clearly expressed this argument in *United States* v. *Butler* (1936):

> It is sometimes said that the court assumes a power to overrule or control the actions of the people's representatives. This is a misconception. . . . When an act of Congress is appropriately challenged in the courts as not conforming to the constitutional mandate the judicial branch . . . has only one duty—to lay the article of the Constitution which is invoked beside the statute which is challenged and to decide whether the latter squares with the former. All the court does, or can do, is to announce its considered judgment upon the question.

Judges should read the Constitution in the narrowest manner, so the argument for restraint goes, avoiding constitutional questions wherever possible.

Taken as a whole, the Constitution serves to foster and encourage the operation of the political process, so Smith and others like him believe. Where there is doubt about what is allowable (as there often will be), judges should defer to decisions made in and through that process. As commentator Ronald Dworkin suggests, the disposition of those who advocate judicial restraint is "skeptical and deferential." In their view, Dworkin tells us, ". . . [C]ourts should allow the decisions of other branches of government to stand even when they offend the judge's own sense of the principles required by broad constitutional doctrines. . . ."

Judicial Activism

For the judicial activist, the Constitution is a statement of moral principles, of those aspirations and ideals that define the political community. It requires the polity to attend, more seriously than it otherwise would, to questions of rights, justice, and legality. Its vagueness is no particular problem; indeed, it is no more vague than any other statement of principles and aspirations. Contemporary judicial activists tend to see the Constitution in terms of its protections of individual rights. The Constitution requires those who interpret it to confront the difficult moral question of what is necessary to advance individual rights in any particular instance. The judge is required to articulate public values. His is never a mechanical task. His proper disposition is philosophical, and his enterprise is to ensure that the political process does not violate principles of the Constitution itself. As Dworkin puts it, ". . . [J]udicial activism holds that courts . . . should work out principles of legality, equality and the rest, revise those principles from time to time in light of what seems to the Court fresh moral insight and judge acts of Congress, the states and the President accordingly."

Judicial Translation and Transformation

The rhetoric of activism and restraint suggests that there is a proper understanding of the nature of the Constitution. Yet if anything is clear, after almost two hundred years of debate on the relationship of the courts to the political process, it is that there is no simple correct answer or resolution that will long satisfy. Indeed, the rhetoric of activism and restraint conveys an inaccurate image of the role of courts in American politics. That mistaken image too narrowly defines the political process to include only the choice of policy, not its judicial interpretation. Hence it erroneously places the courts outside the political process and sees judicial decisionmaking as more or less intrusive into that process. As political scientist Martin Shapiro has said, that image "is just as universally wrong as it is universally held."

Courts and judges are integral parts of the process of politics. The function of courts in American politics is to render judgments, when asked, about what may or may not be decided in and by the majoritarian political process. These judgments are articulated in light of the judge's sense of the values of the polity. And, necessarily, they give new meaning to those values. Politics does not stop when a court's judgments are rendered. Constitutional decisions typically are but moments in ongoing political conflicts, and mark neither their beginning nor end.

To understand the role of courts in American politics, one should focus on the way in which the courts redirect, reshape, and reformulate political issues, on the way they translate competing demands and thus transform political issues. Do judicial decisions advance or inhibit the processes through which a polity finds out and determines its values? Do such decisions make politics wiser, fairer, or more just than it would otherwise be? Do they arrange and rearrange political conflict in ways that help ensure the continuity of a political community in which conflict moves people closer to a better quality of life? These are more relevant questions for students of the courts than are the questions that emerge from the activism/restraint dialogue.

This perspective supplies its own rhetoric, one that suggests a connectedness and continuity between courts and politics, between constitutional litigation and political conflict, and between the language of rights and the reality of power. Tocqueville was right when he recognized, more than 150 years ago, that American culture encourages a consciousness of rights, that the legal profession has a special role in American politics, and that our courts have distinctive and important powers and responsibilities. He was right when he recognized that the combination of those factors creates a special place for law and judges in the political process. He wrote, "scarcely any political question arises in the United States that is not resolved, sooner or later, into a judicial question." But Tocqueville had it only half right. Scarcely any judicial question arises that is not, sooner or later, resolved into a political question.

What courts do when they resolve constitutional questions is, quite consciously, to rearrange the stage on which political conflict is played out. Judges interpret the Constitution so as to put the courts on one side or another of what they know to be continuously changing political balances.

Constitutional questions are not *sui generis* (wholly unique) in American politics. They are often simply political issues moved to what might be called a higher level. It is a mistake to separate constitutional and political issues. The rhetoric of translation and transformation takes us back to the insights of political scientist E. E. Schattschneider and applies them to the courts. Schattschneider argued that the key element in politics is always the level at which conflict is played out and the scope of conflict which is engaged: "... [C]ontestants ... move freely from one level of government to another in an attempt to find the level at which they might try most advantageously to get what they want." This is as true of movement among branches of government as it is true of movement among different levels. Movement of an issue into the courts represents an expansion and intensification of conflict, because the language of rights "universalizes" political claims, vesting them with a certain degree of legitimacy. Judicial decisions rarely move conflict to a lower or more limited level.

Translation and transformation are functions performed in and by all political institutions. When this concept is applied to the courts, it suggests the functional similarity of judicial and political institutions and locates the judicial process *in*—rather than *above* or *outside*—the dynamics of the political process.

The Court's establishment in the 1960s of a constitutionally guaranteed right of privacy provides a starting point for an examination of the processes through which courts translate and transform the nature of abortion politics. The Supreme Court's decision in *Griswold* v.

Connecticut (1965) set the stage for a host of struggles to follow, both judicial and political.

GRISWOLD AND THE RIGHT OF PRIVACY

Connecticut had a long-standing statute that made it a crime for any person, married or unmarried, to use "any drug, medicinal article or instrument for the purpose of preventing conception." In addition, the law made it a crime for anyone to assist another in obtaining or using birth control devices. Estelle Griswold, Executive Director of Planned Parenthood of Connecticut, and Professor C. Lee Buxton of Yale Medical School were both arrested and charged with having dispensed birth control information and advice to married persons in violation of the state law. They were convicted, and their convictions were upheld by the Connecticut courts.

Griswold and Buxton appealed to the Supreme Court, claiming that the state law violated the liberty guaranteed to them by the due process clause of the Fourteenth Amendment. In 1965 the Court held, 7-2, that the Connecticut statute was unconstitutional. Justice William O. Douglas, writing for the majority, argued that the Connecticut law invaded constitutionally protected "zones of privacy," zones protected by "penumbras and emanations," shadows and reflections, of specific provisions of the Bill of Rights.

> [S]pecific guarantees in the Bill of Rights have penumbras, formed by emanations from those guarantees that help give them life and substance. Various guarantees create zones of privacy. The right of association contained in the penumbra of the First Amendment is one. . . . The Third Amendment in its prohibitions against the quartering of soldiers "in any house" . . . is another facet of privacy. The Fourth Amendment explicitly affirms the "right of the people to be secure in their persons, houses, papers and effects. . . ." The Fifth Amendment in its Self-Incrimination clause enables the citizen to create a zone of privacy which the government may not force him to surrender to his detriment.

Douglas went on to argue that the right of married people to be let alone, to pursue "a way of life," falls within those constitutionally protected zones.

Dissenting Justice Hugo L. Black presented a classic case against judicial activism. Black agreed that a right of privacy may in fact be desirable, but he adamantly opposed those who sought justifications for it in the language of the Constitution. To read into the Constitution rights that are not there, he argued, is to weaken the very fabric of constitutional government. "I like my privacy as well as the next one, but I am nevertheless compelled to admit that government has a right to invade it unless prohibited by some specific constitutional provision." Black suggested that the majority opinion reflected the view that

... [T]his Court is vested with power to invalidate all state laws that it considers to be arbitrary, capricious, unreasonable or oppressive. ... If these formulas ... are to prevail, they require judges to determine what is or is not constitutional on the basis of their own appraisal of what laws are unwise or unnecessary. ... Such an appraisal of the wisdom of legislation is an attribute of the power to make laws not of the power to interpret them. The use by federal courts of such a formula or doctrine ... to veto federal or state laws simply takes away from Congress and states the power to make laws. ... So far as I am concerned, Connecticut's law as applied here is not forbidden by any provision of the Federal Constitution as that Constitution was written. ...

By 1968, three years after *Griswold*, the controversy over judicial activism had become a national political issue and an important part of Richard Nixon's presidential campaign. Nixon ran what he called a "law and order" campaign against so-called "rampant permissiveness" in American society. America's problems were largely, though not exclusively, the result of an inversion or abandonment of traditional values, he argued. Along with American Independent Party candidate George Wallace, Nixon suggested that we had become excessively preoccupied with the rights of the deviant or the strange. As a solution Nixon promised "law and order," code words for a return to a more conventional, and restrictive, way of life.

The politics of 1968 were thus dominated, at least partially, by what some then called the "social issue," that is, growing permissiveness in attitudes toward drugs, sex, and social conduct, coupled with an attack on American middle-class values. As Nixon saw it, the courts, through a series of ultraliberal decisions, had contributed to the decline of morals and encouraged the attack on traditional values. They had done so by "seriously hamstringing the peace forces in our society" and by ". . .assuming unto themselves a mandate which is not there, and that is, to put their social and economic ideas into their decisions." Nixon's words—criticizing the Court for overstepping its boundaries and taking an *activist* role in political issues—could as easily have been spoken by Roosevelt, Justice Black, or Attorney General Smith.

Nixon claimed that his opposition to the Warren Court was not based simply on personal disagreement with its decisions but on a belief that the Court had not respected proper judicial procedures or employed appropriate methods in reaching its decisions. Instead, Nixon suggested, it had behaved more like a lawmaking institution than a court. Like Roosevelt, he advocated judicial self-restraint and a narrow reading of the Constitution, what he called "strict constructionism." Nixon promised that if elected he would appoint judges who took less active, reform-minded views of the Court's role in interpreting the Constitution than had the justices of the Warren Court. He promised a court system that would be deferential to the other branches of government, one that would leave the major issues of national policy to the president and Congress. As it turned out, while Nixon was able to appoint four justices to the Court, he was not able to curb its activism. In fact, within five years of Nixon's election, three of those four judges would vote to invalidate state antiabortion legislation. The abortion decisions of the United States Supreme Court, beginning with *Roe* v. *Wade*, provide a major focus for the continuing concern over the proper role of courts in American society, especially for those who contend that the consequences of judicial activism have contributed to the decay of traditional cultural values.

ABORTION POLITICS

"Moral decay," writes the Reverend Jerry Falwell, leader of the Moral Majority, "always precedes political turmoil, economic instability and military weakness in a country." Now "it is time to rise up against the tide of permissiveness and moral decay that is crashing in on our society from every side." For the so-called New Right, a loose coalition of political, religious, and social groups, abortion is the clearest and most dangerous example of that tide of permissiveness and decay. Yet, for others, abortion is necessarily an extension, and part, of a culture of freedom that recognizes the limits of public regulation of private conduct and respects the right of individuals to make those choices which most centrally affect their own lives. For them abortion is synonymous with freedom, with liberation, if you will, especially the liberation of women. It is these contrasting images of American society—moral decay versus a strengthening of freedom—that have consistently surrounded the controversy over abortion.

Many who write about abortion focus exclusively on the Supreme Court's 1973 decision to permit abortion in *Roe* v. *Wade*, holding it up as the centerpiece of that controversy. This is not a wholly mistaken approach, but it is wrong to conclude that the abortion controversy either began or ended with *Roe*. The issue of abortion emerged as a major political issue during the late 1960s. Prior to that time, abortion—the very word and idea—had such unpleasant connotations that it found no place on the political agenda. Moreover, it was and remains a no-win political issue, intensely divisive with no apparent, or satisfactory, middle ground. It is an issue that cuts across partisan lines. Only with the boundary-breaking demands for personal freedom of the 1960s was abortion put on the public agenda. Only with the reemergence of a serious gender-based political consciousness was the energy available to create and sustain a momentum for the reform of antiabortion laws. Only with an appeal to the sanctity of the doctor-patient relationship and the best traditions of American civil libertarianism did a coalition emerge that was sufficiently vocal to acquire political attention.

At the time when abortion politics emerged, every state had criminal statutes forbidding the intentional termination of pregnancy. (The single allowable exception, in most state laws, was to save the life of the mother.) Many of those statutes were first written in the 19th century, such as Connecticut's criminal statute pertaining to abortion written in 1821. That law made it a crime to abort a fetus after what is called "quickening," the time at which there is fetal movement in the womb. Following Connecticut's lead, New York passed a law making it a misdemeanor to abort the unquickened fetus and manslaughter to abort a quickened fetus. Most states initially followed New York's lead in treating abortion differently at different stages of pregnancy. However, by the turn of the century most antiabortion statutes were revised to drop the quickening distinction and increase the penalties for violations. These laws, it was argued, were necessary to protect women from the then hazardous and unsafe procedures associated with abortion. Little evidence exists to suggest that the enactment of antiabortion statutes precipitated the kind of moral and cultural conflict that characterizes contemporary abortion politics.

TOWARD LIBERALIZATION

There have been three stages of abortion politics since the late 1960s, stages without easily separable boundaries but with clear differences in emphasis. The first stage involved a movement to liberalize restrictions on abortion and recognize additional exceptions to the general prohibition against it. At this stage the legitimacy of antiabortion legislation was not seriously debated. The second stage was marked by increased attention to the constitutional dimension of the abortion controversy and by a demand that abortion be recognized as a purely "private choice." This stage was prompted by the Supreme Court's recognition of the claim to privacy in matters affecting sexuality as a fundamental right, a claim vindicated in the *Griswold* case in 1965. The third stage is the current one of reaction against the extension of the right of privacy to include a woman's decision whether or not to carry an unborn child to term. In this stage there has been a movement to restrict the right to abortion and to seek constitutional change to again prohibit it altogether, except in cases involving rape or incest. In each of these stages prochoice (those asserting a woman's right to have an abortion without state intervention) and antiabortion forces have moved their conflict back and forth between legislatures and courts and between the state and the federal level. At each stage courts have been intimately involved in the strategic maneuvering surrounding abortion politics.

Liberalization of abortion laws carrying criminal penalties began with the adoption of the American Law Institute's model abortion statute. The ALI, a group of lawyers interested in the modernization of law and legal procedure, adopted a Model Penal Code in 1962 containing suggested revisions in antiabortion laws. The revisions allowed abortions in cases of rape or incest or to protect the health and well-being of the mother. The ALI's commentary on its proposed model statute suggested that antiabortion laws were primarily the product of outdated Christian religious dogma and reflected a rigid view of the interests of society in protecting the unborn. Beginning in 1967 and continuing until *Roe* v. *Wade* (1973), 19 states changed their antiabortion laws to bring them into conformity with the ALI proposal. Four states—Alaska, Hawaii, New York, and Washington—went well beyond that proposal and repealed criminal penalties for all abortions performed by a licensed physician on grounds of medical necessity.

Doctors, Lawyers, and Planned Parenthood

The primary forces behind the initial movement for liberalization were drawn from three professional groups—doctors, lawyers, and public health workers. By the end of the 1960s, important segments of the medical profession had come to see antiabortion legislation as an invasion of their professional autonomy. That legislation seemed to place doctors in the position of having to respect and follow a law that often conflicted with their own judgment concerning the best interest of a patient. Alternatively, they could and often did disregard such laws to render what they considered sound medical care. Antiabortion laws, it seemed to many of them, made reputable professionals into criminals for exercising and using their special knowledge and skill. In addition, antiabortion laws created a black market for medical services. Women were driven to illicit practitioners and deprived of competent medical care. As a result, state medical associations and other organizations of physicians played active roles in prompting legislative consideration of liberalization. Abortion was portrayed not as a moral issue, but as one of professional competence, freedom, and unwarranted state regulation.

Organized medicine, as represented by the American Medical Association, played an important role in legitimating the campaign for liberalization. In 1967 the AMA's House of Delegates approved a resolution supporting the activities of physicians aiding and promoting legislative consideration of changes in abortion laws. At the same time, its Committee on Human Reproduction endorsed legislative proposals to permit abortions to protect maternal health, to prevent the birth of a seriously deformed child or a child conceived through rape or incest so long as such procedures were certified as necessary by three physicians and performed in accredited hospitals. When the House of Delegates adopted the Committee's resolution in 1970, it suggested that liberalization would place abortion more squarely within "the standards of sound clinical judgment, which together with informed patient consent should be determinative according to the merits of each individual case."

The doctors' campaign in favor of abortion reflected the strength of professionals in America and the growing perception that professionalism meant doctors ought to be given a key role in policy decisions relating to health care. Professionalism without professional autonomy, so the argument goes, means little. The state has a legitimate role, in conjunction with the medical profession, in establishing standards for licensing competent professionals. But once those professionals have been authorized by the state to practice, they must be allowed to make all necessary medically justifiable decisions. In its initial incarnation, the doctors' attack on antiabortion legislation took the form of an argument for professional control rather than an argument for personal freedom. Abortion was seen as a medical not a moral matter, a matter in which political and legal considerations had no place.

Joining with the doctors was the major organization of civil liberties lawyers in the United States, the American Civil Liberties Union. The ACLU came to the campaign for liberalization as part of its more general interest in expanding the protections of the Bill of Rights. To the ACLU, abortion was clearly a matter of personal rights, a matter in which the state ought to leave women alone to exercise their individual freedom. Long active in litigation to recognize and define a new series of constitutionally protected fundamental rights, the ACLU had been, in large part, responsible for the successful litigation of *Griswold*.

Three years after *Griswold*, in 1968, the ACLU announced that it considered a woman's decision concerning reproduction to be included in the constitutionally protected right of privacy and that it would work for liberalization (and eventual repeal) of antiabortion legislation. It took as its constituency or client group women—especially poor women—whose reproduction decisions were unduly infringed by state legislation. Working with representatives of women's groups, leaders of the ACLU described the abortion issue as an issue that struck at the heart of the Constitution's protection of individual freedom.

The call for professional autonomy and personal liberty was underlined with an argument about sound social policy. By placing the abortion issue in the general framework of concerns for population growth and overpopulation, proponents of liberalization formed an alliance with public health professionals and with the Planned Parenthood Federation of America. Historically, Planned Parenthood had been committed to the formulation of a rational population policy, a commitment that had made the organization a major sponsor of birth control and contraception as well as an ally of the ACLU in the successful constitutional litigation against state anticontraception legislation. Yet well into the 1960s Planned Parenthood, both in America and other nations, opposed abortion "because of its effects on the life and health of women who undergo it and their future children."

By the end of the decade, however, Planned Parenthood in America was an active proponent of liberalization. This change of position was, to some extent, the result of an attack on traditional birth control advocates by radical proponents of Zero Population Growth. The ZPG movement labeled Planned Parenthood an obstacle to the adoption of necessary measures to deal with the so-called "population bomb"; fine moral distinctions appeared irrelevant to them, given the world population picture. Planned Parenthood responded to this challenge by changing its position and allying itself with the proabortion coalition. This shift prevented a substantial erosion in its position among population control advocates, satisfied its allies in the ACLU, and was made respectable by the position of organized medicine.

Conflict Among Religions

The campaign for liberalization took as its primary targets state legislatures across the country. Active information and lobbying campaigns were mounted, with testimony, evidence, and legal argument presented to scores of legislative committees. That campaign did not, however, go unopposed. In many states, "Right to Life Committees" were formed to try to prevent any further liberalization and encourage even stiffer laws. In addition, coalitions of religious groups formed for similar purposes. Indeed, perhaps the most vocal and persistent opposition was mounted by the Catholic Church.

In state after state, Catholic clergymen issued statements denouncing advocates of liberalization and opposing legislative reforms. They openly called upon the faithful to oppose abortion reform and to abide by the Church's ban on all artificial methods of contraception. One result of the Catholic Church's outspoken campaign, however, was to energize other religious groups, groups both sympathetic to abortion reform and opposed to the open involvement of the Catholic Church in political matters. Thus, in 1967, the American Baptist Convention issued a statement urging liberalization, and the Protestant Council and the Federation of Reform Synagogues of New York criticized the Catholic Church's involvement in and opposition to abortion reform in that state.

While most of the energies on both sides were concentrated on legislative reform, there were initially a few lawsuits that raised significant abortion issues, one of the earliest being a case that the New Jersey Supreme Court decided in March 1967. In that case a married couple sued a physician for malpractice resulting from his failure to warn the woman, who had been exposed to German measles, that she might have a deformed child. The Court, while upholding the lower court judgment in favor of the doctor, suggested that such information could not have led to any alternative procedure since, in its view, the right to life of even a defective fetus is more compelling than the parent's wish for an abortion.

From the Legislatures to the Courts

By the end of the 1960s, courts were more actively and directly involved in the struggle for liberalization. In Washington, D.C., a claim was made that the District of Columbia's abortion law allowing abortions when "necessary for the preservation of the mother's life or health," was unconstitutionally vague.

That claim proved to be particularly significant in the history of abortion politics for three reasons. First, it marked the beginning of a substantial increase in judicial activity in the abortion controversy, activity that soon became a regular part of the political strategy of prochoice forces. Second, it promoted a transition from the stage of liberalization to the stage of freedom of choice. (It is noteworthy that the same constellation of political forces that *advocated* liberalization by state legislatures would later turn to the federal courts to *attack* liberalized laws.) Third, it set the stage for the Supreme Court's first abortion decision in 1971.

The *Vuitch* Case

Dr. Milan Vuitch, a physician in Washington, D.C., was indicted for performing abortions. Before trial he moved to dismiss the indictment on the grounds that the law under which he was being prosecuted was unconstitutionally vague and that it required him to prove his innocence rather than requiring the government to prove his guilt. Judge Gerhard Gesell, a federal district court judge, granted that motion. Subsequently, the United States appealed to the Supreme Court, and the Court reversed Gesell's decision. Justice Black, writing for the majority, argued that while the D.C. law incorporated a general exception for abortions "necessary" to preserve maternal life or "health," it remained the responsibility of the prosecution "to plead and prove that the defendant is not within the exception"; thus, the statute did not violate Dr. Vuitch's right to the presumption of innocence. Moreover, Black found that the word "health" could be broadly construed to include "mental and physical well-being" and, as a result, it presented no problem of vagueness insofar as the defendant was concerned.

Dr. Vuitch, with the aid of an *amicus curiae* (friend-of-the-court) brief submitted by the ACLU, also argued that the abortion statute was an unconstitutional invasion of the privacy of the doctor-patient relationship, a privacy recognized and protected by *Griswold* in 1965. Black, however, refused to reach the privacy claim since it had not been the basis for Judge Gesell's action. Nevertheless, Justice Douglas, writing in dissent, argued that the claim should be adjudicated. Douglas, who had written the majority opinion in *Griswold*, stated that the D.C. abortion law was *both* unconstitutionally vague and an abridgment of the right of privacy. He suggested that a doctor could not know what considerations would constitute valid health reasons under the law. "Would any unwarranted pregnancy [be] a health factor because it is a source of anxiety and stress?" he asked. Yet, for Douglas, the real issue was privacy. He argued that the right to decide whether to have an abortion should be included within constitutionally protected zones of privacy. "Abortion," Douglas suggested, "touches intimate affairs of the family, of marriage, of sex which ... involve rights associated with several constitutional rights.... There is compelling personal interest in marital privacy and in the limitation of family size." Douglas found in the Constitution protection for the difficult moral consideration involved in the decision to have an abortion. As he put it, "The subject of abortion ... is one of the most inflammatory ones to reach the Court. People instantly take sides.... The issue is volatile; and it is resolved by the moral code which an individual has." Subsequent events would prove the accuracy of Douglas's analysis of the nature of the abortion issue.

The *Vuitch* decision clearly precluded one line of attack by those seeking to move from liberalization to freedom of choice even as it indicated that there were some on the Supreme Court willing to entertain the broadest possible constitutional arguments. Meanwhile the push toward liberalization and eventual repeal continued. Established groups joined or were drawn into it. In 1968, both the American College of Obstetricians and Gynecologists and the American Public Health Association became active supporters of liberalized abortion laws. The following year an organization of women's rights activists called the Congress to Unite Women urged the repeal of all antiabortion laws. Women began to perceive the limitations of liberalization as the goal and to move the focus of conflict to the freedom of choice issue. They were joined in this effort by another new organization, the National Association for the Repeal of Abortion Laws, an association of civil libertarians and liberal religious groups, whose mission was to overcome Catholic resistance to abortion reform and support the recognition of a constitutional right to abortion.

Despite the broadening scope of the abortion controversy, it did not play a prominent part in the 1968 presidential election campaign. This was, however, to be the only presidential election in the next decade and a half about which that could be said.

TOWARD FREEDOM OF CHOICE

By 1970 the abortion reform movement was clearly set on a two-track course—one track involved the push for continued liberalization in state legislatures, the other the pursuit, through litigation, of a constitutional right to abortion. The movement of the controversy into the courts proved to be a valuable resource in the liberalization campaign in some states, while in others it turned out to be an obstacle. Abortion reform groups used the threat of judicial intervention and the spectre of judges ready to go beyond the ALI model statute to encourage recalcitrant legislators to reform their abortion laws. Yet in other states sympathetic legislators seeking to avoid the political turmoil building around the abortion issue argued that no reforms should be undertaken until there was a judicial resolution of the question of the constitutional status of abortion. These divergent outcomes in the abortion controversy illustrate the general difficulty of managing and using the threat or prospect of litigation to achieve political goals.

By 1972 the movement to liberalize abortion had succeeded in persuading many state legislatures to alter their antiabortion statutes. At the same time, prochoice and antiabortion coalitions had filed suits in state and federal courts across the country challenging liberalized as well as traditional statutes. Suits were brought in California, Wisconsin, New Jersey, Minnesota, Louisiana, Pennsylvania, Illinois, Connecticut, Florida, Georgia, Missouri, and Texas, with mixed results. Judges in Minnesota, Louisiana, and Pennsylvania upheld their state antiabortion laws, while judges in other states found such statutes unconstitutional. The most sweeping decisions were made in Connecticut and Texas where federal judges, adopting Justice Douglas's reasoning in *Vuitch*, found that decisions concerning abortion fell within the constitutionally protected right of privacy. Elsewhere, however, laws were enacted and lawsuits were filed to limit the effects of liberalization. In Philadelphia, for example, attorneys representing the National Federation of Catholic Bishops sought to prevent a public hospital from performing abortions. In New York City the Department of Public Health issued a regulation requiring that the name and address of a woman undergoing an abortion be placed on a death certificate issued for the fetus. (This regulation later was challenged successfully in court.)

The back and forth movement of the abortion issue between legislatures and courts is nowhere better illustrated than in the state of

Connecticut. During 1970 and 1971, bills were introduced in the Connecticut General Assembly to liberalize the law prohibiting all abortions except those necessary to save the life of the mother. Those attempts at liberalization, however, were defeated. In early 1971 a suit was filed by a group called Women Versus Connecticut, which sought to have the state's antiabortion statute declared unconstitutional. In the spring of 1972, a three-judge federal court found the law in violation of the right of privacy recognized under the Ninth Amendment to the Constitution, which the Court construed as reserving certain rights to the people. Almost immediately Governor Thomas Meskill announced his intention to call a special session of the Connecticut legislature to enact a new antiabortion law.

The new law he proposed would recognize the right of the unborn to equal protection under the law and would impose criminal penalties on both women seeking abortions and doctors performing them. Prochoice and antiabortion forces mounted major campaigns, with the prochoice position favoring legislation on the ALI model. The prochoice position prevailed in the state Senate, but not in the state House of Representatives. Governor Meskill threatened to veto legislation unless it forbade all abortions except those necessary to save the life of the mother. One week later, the Senate reversed its earlier vote and endorsed the Meskill version, thus returning Connecticut to its position prior to the court decision. The new law differed from the old law only in the preamble, which emphasized the intention to protect the fetus's right to life.

Two months later Women Versus Connecticut was back in federal court seeking to enjoin enforcement of the state's new law. In September, the federal court found the new law an unconstitutional abridgment of the rights of women "to privacy and personal choice in matters of sex and family life." The state immediately filed an appeal to the U.S. Supreme Court, asking that it grant a stay to prevent the federal district court from interfering with enforcement of the new state law. The Court granted the state's request pending a full hearing and consideration. The issue remained there until the Court handed down its ruling in *Roe v. Wade* on January 23, 1973, some four months later.

The overall success of the liberalization campaign helped to intensify opposition to abortion reform, particularly within the Catholic Church. Cardinal Cooke of New York City led a campaign to overturn New York's liberalized law. Other Catholic clergymen threatened excommunication for doctors and nurses performing abortion or parishioners active in the campaign for liberalization. In some cases, the abortion issue split religious groups—Orthodox and Reform Jews, for example—but in general it politicized America's religious community: the Greek Orthodox Archdiocese of North and South America supported the position of the Catholic Church, and the Southern Baptist

Convention, the United States Southern Presbyterian Church, the United Methodist Conference, and the United Church of Christ all supported abortion reform.

While most liberalization activity was carried on at the state level, abortion politics was beginning to have an impact in Washington, D.C., as well. In 1970, for example, the United States Department of Defense, largely at the urging of the Department of Health, Education and Welfare, issued a policy statement concerning abortions for American military personnel and their dependents. That statement permitted abortions to be performed in military medical facilities for reasons of "mental health . . . without regard to local law." Eight months later, however, President Nixon rescinded that policy, saying that he could not "reconcile unrestricted abortion . . . or abortion on demand with my personal belief in the sanctity of human life."

Nixon's antiabortion position was demonstrated further in the spring of 1972 when he announced his support for the New York State campaign to repeal the recently liberalized abortion law. Later that year, a National Commission on Population and the American Future, dominated by presidential appointees, recommended that ". . . women should be free to determine their own fertility, [and] that the matter of abortion should be left to the conscience of the individual." The commission's recommendation added significantly to the impetus for freedom of choice, and it was quickly endorsed by the National Association for the Repeal of Abortion Laws. Nixon himself, however, rejected the commission's recommendation.

By the spring of 1972, presidential candidates had moved to position themselves on the abortion issue. For Nixon the choice was easy. For George McGovern, then seeking the Democratic presidential nomination, it proved considerably more difficult. He was caught between two very diverse components of the Democratic coalition: its traditional Catholic supporters, on the one hand, and women's groups and other social issue activists on the other. He suggested that abortion was properly a matter for state regulation and indicated that he had no personal view on its propriety. His statement drew immediate criticism from both sides and led to a fierce fight at the Democratic National Convention over the inclusion of a prochoice recommendation in the party platform, a position rejected by the convention as a whole. The target of demonstrations by both prochoice and antiabortion groups, McGovern's equivocation about abortion came back to haunt him during the entire campaign.

Ironically, freedom of choice is at least indirectly the legacy of Richard Nixon. During his first term, Nixon had the unusual opportunity to appoint four justices to the United States Supreme Court:

Warren E. Burger, Harry A. Blackmun, Lewis F. Powell, Jr., and William H. Rehnquist. At the time of their appointments, Nixon described each of them as firmly within the camp of strict constructionism that he had promised during his campaign. Yet, in January 1973, when the Court announced decisions in cases challenging abortion laws in Texas and Georgia, all the Nixon-appointed justices but Rehnquist endorsed the prochoice position first advocated by Justice Douglas in *Vuitch*.

RECOGNIZING ABORTION RIGHTS

In late 1970 a three-judge federal court in Dallas, Texas, ruled that the Texas antiabortion statute, making it a crime to "procure an abortion" except when "attempted by medical advice for the purpose of saving the life of the mother," was both unconstitutionally vague and a violation of the right of privacy protected by the Ninth and Fourteenth Amendments. The court granted a declaratory judgment to that effect but refused to grant an injunction against Wade, the district attorney of Dallas, Texas. The three plaintiffs were an unmarried pregnant woman (called Roe by the court), a physician who had two abortion prosecutions against him, and a childless married couple who alleged that the state law might pose a danger to the wife's health should she conceive.

After the district court's ruling, Wade announced that he would continue to enforce the law. As a result, all three plaintiffs appealed to the U.S. Supreme Court asking that the injunction be granted. The state of Texas also appealed, seeking to overturn the district court's declaratory judgment. The Supreme Court consolidated this case, *Roe* v. *Wade*, and a similar challenge to the Georgia antiabortion statute brought by an indigent married woman who had been denied an abortion after eight weeks of pregnancy.

With the Court's decision to confront the abortion issue, a wide array of prochoice and antiabortion groups mobilized. Briefs supporting the prochoice position were filed on behalf of Planned Parenthood, the California Committee to Legalize Abortion, the National Organization of Women, Zero Population Growth, the American College of Obstetricians and Gynecologists, American Psychiatric Association, the American Medical Women's Association and the New York Academy of Medicine. These proponents of liberalization carried forward Douglas's right of privacy argument and also argued that antiabortion statutes unduly interfered in the doctor-patient relationship.

Briefs in support of the Texas and Georgia laws were filed by several groups, including Americans United for Life, the National Right to Life Committee, and the attorneys general of Arizona, Connecticut,

Kentucky, Nebraska, and Utah. These briefs claimed: "The crux of the moral and legal debate over abortion is, in essence, the right of the woman to determine whether or not she should bear a child versus the right of the child to life. The proponents of liberalization ... speak of the fetus as a 'blob of protoplasm' and feel it has no right to life until it has reached a certain stage of development.... [However], from conception the child is a complex, dynamic, rapidly growing organism."

After twice hearing oral argument, the Court ruled that state criminal abortion laws that exempted only a life-saving procedure and paid no heed to different stages of pregnancy violated the due process clause of the Fourteenth Amendment. The Court, with Justice Blackmun writing for a 7-2 majority, found that the "right of privacy ... is broad enough to encompass a woman's decision whether or not to terminate her pregnancy." Nevertheless, the Court did not agree with the prochoice argument that a woman's right to terminate pregnancy is absolute; instead it recognized legitimate—indeed compelling—state interests in the protection of maternal health and the potential life of the fetus. Those interests, Blackmun argued, grow during the time of the pregnancy and become compelling at different stages.

Blackmun developed a "trimester theory" of fetal development. He suggested that during the first three months the risks of abortion were no greater than the risks of carrying the child to term. As a result, "any interest of the state in protecting the woman from an inherently hazardous procedure ... has largely disappeared." During the second trimester, health risks increase and, as a result, "a state may regulate the abortion procedure to the extent that the regulation reasonably relates to the preservation and protection of maternal health."

With respect to the state's interest in the potential life of the fetus, Blackmun could find no justification for including the fetus within the broad scope of the Constitution's protection of "persons." However, there remained the difficult question of whether the fetus represented a life which the state could justifiably act to protect. Blackmun acknowledged that the Court was itself in no position to "resolve the difficult question of when life begins." He wrote in the opinion, "When those trained in the respective disciplines of medicine, philosophy, and theology are unable to arrive at any consensus, the judiciary ... is not in a position to speculate as to the answer." Nevertheless, the Court found the state's interest in protecting the potential life of the fetus to be compelling when the fetus became "viable," that is, when it "presumably has the capacity for meaningful life outside the mother's womb," after approximately 24 weeks of pregnancy. Thus, at the end of the second trimester the state justifiably and constitutionally might proscribe abortion except where it is necessary to preserve maternal life and health.

The Court's decision in *Roe* v. *Wade* went considerably beyond the position of the ALI. It created a period of pregnancy during which abortion decisions would be regarded as a "private choice," a matter to be left beyond the reach of state regulation. As Douglas wrote in an opinion concurring with the result in *Roe* and its companion case, *Doe* v. *Bolton*, "freedom of choice in the basic decisions of one's life" is guaranteed by the word "liberty" in the Fourteenth Amendment. "Unwanted children," he argued, "deprive a woman of her preferred lifestyle and force upon her a radically different and undesired future." Thus, as he saw it, the Court's decision guaranteed women the right to choose their lifestyles and shape their futures without state interference.

Justices White and Rehnquist dissented from the Court's decision because as Rehnquist said, "The decision here to break pregnancy into three distinct terms and to outline the permissible restrictions the state may impose in each one ... partakes more of judicial legislation than it does of a determination of the intent of the drafters of the Fourteenth Amendment." For Rehnquist, the decision in *Roe* was a blatant example of the kind of judicial activism that he believed should be curtailed. For White, what was most unacceptable was the balance which the Court struck between the competing interests of the mother and the unwanted fetus. According to the majority's decision, what the Constitution values most highly is the "convenience, whim or caprice of the putative mother." As White saw it, "In a sensitive area such as this, involving as it does issues over which reasonable men may easily and heatedly differ, I cannot accept the Court's exercise of its clear power of choice by interposing ... a barrier to state efforts to protect human life.... This issue ... should be left with the people."

RESTRICTING THE REACH OF ABORTION RIGHTS

On first look it would appear that the Court's decision in *Roe* effectively put an end to abortion politics. Not only had the Court invalidated state-imposed restrictions on abortion during the first trimester, it had, in effect, written a new model abortion statute. But because most states, even those with recently liberalized laws, had not incorporated anything like the Court's trimester approach, the abortion issue returned to the legislatures. Once again, the issue moved from the legal process back to the political process.

In the months following the *Roe* decision, most state legislatures acted to bring their laws into conformity with the Court's ruling. But rewriting abortion legislation provided antiabortion groups an opportunity to try to restrict the reach of the newly recognized rights. Pressure from religious groups also was brought to bear. For example, Catholic priests in Marlboro, Massachusetts, refused to baptize the child of a well known abortion activist, and the Catholic Bishop of San Diego, California, ordered the priests of his diocese to refuse communion to known members of the National Organization for Women unless they renounced that group's stand on abortion.

In addition, attention was focused on public and private hospitals to get them to refuse to perform abortions. The constitutionally protected right to *have* an abortion did not, so the antiabortionists argued, require any doctor or hospital to *perform* an abortion. In fact, New Jersey passed a law specifically authorizing doctors and hospitals to refuse to perform abortions for reasons of conscience. In other states antiabortion forces mounted extensive lobbying campaigns to promote other types of legislative restrictions on abortion. Florida, Pennsylvania, and Massachusetts enacted legislation requiring spousal consent for married women and parental consent for unmarried minors before abortions could be obtained. Virginia made it a criminal offense to publish advertisements for abortion services; New York and Connecticut state welfare departments issued regulations prohibiting the use of state funds for abortion.

At the same time, Congress began to consider and enact similar restrictions. In late 1973, Congress passed legislation to restrict the use of federal funds for research on any aborted fetus. That same year Senator James L. Buckley of New York introduced an amendment to forbid use of federal Medicaid funds for abortion. This attempt to cut off federal benefits would become the major focus of antiabortion activity over the next several years. Greatly distressed that the Constitution, as read by the Supreme Court, permitted abortion, antiabortion groups strongly opposed the use of federal (and state) taxes to finance abortions for those who could not otherwise afford them. A prohibition on state interference with a so-called personal right should not, they argued, be turned into state support, or facilitation, of the now permitted "private choice." Finally, in mid-1973, Buckley and six other senators introduced legislation to amend the Constitution to prohibit all abortions except those necessary to save maternal life. Antiabortionists contended that such an amendment was necessary to save the Constitution from those who had no respect for life itself. In the future, energies would be simultaneously devoted to restricting the reach of abortion rights and eliminating them entirely.

The renewal and success of antiabortion movements, especially at the state level, prompted a quick response from the prochoice coalition. Organizers worked to ensure that those who had fought for abortion rights did not disband or become complacent in the wake of their 1973 victory in *Roe*. The National Association for the Repeal of Abortion Laws reconstituted itself as the National Abortion Rights Action

League and announced that it would join with the ACLU to get courts to overturn any and all restrictions on abortions. Their first efforts were lawsuits in seven states to compel hospitals to perform abortions. Other suits were brought challenging spousal and parental consent laws on the grounds that they constituted an undue interference with the exclusive right of women and their doctors to make decisions concerning abortions during the first trimester. (This litigation resulted in favorable judgments in Florida, Louisiana, Pennsylvania, and Massachusetts.) Prochoice groups even tried to use the judicial system to attack organized Catholic opposition to abortion. Thus, Women's Lobby, a Washington-based group active on behalf of women's rights, filed what would prove to be an unsuccessful suit in the federal district court challenging the tax-exempt status of the United States Catholic Conference. The suit alleged that that group's activities against abortion revealed it to be primarily a political rather than a religious organization.

The Supreme Court's decision in *Roe* transformed the abortion issue from one of legislative reform to one of constitutional rights. It seemed, at first, to shift the balance of power in favor of the prochoice coalition, which would no longer have to carry the burden of promoting reforms. That burden now shifted to antiabortion groups, which attempted to use their influence in arenas where they had formerly been able to exert control, primarily state legislatures. Finally, the *Roe* decision facilitated a translation of the abortion issue from legal to moral terms. Because it foreclosed legal prohibition of abortion, antiabortion groups had to cast their activities as a moral crusade, a crusade on behalf of American values.

Picking up the rhetoric of Justice White's dissent, antiabortion forces were able to coalesce around the issue of life itself. They were able to successfully portray themselves as defenders of the unborn, of the future of humanity. They were able to exploit Blackmun's ambivalence about the status of the fetus and claim—as he had acknowledged—that the Supreme Court had no competence to decide when life begins. Because the Court went beyond the mere prohibition of antiabortion legislation to present its own arguments about maternal health and fetal life, it exposed itself (and the prochoice coalition) to the charge that it (and they) were simply reading their own moral preferences into law.

Even those otherwise sympathetic to abortion were critical of the Court's decision in *Roe*. Harvard Law Professor John Hart Ely expressed this position best. "Laws," he said,

> prohibiting the "use" of soft drugs or, even more obviously, homosexual acts between consenting adults can stunt "the preferred lifestyles" of those against whom enforcement is threatened. . . . It is clear that such acts harm no one besides the participants. . . . Yet such laws

survive on the theory that there exists a societal consensus that the behavior involved is revolting or at any rate immoral.... Whether the anti-abortion legislation cramps the lifestyle of an unwilling mother more significantly than anti-homosexual legislation cramps the lifestyle of a homosexual is a close question. But even granting that it does, the other side of the balance is very difficult.... Abortion ends the life of a human being other than the one making the choice ... that the life plans of the mother must ... prevail over the state's desire to protect the fetus ... does not follow from the judgment that the fetus is not a person. Beyond all that, however, the Court has no business getting into that business.... What is frightening about *Roe* is that ... [abortion] is not inferable from the language of the Constitution, the Framers' thinking respecting the specific problem at issue, [or] any general value derivable from the provisions they included.... At times the inferences the Court has drawn from the values the Constitution marks for special protection have been controversial, even shaky, but never before has its sense of an obligation to draw one been so obviously lacking.

Charges like these legitimated the attempts by antiabortion groups to turn abortion politics into a contest of competing moral visions and lifestyle preferences. As a result, what was a legal victory for the prochoice coalition quickly was turned into a political liability.

The *Roe* decision became a central focus and symbol for abortion politics. In the social context of the early 1970s, it placed the law and the Constitution firmly on the side of those who desired a freer, more open society. Like all legal decisions in moral controversies, it was an important public affirmation of the worth of one set of cultural values, in this case an affirmation of those who thought women should be more fully emancipated and that the culture as a whole should be more cosmopolitan. This affirmation is itself an important resource in the struggle for prestige and dominance within the society.

For antiabortion groups *Roe* posed a threat to their position within the larger culture. As sociologist Joseph Gusfield wrote, "The public support of one conception of morality at the expense of another enhances the prestige and self-esteem of the victors and degrades the culture of the losers." The Supreme Court's legitimation of the desire of women to exercise control over childbearing decisions poses a serious threat to those who believe that the health of America depends on the strength of its family life.

Abortion as an Electoral Issue

The apparent victory of the prochoice camp in *Roe* served to mobilize and energize antiabortion groups in a coordinated national effort to restrict and revoke abortion rights, to mold public opinion and influence elections, and to win legislative victories. Abortion politics now took to the streets. Antiabortion groups sponsored a march on

Washington, D.C., commemorating the anniversary of the 1973 *Roe* decision. Every year, from 1974 to the present, the National March for Life Committee has turned out thousands of people for rallies and demonstrations to express moral outrage at the Court's decision and to voice support for a prolife constitutional amendment.

In addition to providing such dramatic reminders of their influence, antiabortion groups began to undertake active roles in electoral politics. First in a few states and then at the national level, abortion was turned into an important voting issue. Early in 1976 a coalition of Roman Catholic bishops unveiled a plan to establish groups within each congressional district to monitor the voting of each member of Congress on abortion issues and to mobilize support against those who were not firmly prolife. In some states prolife candidates tried, albeit with little success, to win Democratic or Republican congressional or senatorial nominations. At the presidential level antiabortion groups were active in state primaries in opposing candidates such as Democratic Senator Birch Bayh, a noted liberal on social issues. There was, however, virtually no comparable proabortion electoral activity. (This asymmetry, partially attributable to the differential impact of *Roe* on abortion politics, was to be equally apparent in the 1978 and 1980 elections.)

Later in 1976 more than 10,000 demonstrators marched on the Democratic National Convention, demanding that it include a prolife constitutional amendment in its platform. But the convention followed the lead of its nominee, Jimmy Carter, and did not support such an amendment. Taking a position reminiscent of McGovern's stand in 1972, Carter said that while he was opposed to abortion as a matter of personal conscience, he could not support a change in the Constitution. However, he did indicate his opposition to the use of federal funds to finance abortions for poor women. Again the Democratic nominee tried to find a middle ground and, in so doing, satisfied neither prochoice nor antiabortion groups. Republican candidate Gerald Ford campaigned on a platform much closer to the position of the antiabortion coalition, endorsing a constitutional amendment to return control of abortion to the states.

Antiabortion groups continued to intensify their electoral activities after the 1976 election. The National Right to Life Convention announced in 1977 that it would work to defeat any member of Congress who did not support pending legislation to ban the use of federal Medicaid funds for abortion. The group carried out its plan during the 1978 congressional elections and scored a major victory in Iowa, where it was credited with contributing to the defeat of liberal Senator Dick Clark. The Iowa result served notice of the capacity of antiabortion groups to mobilize a substantial "single-issue vote" and provided a significant boost to the ambitions of the prolife cause.

During the 12 months following the 1978 election, the Life Amendment Political Action Committee (a relative newcomer to abortion politics), the National Conservative Political Action Committee, and a coalition of other antiabortion and ultraconservative political groups joined together with the announced intention of defeating five liberal senators running for reelection in 1980. Among those targeted for defeat were George McGovern and Birch Bayh, who had become leading opponents of moves to restrict abortion rights. But the real strength of the antiabortion political movement emerged only in late 1979 and early 1980 with the creation of the Reverend Jerry Falwell's Moral Majority, an alliance of fundamentalist religious groups.

The Moral Majority sought to energize the newly popular television evangelical preachers and encourage them to develop an active political role. With great success, Falwell urged ministers to see the intimate connection between morality and politics, to lead their congregations in political as well as religious matters. The Moral Majority was not, however, the only group to take this position. Others, such as the Christian Voters Victory Fund, supported a so-called "Christian crusade" in the 1980 election. These groups saw the electoral process as the best channel to achieve their moral, social, and cultural goals. They argued that political leaders who supported abortion and tolerated other forms of "immoral" social activity should not hold public office. The Moral Majority portrayed abortion as a sin, as perhaps the most visible element in America's cultural decay. They saw abortion and that cultural decay as threats to their way of life and directly antithetical to the teachings of the Bible. As Professor Sheldon Wolin wrote, they embodied a fundamentalist reaction, a reaction based on the fundamentalist belief in separation:

> We practice separation from the world and all its entanglements. We refuse to conform to the standards of a sinful society—and yet they [the fundamentalists] remain in the world, living as others do in the midst of a technological and a grossly material culture. They are threatened . . . by a relentlessly modernizing society that exposes their most cherished beliefs as archaic. . . .

The results of the 1980 election left antiabortion groups basking in the glow of victory; Falwell claimed that the Moral Majority alone had registered over three million new voters and spent over four million dollars. In Ronald Reagan they had a president much more sympathetic to their cause than Nixon, Ford, or Carter had been. The astonishing defeat in 1980 of most of the senators who had been targeted by antiabortion groups meant that Congress would be even more receptive to the views of those groups than it had been in the past.

Challenging State Reactions to *Roe*

While the antiabortion coalition emerged as a major force in electoral politics, prochoice groups continued to work, primarily through the courts, to overturn post-*Roe* state laws restricting abortion rights. Those laws often took one of two forms, requirements of spousal or parental consent or restrictions on the use of public funds for abortion. Between 1973 and 1980 the constitutionality of those restrictions was challenged in state and federal courts across the country, and the United States Supreme Court made more than half a dozen major decisions concerning the reach of abortion rights.

The first of these rulings, in 1976, came out of a challenge brought by Planned Parenthood to a Missouri statute. That statute, passed to bring state law into conformity with *Roe*'s requirements, defined viability (the critical point in *Roe*'s definition of abortion rights) as the point at which "the life of the unborn child may be continued indefinitely outside the womb by natural or artificial life support." Furthermore, it required that women seeking abortions must consent in writing and that the doctor performing the abortion must obtain written consent from the spouse, in the case of married women, or from parents, in the case of minors. The law required doctors to exercise care to preserve all fetal life, declared any fetus surviving an abortion to be a ward of the state, and prohibited saline abortions after the first 12 weeks of pregnancy.

This law was challenged in federal district court as an unconstitutional restriction of women's abortion rights, but the district court ruled in favor of the state. The case reached the Supreme Court as *Planned Parenthood* v. *Danforth*. The Court, in its first major post-*Roe* abortion decision, ruled unconstitutional, 5-4, those provisions of law requiring spousal or parental consent as well as those requiring doctors to preserve fetal life and prohibiting the use of the saline method of abortion. All other provisions were upheld. Justice Blackmun, again writing for the majority, found the law's imposing structure for control and regulation of abortion *at all stages of pregnancy* to be unacceptable. He argued that the consent requirements could not be justified as a way of strengthening the institution of marriage. The Constitution, he wrote, did not allow husbands a "veto power" over the abortion decision. Similarly, requirements for parental consent could not be justified as a way of strengthening the family. The effect of this requirement was to give third parties control over the decisions of doctors and patients. Therefore, Blackmun concluded, the Constitution prohibited "blanket provisions" requiring parental consent.

To antiabortion groups, the phrase "blanket provisions" seemed to leave the door open for some types of parental consent requirements.

They busily set to work in several states to push for the enactment of such requirements. In 1979, three years after *Planned Parenthood* v. *Danforth*, the Supreme Court in *Bellotti* v. *Baird* ruled that such requirements would be constitutional in cases where it could be shown that the minor child was neither mature nor well informed enough to responsibly make a decision to have an abortion. In addition, consent statutes had to provide some alternative procedure through which consent could be obtained.

In the case of the Massachusetts statute challenged in *Bellotti*, that alternative procedure involved an appeal to the courts. However, Justice Powell, writing for the minority, found that the Massachusetts statute unduly infringed upon the right to obtain an abortion because it permitted parents and courts to withhold permission from "mature and competent minors." Yet, Powell recognized that narrowly drawn parental consent requirements, because they were supportive of the parental role, were "important to the child's chance for full growth and maturity that make eventual participation in a free society meaningful and rewarding."

Two years later, in 1981, the Court upheld a parental consent requirement enacted in Utah that was challenged by an unmarried woman living with, and dependent upon, her parents. The majority ruled that that law served important state interests in protecting and promoting the integrity of the family. As Justice Stevens wrote in a concurring opinion, "The possibility that some parents will not react with compassion and understanding upon being informed of their daughter's predicament ... does not undercut the legitimacy of the state's attempt to establish a procedure that will enhance the probability that a pregnant young woman will exercise as wisely as possible her right to make the abortion decision." Thus, not 10 years after *Roe*, proponents of abortion rights found the Supreme Court—which had first articulated those rights—upholding state restrictions in the name of family integrity and using language similar to that used by the Moral Majority in its condemnation of abortion.

Financing Abortion Rights

As important as these cases were in demonstrating the Court's willingness to restrict abortion rights, the first and more important indication came in 1977 rulings concerning states' attempts to prevent state welfare funds from being used to finance abortions. As noted previously, one major strategy of the antiabortion coalition was to ensure that the government itself, although it could not constitutionally restrict abortions, did not facilitate the exercise of abortion rights. Almost immediately after *Roe*, state legislatures or welfare administrators began to prohibit use of welfare funds for abortion. Again the strategy of abortion advocates was to seek judicial redress, claiming that denial of state aid to poor women violated the Fourteenth Amendment's guarantee of equal protection of the law. What good was a right if it could not be exercised by those without financial resources? Moreover, as they saw it, since state funds still would be available to pay for the expense of childbirth, cutting off state aid for abortion meant that states were using financial leverage to compel women to bear unwanted children.

By 1977 two cases had reached the Supreme Court in which those claims would be adjudicated. The first, *Maher* v. *Roe*, concerned a Connecticut welfare department regulation limiting state Medicaid benefits for first-trimester abortions to those certified by a licensed physician as "medically necessary." A three-judge district court had found that requirement to be a violation of equal protection. The court argued: "The state may not justify its refusal to pay for one type of expense arising from pregnancy on the basis that it morally opposes such expenditures. To sanction such a justification would be to permit discrimination against those seeking to exercise a constitutional right on the basis that the state simply does not approve of the exercise of that right."

In a similar case in Connecticut, *Beal* v. *Doe*, a federal court ruled that regulations limiting eligibility for Medicaid assistance for abortions to those certified as "medically necessary" did not conflict with the federal statute establishing the Medicaid program, but did violate the equal protection clause of the Fourteenth Amendment.

In both cases, however, the Supreme Court upheld the state regulations. Justice Powell, who authored both opinions, noted that *Roe* did not declare an unqualified constitutional right to an abortion. In his view the right protected women only from "unduly burdensome" interference. In neither case did the Court find the regulations to amount to such interference. As Powell put it, "The state merely makes childbirth a more attractive option without imposing restrictions on abortion rights that were not already there. . . . There is a basic difference between direct state interference with a protected activity and state encouragement of an alternative activity. . . ." Moreover, Powell observed, echoing arguments for judicial restraint, "When an issue involves policy choices as sensitive as those implicated by public funding of nontherapeutic abortion, the proper forum for their resolution is the legislature."

The Court found that the equal protection provision does not require the state to fund the exercise of constitutional rights for those who cannot otherwise afford to do so, and that state regulations like those of Connecticut and Pennsylvania do not impinge on the right of privacy. The Court indicated that the right of privacy implies no limit on state authority to make judgments favoring childbirth and that Title XIX of the Social Security Act, which established Medicaid, allows states to establish reasonable standards for determining the nature and extent of state assistance.

For Justices William J. Brennan, Jr., and Thurgood Marshall, who along with Justice Blackmun, dissented in *Maher* and *Beal*, as well as for the prochoice coalition, these decisions seriously eroded the constitutional right recognized in *Roe*. As Brennan wrote, "The Court's construction can only result as a practical matter in forcing penniless pregnant women to have children they would not have borne if the state had not weighted the scale to make their choice to have abortions substantially more onerous." Justice Marshall was even more direct in criticizing the Court's position:

> It is all too obvious that the government actions in these cases ostensibly taken to "encourage" women to carry pregnancies to term are, in reality, intended to impose a moral viewpoint that no state may constitutionally enforce. Since efforts to overturn those decisions have been unsuccessful the opponents of abortion have attempted every imaginable means to circumvent the commands of the Constitution and impose their moral choices on the rest of the society. The present cases involve the most vicious attacks yet devised. . . . The enactments challenged here brutally coerce poor women to bear children whom society will scorn for every day of their lives. . . . I am appalled at the ethical bankruptcy of those who preach a "right to life" that means, under present social policy, a bare existence in utter misery for so many poor women and their children.

Moreover, Marshall clearly recognized that the Court's decisions would alter the balance of abortion politics, that those decisions would be taken as an "invitation to public officials, already under extraordinary pressure from well-financed and carefully orchestrated lobbying campaigns, to approve more such restrictions."

Marshall's predictions were borne out. The decisions in *Maher* and *Beal* meant that the prochoice coalition could no longer rely on the courts to reverse unfavorable political decisions. Once again, the Court transformed the shape of abortion politics. It removed the aura of constitutional legality from the arsenal of prochoice groups and put them, or so it seemed, on the wrong side of the legal as well as moral argument. It translated the abortion conflict back into 50 different conflicts by allowing each state to fashion its own regulations. As Schattschneider observed, this change of arena is often decisive. Antiabortion groups already had proven their power at the state and local level where their ability to mobilize intense opposition to abortion could be felt most. These decisions put the proabortion coalition on the defensive and forced them to fight from a weakened position. Finally,

Maher and *Beal* established two levels of abortion rights, the right to freedom of choice for those who could afford abortions, and a return to the pre-*Roe* condition of liberalized rights for the poor. They transformed the issue more clearly into a conflict between welfare-state liberals, on the one hand, and fundamentalist and traditional conservatives on the other. The issue of state funding support split the prochoice coalition, divorcing the more conservative advocates of noninterference with individual rights and delivering them into the hands of antiabortion groups now opposing a further extension of welfare state interventionism.

As Justice Marshall feared, the decisions in *Maher* and *Beal* aided those who had been trying to persuade Congress to restrict funding for abortion at the same time the states were doing so. Efforts toward that end began almost immediately after *Roe*, but they did not come to fruition until 1976, when Congress enacted a provision strictly limiting federal Medicaid payments for abortion in an appropriation for the Department of Health, Education and Welfare. That bill was vetoed by President Ford, who claimed that Congress had appropriated too much for HEW.

Congress, with little debate about the cutoff amendment, overrode the President's veto. Almost immediately, however, the National Abortion Rights Action League—as well as the United Methodist Church, the New York City Health and Hospitals Corporation, and a Medicaid recipient, Cora McRae—filed suit in Brooklyn, New York, to enjoin the secretary of HEW from implementing the Medicaid cutoff. Federal Judge John Dooling issued a temporary restraining order citing the irreparable damage that would be done to poor women if the cutoff were carried out while litigation was pending. The litigation was unresolved and the judge's order still pending when the year ended.

The election of Jimmy Carter brought a supporter of the antiabortion position on federal aid to the White House. When challenged to justify his support of that position, in light of its apparently unfair treatment of poor women, Carter said, "... there are many things in life that are not fair ..." and that "the government should not foster equality where morality is at issue." At the same time, Congress was considering an amendment to the new HEW appropriations bill, proposed by Representative Henry Hyde, R-Ill., to prevent Medicaid payments for abortion. While that consideration was under way, Judge Dooling lifted his 1976 order after finding that the language of the proposed cutoff was not unconstitutionally vague. (He reserved judgment, however, on other claims.)

By the fall of 1977, Congress was deadlocked, not over the cutoff issue itself but rather over what exceptions should be allowed. The House had passed legislation forbidding use of federal funding for abortions except to save maternal life. The Senate had passed similar legislation but would have permitted the use of federal money in cases of rape and incest as well. A House-Senate conference committee, after working for five months to try to reconcile these positions, finally agreed in November to allow the use of funds to preserve maternal life and to fund procedures to "help avert pregnancy" for victims of rape or incest.

As part of its annual appropriations process, Congress reenacted the Hyde Amendment, first in 1978 and then again in 1979, after finding itself deadlocked because of different language in the House and Senate versions. That deadlock was resolved when the House agreed to Senate language permitting the use of Medicaid funds for cases of rape and incest. However, in January 1980, Judge Dooling rendered a final judgment that struck down all versions of the Hyde Amendment as violating the equal protection clause, unconstitutionally abridging the abortion rights of poor women, and abridging the free exercise of religion by favoring the dogmas of the Catholic Church.

The issue of the constitutionality of the Hyde Amendment's cutoff of federal Medicaid funds reached the Supreme Court later in 1980 in the case of *Harris* v. *McRae*. The Court, in overturning Dooling's decision, found that the Hyde Amendment did not violate the First or Fifth Amendment or infringe on constitutionally protected abortion rights. Echoing the language of *Maher* and *Beal*, Justice Stewart wrote,

> The Hyde Amendment . . . places no governmental obstacle in the path of a woman who chooses to terminate her pregnancy, but rather, by means of unequal subsidization of abortion and other medical services, encourages alternative activity deemed in the public interest . . . [and] that it simply does not follow that a woman's freedom of choice carries with it a constitutional entitlement to the financial resources to avail herself of the full range of protected choices.

Stewart resisted the argument that the Hyde Amendment, like its counterparts in the various states, would create two different categories of abortion rights. Moreover, he viewed the constitutionally protected right to an abortion as a guarantee of noninterference rather than a guarantee of government responsibility to remove obstacles to the exercise of rights by particular groups of citizens. As he saw it, "The Hyde Amendment leaves an indigent woman the same range of choice in deciding whether to obtain an abortion as she would have had if Congress subsidized no medical costs." (Of course, that was a purely hypothetical argument since the issue before the Court was whether Congress, having made the decision to subsidize such costs, could favor one type of medical treatment over another.)

Stewart's opinion turned upon the belief that requiring the government to pay for abortions under Medicaid "would mark a drastic change in . . . the Constitution," a change that would use the equal protection clause to guarantee that all categories of citizens were provided the resources necessary to ensure a meaningful choice concerning the uses of their legal rights. The position of prochoice groups, Stewart contended, turned the Constitution on its head. In addition, the Court dismissed the argument that the Hyde Amendment violated the establishment clause of the First Amendment: ". . . we are convinced that the fact that funding restrictions in the Hyde Amendment may coincide with the religious tenets of the Roman Catholic Church does not, without more, contravene the Establishment Clause."

Brennan, in dissent, argued that Stewart had misconstrued the issue, that the question of whether the government was under an affirmative obligation to provide access to abortions for poor women was not at issue. To Brennan, the Hyde Amendment represented "an attempt by Congress to circumvent the dictates of the Constitution and achieve indirectly what *Roe* v. *Wade* said it could not do directly," namely, to prohibit abortion. By funding all of the expenses of childbirth but none of the expenses of an abortion, the government, in Brennan's words, "literally makes an offer that the indigent woman cannot refuse." Brennan warned:

> [T]he discriminatory distribution of the benefits of government largesse can discourage the exercise of fundamental liberties just as effectively as can an outright denial of those rights through criminal and regulatory sanctions. Implicit in the Court's reasoning is the notion that so long as the government is not obligated to provide its citizens with certain benefits or privileges, it may condition the grant of such benefits on the recipient's relinquishment of his constitutional rights.

McRae represented a major victory for the antiabortion coalition. Combined with the results of the 1980 election, the tide seemed to turn against the proponents of abortion rights across the entire spectrum of political and legal institutions. What had started out more than a decade earlier as a push for liberalization—a movement which had gotten its greatest apparent boost from the Supreme Court—had been dealt yet another severe blow. The Court, now echoing the language of judicial restraint, was unwilling to prevent through the legal process what could not be prevented through the political process.

Harris v. *McRae* did not by any means end abortion politics. It marked only the end of another stage, the stage of taking back much of what *Roe* seemed to promise, the stage in which antiabortion forces reasserted their influence. Furthermore, *McRae* shifted the focus of antiabortion groups ever more securely toward the Congress and the process of amending the Constitution. Virtually all that was left in the way of a complete reestablishment of the pre-*Roe* status quo was *Roe* itself, a decision that removed from state legislatures the power to regulate and prohibit abortion.

By the spring of 1982 even *Roe* seemed in jeopardy. In March, the Senate Judiciary Committee for the first time approved a proposal to amend the Constitution to enable Congress and the states to ban abortions. That amendment, sponsored by Republican Orrin Hatch of Utah, would give Congress and the states "concurrent power to restrict and prohibit abortion" and would allow more restrictive state legislation to prevail. (A similar measure has been introduced in the House of Representatives.) The committee's vote marked yet another defeat for antiabortion groups including Planned Parenthood, the American Civil Liberties Union, and the National Abortion Rights Action League, all of whom had vigorously opposed it. Paradoxically, some antiabortion groups did not support the Hatch Amendment because they felt it did not go far enough. Instead, they favored a proposal that would write into law a definition of life as beginning at conception.

SOME QUESTIONS TO EXPLORE

Surely there can be no doubt, at least in the case of abortion, of the shifting and often imperceptible boundaries of law and politics. Courts were used as but one among many arenas in which the abortion conflict was played out. Judicial decisions were rarely final or indeed enduring. The abortion issue bounced back and forth among the three branches of government without any clear delineation of where particular decisions would be made. The key role of the courts in abortion politics was in transforming and translating that conflict, shaping and redefining it, posing new strategic dilemmas for losers and new opportunities for winners. But as the reaction to *Roe* demonstrated, even those transformations could not be fully comprehended or controlled.

In the case of abortion, what looked like a decision favorable to one side became its major liability. What had been, before *Roe*, intense, political conflicts at the state level became, after *Roe*, a major focus of cultural conflict on the national level. Judicial decisions, because they seem definite and are accompanied by more or less persuasive statements of reasons, give a clarity and focus to issues in conflict that are not often attained elsewhere in the political system. By invoking the language of rights, those decisions add a moral coloration to all political issues. Where the issue already has such a context, as with abortion, the judiciary often short-circuits the process of incremental adjustment and adds rhetorical fuel to the conflict over volatile social issues. Courts transform conflicts by translating the language in which conflict is carried on and by altering the terms on which those conflicts will be conducted outside the judicial process.

Judicial power is important in giving shape and form to American politics. Yet judges are, at best, only indirectly accountable. This combination of power and limited accountability has contributed to a long-standing concern about the compatibility of courts and democracy. Thus, we might ask, *do courts contribute to or weaken democratic political processes?* Some have answered this question by suggesting that courts contribute to democracy precisely because they are not themselves democratic. They provide stability and continuity that might otherwise be lacking. In addition, judicial decisions may legitimate actions by the popularly elected branches of government. When political decisions are found to be constitutional—as is generally the case—popular belief is that the appropriateness and propriety of democratic politics may be strengthened.

Alternatively some believe that courts frustrate and weaken democracy by concentrating great power in the hands of judges and by removing some of the most important political decisions from the people and their elected representatives. Adherents to this view argue that judicial review is an insult to the capacity of people to rule themselves and abide by rules which, in effect, the people have made to govern the political process.

But these general questions take us far afield from the abortion issue. As suggested earlier, the Supreme Court's major abortion decision—*Roe* v. *Wade*—has been the subject of considerable controversy, much of it directed at the quality of the Court's reasoning. *Is that reasoning appropriate for a court of law?* Should the courts make decisions in the absence of clear legal standards? What would happen to abortion rights if medical technology advances to the point where the fetus can be sustained outside the womb after three months or after six weeks? Advocates of abortion rights can take little comfort from a decision that so clearly tied those rights to the state of scientific knowledge. Moreover, they find themselves having to defend the language and logic of Blackmun's majority opinion, which many supporters of abortion find wanting.

What is the proper role of religion in politics? The abortion issue illustrates the complex interrelationship of religious and political questions. Religious groups play an active and continuing role in the abortion controversy. The First Amendment's separation of church and state prevents state sponsorship of religion; it does not prevent political activity by religious groups. Still, one might ask whether that activity is desirable or undesirable. Religious groups have been and remain involved in a broad range of political issues, ranging from civil rights to environmentalism to nuclear disarmament. The traditional fear of mixing religion and politics was based on the assumption that political involvement arising from religious conviction would produce intense political conflict. Yet perhaps religious groups have a special and valuable perspective to bring to politics; perhaps they contribute to a politics which, on the whole, is more concerned with questions of right or wrong than it would otherwise be.

Finally, one might ask *what happened to bring abortion politics to the point where even the modest victories of the liberalization effort are in jeopardy?* Consider the following explanation. Much of the blame (if blame is the right word) belongs with the prochoice forces themselves; much can also be laid at the door of the Supreme Court. In politics, so the saying goes, timing is everything. The prochoice coalition pushed too far, too fast. The Court in *Roe* stepped too far out in front of the culture, and, in so doing, helped to transform the victories of liberalization into defeats at the hands of those opposed to all abortion rights. Prochoice groups did not realize the power of the symbolic avalanche that would bury them after *Roe* v. *Wade.* They did not see their cause for what it was, a frontal assault on conventional morality. As a result, they did not take the time necessary to consolidate their early gains, but rather like an overly eager general, charged ahead to what looked like a final victory only to find the enemy more united and stronger than ever.

In the final analysis, the shifting fortunes of abortion politics cannot be attributed to the actions of any group or institution, but rather to the rhythms of the larger culture. Perhaps no strategy of advance could have consolidated abortion rights. Perhaps the changing fate of abortion rights reflects the apparent, although not yet final, judgment of American society on the latest cycle of cultural liberation.

SOURCES AND READINGS

This study is based on a wide variety of sources, including court decisions concerning abortion and related issues and briefs filed in those cases, as well as books and articles concerning abortion politics and the nature of the judicial process.

Among the most important Supreme Court decisions are *Griswold* v. *Connecticut,* 381 U.S. 479 (1965), which recognized the constitutionally protected right of privacy, and *Eisenstadt* v. *Baird,* 405 U.S. 438 (1972), which further extended it. Other significant decisions concerning abortion rights include *U.S.* v. *Vuitch,* 402 U.S. 62 (1971); *Roe* v. *Wade,* 314 F. Supp. 1217 (ND Tex, 1970); *Doe* v. *Bolton,* 319 F Supp. 1048 (ND GA, 1970); *Roe* v. *Wade,* 410 U.S. 113 (1973); *Doe* v. *Bolton,* 410 U.S. 179 (1973); *Planned Parenthood* v. *Danforth,* 428 U.S. 52 (1976); *Singleton* v. *Woulff,* 428 U.S. 106 (1976); *Bellotti* v. *Baird,* 428 U.S. 132 (1976); *Poelker* v. *Doe,* 432 U.S. 519 (1977); *Maher* v. *Roe,* 432 U.S. 464 (1977); *Beal* v. *Doe,* 432 U.S. 438 (1977); *Bellotti* v. *Baird,* 443 U.S. 662

(1979); *McRae* v. *Matthews*, 421 F Supp. 533 (1976); *Harris* v. *McRae*, 100 S. CT 2671 (1980); *Williams* v. *Zbabz*, 100 S. CT 2694 (1980); and *H.W.* v. *Matheson*, 101 S. CT 1164 (1981).

There are, unfortunately, relatively few systematic treatments of abortion politics. The best is John Noonan, *A Private Choice* (New York: The Free Press, 1979). Other useful works concerning the politics, morality, or legality of abortion include James Mohr, *Abortion in America* (New York: Oxford University Press, 1978); Robert Destro, "Abortion and the Constitution," *California Law Review*, 63 (1975): 1250; Michael Perry, "Abortion, Public Morals and the Police Power," *U.C.L.A. Law Review*, 23 (1976): 689; Richard Epstein, "Substantive Due Process by Any Other Name," *Supreme Court Review* (1973): 159; Charles Rice, "Dred Scott Case of the Twentieth Century," *Houston Law Review*, 10 (1973): 1059; Harriet Pilpel and Dorothy Patton, "Abortion, Conscience and the Constitution," *Columbia Human Rights Law Review*, 6 (1974-1975): 289; Alan Guttmacher, "Symposium - Law, Morality and Abortion," *Rutgers Law Review*, 22 (1968): 415; and Bernard Nathanson, *Aborting America* (Garden City, N.Y.: Doubleday, 1979). See also Eva Rubin, *Abortion, Politics and the Courts* (Westport, Ct.: Greenwood Press, 1982).

Perhaps the best treatment of the implications of abortion for an understanding of the role of the courts in American society is John Hart Ely, "The Wages of Crying Wolf," *Yale Law Journal*, 82 (1973): 920. The author's own understanding of abortion politics has been most influenced by Joseph Gusfield, *Symbolic Crusade* (Urbana: University of Illinois Press, 1964) and by E. E. Schattschneider, *The Semisovereign People* (Hinsdale, Ill.: The Dryden Press, 1975).

Works on the role of courts in American politics and society, of course, are much more numerous. Among the most important are Alexander Bickel, *The Least Dangerous Branch* (Indianapolis: Bobbs-Merrill, 1962); Charles Black, *The People and the Court* (New York: Macmillan, 1961); Archibald Cox, *The Role of the Supreme Court in American Government* (New York: Oxford University Press, 1976); Donald Horowitz, *The Courts and Social Policy* (Washington, D.C.: Brookings Institution, 1977); Lon Fuller, "The Forms and Limits of Adjudication," *Harvard Law Review*, 92 (1979): 353; Ronald Dworkin, *Taking Rights Seriously* (Cambridge, Mass.: Harvard University Press, 1977); Richard Neeley, *How Courts Govern America* (New Haven: Yale University Press, 1981).

Controversy concerning the role of the courts is exemplified in Nathan Glazer, "Toward An Imperial Judiciary," *Public Interest*, 41 (1975): 104; Ralph Cavanagh and Austin Sarat, "Thinking About Courts," *Law & Society Review* 14 (1980): 371; and Jethro Lieberman, *The Litigious Society* (New York: Basic Books, 1981). The author's perspective on the relationship of courts and politics has been particularly influenced by Stuart Scheingold, *The Politics of Rights* (New Haven: Yale University Press, 1974); Martin Shapiro, "Judicial Activism," in *The Third Century*, ed. Seymour Martin Lipset (Stanford, Ca.: Hoover Institution Press, 1979); and Lynn Mather and Barbara Yngvesson, "Language, Audience and the Transformation of Disputes," *Law and Society Review*, 14 (1980): 775.

5

Political Parties

Another Machine Withers Away: For Better? For Worse?

Gerald M. Pomper, Rodney Forth, and Maureen W. Moakley

When parties can't get offices, they'll bust. They ain't far from the bustin' point now.... How are you goin' to keep up patriotism if this thing goes on? You can't do it. Let me tell you that patriotism has been dying out fast for the last twenty years. Before then when a party won, its workers got everything in sight. That was somethin' to make a man proud. Now, when a party wins and its men come forward and ask for their rewards, the reply is, "Nothin' doin', unless you can answer a lot of questions about Egyptian mummies."... Sad indeed is the change that has come over the young men.
—George Washington Plunkitt, of New York's Tammany Hall

This statement of practical philosophy dates from the beginning of this century, but it could have been expressed in the fall of 1979, when an official we will call Kelley* was indicted by a federal grand jury. The indictment charged that Kelley, in return for cash contributions and service to his local political party, had provided jobs in his agency, promotions, and salary increases. Kelley denied the charges and, a year

---

* Because the material in this chapter is sensitive and was acquired with firm promises of confidentiality, we disguise all names and places. No person named Kelley was actually connected to the case.

later, the case was thrown out of court by a federal judge. The dismissal of the charges was upheld on appeal.

Kelley's operations are worth attention because they raise more general issues about the nature and future of American political parties. Kelley readily admitted that his agency appointed people to their jobs on the basis of party work. He took this to be established and legitimate practice. If he were more of a scholar, he might have cited Andrew Jackson as advocating the principle that "To the victor belong the spoils." In contrast, attorneys for the prosecution were critical not only of Kelley's alleged corruption, but of the basic premise that partisan activity was relevant to public employment. They might have cited another aphorism, "There is no Republican or Democratic way to clean the streets."

Kelley and his prosecutors basically disagreed about what an American political party is and should be. To Kelley, a party is a *private* organization; to his opponents, a party is a *public* agency. Each side could present a good argument because parties have an ambiguous character—they are both partially private and partially public. This argument will be a recurring theme in the following examination of three topics: (1) parties in general; (2) one specific party organization; and (3) current changes in American national parties.

In some ways, parties can be considered private organizations, created and maintained in order to suit the purposes of their members. In this view, parties are just like corporations or unions, which exist to get more profits for stockholders or better working conditions and higher wages for workers. We do not expect corporations or unions to be public-spirited most of the time, and so we are skeptical toward them. Similarly, our wariness toward the parties is based in part on our distrust of the parties' evident selfishness.

On the other hand, parties are clearly public institutions, directly involved in our governmental process. Presidents and governors are nominated by parties and elected under party labels and on behalf of party programs. Congress and the state legislatures are structured along party lines, and partisan ties are a major means by which coordination is achieved among the fragmented institutions of American government. Through their programs, leaders, and negotiations, parties help to channel and translate public wishes into public policy. Their legitimacy is widely accepted, and they enjoy a certain public respect.

Parties, then, are private-minded, self-interested organizations that also manage to serve a public purpose. To win elections, parties, like the individual candidates who run under their banners, must satisfy their constituents' demands. Thus, as Anthony Downs argued, "parties formulate policies in order to win elections, rather than win elections in order to formulate policies." Here the analogy to corporations is very close. General Motors, for example, does not produce fuel-efficient cars because it is primarily concerned with preserving the world's diminishing oil supplies. Rather, it has retooled to emphasize small cars in order to meet consumers' current demands. In the process of preserving its own profits, however, it is indirectly meeting public policy needs as well.

Traditional urban parties, or "machines" such as Kelley's, epitomize the private-minded party in its most extreme form. This case study describes a particular machine, its present state of decay, and a new kind of organization—which we term a policy party—that is fast replacing it. In the latter part of the study, we consider the relevance of these two kinds of parties to aspects of national politics. Throughout this examination, keep in mind one basic question: What is the most *feasible* (if not necessarily the ideal) way to organize politics?

TWO KINDS OF PARTIES

Party Machines

The private-minded party is primarily concerned with the success of the organization itself. Its emphasis can be satirically described, in the words of humorist Ambrose Bierce, as "a strife of interests masquerading as a contest of principles" or "the conduct of public affairs for private advantage." Members of this kind of party are typically portrayed as interested primarily in their own advancement and the money and power to be derived from politics. To get these rewards, they form alliances with others, exchanging favors, making "deals" and compromises. If the voters want certain policies—higher welfare payments or disarmament, for example—the parties will push these programs. If the voters change their minds—now favoring lower taxes or a stronger military—the parties will revise their programs accordingly.

The urban political machine is the closest approximation of this abstract construct. People work for and contribute money to machines in return for material benefits, such as getting a job or a contract from the local government. Patronage—the appointment of party workers to public jobs—is critical to the machine. As Milton Rakove observed, "An effective political party needs five things: offices, jobs, money, workers, and votes. Offices beget jobs and money; jobs and money beget workers; workers beget votes; and votes beget offices. In Chicago and Cook County, Illinois, Democratic control of all major offices insures that the Republican party will have difficulty generating workers, voters and money."

To evaluate machines one must consider not only the narrow objectives of their members, but their impact on the general population. The evils of machines are widely known: corruption, financial waste, a lack of vision for reform. But the positive effects of machines are usually given less recognition. It can be argued that, although unintended, they have had several genuinely beneficial aspects. Three of these are especially important:

(1) Machines often provided a means of social mobility for immigrant ethnic groups, the poor, and the disadvantaged. They integrated new citizens into the American electoral system without destroying their cultural identity. As William Shannon wrote in *American Irish*, machine politicians

> organized the Irish voters as a battering ram to break the power of a hostile majority. They put an end to elementary forms of discrimination such as the exclusive use of the King James Bible in the schools. . . . Next, they fought for the appointment of Irish as schoolteachers and as policemen and firemen. Finally, they sought to take all political power into their own hands.

(2) The machine provided a means to mobilize political power for collective purposes. As a disciplined organization, it could apply its considerable strength on behalf of popular demands. With few inherent policy interests of its own (other than protecting its power), the machine was open to adopting the position of any group with votes at hand. With control over public jobs and nominations to elective office, it could easily get approval of these demands from legislators and administrators. A neighborhood playground or a new fire station was the usual fare of the machine—small, highly visible accomplishments important in the daily lives of its constituents. At other times, the machine thought more grandly and exercised its muscle to provide such far-reaching social projects as the New York subway system or the Jersey City Medical Center, which once provided an excellent and free system of community medical care.

(3) Most notably, machines comforted their constituents. Beyond the famous gifts of Thanksgiving turkeys and Christmas buckets of coal to constituents, there were emotional supports and personal ties to overcome the cold formality of bureaucracy and the impersonal applications of rules and regulations. As boss Martin Lomasny of Boston explained, "I think that there's got to be in every ward somebody that any bloke can come to—no matter what he's done—and get help. Help, you understand; none of your law and your justice, but help."

In many ways, the machine acted as a primitive but humane social welfare service. As Plunkitt of Tammany Hall put it:

> What tells in holdin' your grip on your district is to go right down among the poor families and help them in the different ways they need help. I've got a regular system for this. If there's a fire in Ninth, Tenth or Eleventh Avenue, for example, any hour of the day or night, I'm usually there with some of my election district captains as soon as the fire engines. If a family is burned out I don't ask whether they are

Republicans or Democrats, and I don't refer them to the Charity Organization Society, which would investigate their case in a month or two and decide they were worthy of help about the time they are dead from starvation. I just get quarters for them, buy clothes for them if their clothes were burned up, and fix them up 'till they get things runnin' again. It's philanthropy, but it's politics too—mighty good politics.

Policy Parties

Another (and more noble) conception of parties was best stated by Edmund Burke, an English statesman of the late 18th century. He defined a political party as "a body of men united, for promoting by their joint endeavors the national interest, upon some particular principle in which they are all agreed." The emphasis here is on public policy objectives. Parties should stand for something and not seek office simply for their own sake. They should hold fast to their principles because they have a program to achieve. Ideally, parties should be public-minded groups which "bring forth programs to which they commit themselves" and which are organized so that they "possess sufficient internal cohesion to carry out these programs."

In this type of "policy party," material motives are regarded as selfish and deplored while the loftier motive of "good public policy" is revered. The machine is condemned as an "organization for plunder," and patronage appointments are specifically rejected. As one leader of a local party of this type declared,

> We believe that we must eliminate the control by party officers over appointive positions. The only people who should control appointive positions should be elected officials. . . . I know we are accused of being impractical and naive. . . . But it is a philosophy. . . . And we must have such a philosophy. Patronage is an obvious fraud and it is illegal. It is not right for party officials to take public money to perform party duties.

People participate in policy party activity because they see themselves as "good citizens" promoting good causes, not because they seek direct benefits for themselves from their party's policies. The stress on policy goals is reflected in one California political activist's explanation:

> You must realize the importance of these Issues Conferences to us. They may hurt us in some races, although I don't think they do. But we have to have these issues to get us to work. We're volunteers. We have to have the feeling we are working for a cause in which we believe in order to work at all. . . . If we didn't have this cause to believe in . . . we wouldn't work at all.

A policy party further emphasizes extensive popular participation within the party itself. Policy goals are expressions of the rank-and-file membership; they are embodied in leaders selected by the membership to carry out these policies. Leaders are judged, then, not simply on their ability to win elections, but to articulate and to achieve the party program.

Participation in the policy party and its internal offices, and the status and intimacy it provides, are the incentives for people to contribute time, activity, and money to the group. With the lure of jobs and patronage considered unacceptable, participation and policy become the primary inducements to party work. A great portion of the organization's life is devoted to meetings, conferences, and debates on policy questions, and to internal elections for various offices, all conducted under elaborate procedures to ensure "democratic" involvement.

The policy party model has considerable standing in American history and practice. Minor or "third" parties (contending with the two major parties in the American system) are usually policy parties. Although very diverse in their views, they are similar in their emphasis on a particular ideology or program to which they are deeply committed. Within the two major parties as well, there are recurrent emphases on policy objectives, even at the cost of electoral victory. For example, the Republican party nominated Barry Goldwater for president in 1964 not so much in the expectation of success, but in order to further his conservative principles by offering the electorate "a choice, not an echo." In 1972, the Democrats nominated George McGovern, even though he was a relatively extreme liberal, as an endorsement of his opposition to the Vietnam War.

American law also shows a preference for the policy party. To limit machines, state statutes regulate many details of party operations and seek to broaden participation within these organizations. In nominating candidates—arguably their most important function—American parties are not permitted to handle their own selections. Instead, nominees are typically chosen by direct primary elections in which the rank-and-file voters, who participate in determining the Democratic or Republican candidate, incur no further obligation to give the party anything— time, money, or even their votes in the ensuing general election. Further actions to limit the independent power of party leaders include removing most government jobs from patronage, eliminating party labels in elections to local office, and curbing financial contributions to parties.

Comparing the Two Parties

These two kinds of organizations, machines and policy parties, are only abstractions. In real life, no machine, and no human, ever operates simply and logically on the basis of self-interested calculation. Politicians, like the rest of us, also have emotions, personal loyalties, and principles that complicate their behavior and scholars' analyses. In real life, few policy activists are concerned simply and solely with ideology and issues. To achieve public goals, they also must be concerned with public jobs.

Nevertheless, the emphases of these two kinds of parties are quite distinct. To summarize, consider the different responses to some basic questions about politics, first by the representative of the abstract party machine and then by the abstract policy party:

Q: *Who will staff government agencies?*
A: Those who work for the party that wins control of government.
or
A: Persons chosen for their competence in the policy area.

Q: *What policies will the government follow?*
A: Whatever policies the party finds necessary to promise and fulfill in order to get votes.
or
A: Those that are advanced by the party, after internal discussion, and approved by the voters in an issue-oriented election.

Q: *How is party unity achieved?*
A: By promises of personal political advancement or threats to remove people from power.
or
A: By agreement on matters of principle.

Q: *How are campaigns financed?*
A: By contributions to the party from persons who hope to gain personal advantages.
or
A: By contributions of citizens in support of policy programs.

Q: *Who receives party nominations?*
A: Those who are most likely to help the party win the election.
or
A: Those who best express party principles.

Q: *How are nominations made?*
A: By negotiation among party leaders exercising party discipline.
or
A: By a broad-based endorsement of the party membership.

Q: *How are elections conducted?*
A: By a united party, seeking the jobs of government, which enlists the personal loyalties of voters to their local party leaders.
or
A: By persons dedicated to the party program, who persuade voters to support their cause.

ONE MACHINE

The Setting

We now move from abstractions to a real party organization in a densely populated county in the northeastern United States. Tyrone County, to give it a name, contains a large central city, Bradford, which has a decaying industrial base and a declining population (now comprising less than one-fourth of the total county). The city's electorate was once dominated by the Irish, who had first settled there during the massive waves of immigration which ended after the first World War. As the Irish prospered and climbed the social ladder, they moved out to join white Anglo-Saxon Protestants in the surrounding suburbs. Later, Jews, Italians, and eastern European immigrants also settled in these suburbs, making Tyrone County a typically northeastern salad bowl of diverse ethnic groups. The whites departing from Bradford were replaced by new migrants, blacks from the South seeking jobs and racial equality, and Puerto Ricans. By the time of our study, these racial minorities comprised about two-thirds of Bradford's population and more than 40 percent of the county.

Politically, too, the area was changing. Until the 1950s, the county had generally voted Republican, although there was a significant Democratic opposition, concentrated in Bradford. With the movement of population, however, the political tide changed. As the various white ethnic groups moved from Bradford to its suburbs, they took their Democratic party loyalties with them. The new migrants to Bradford itself were even more strongly Democratic than the previous residents. Bradford became an overwhelmingly Democratic city in the 1960s and political power passed to the new ethnic groups when a black mayor was elected in the middle of the decade. At this time, the county also came under Democratic control, with the party successfully presenting a "balanced ticket" that included candidates of Irish, Italian, Polish, Jewish, and black ethnic origins. Republican strength was confined to the more distant and affluent suburban areas, whose expensive shops, wooded homes, and exclusive clubs contrasted sharply with the crowded single-family homes of the older suburban towns and with the abandoned tenements of Bradford.

Democratic success was aided by the governmental structure and the party organization. For governmental purposes, the county was considered a single unit. Its delegation to the state legislature was elected as a bloc, and all members of the county legislative body were chosen by the total Tyrone electorate, as were a number of administrative officers, including Kelley, the county counsel. This system of at-large elections meant that the county party was the crucial organization for nominating candidates. Popularity in one city or region within the county was insufficient—a candidate had to carry the entire county. The county party organization, in turn, used its support of candidates to represent its diverse population through the device of the balanced ticket, by which the claims of competing ethnic factions were given official recognition. Kelley himself was chosen for his office, among other reasons, because it seemed appropriate to give this position to the Irish who had long held it.

The Effective Machine in Operation

When the Democrats first achieved dominance in Tyrone, they (and the Republicans before them) exemplified the traditional machine. There was a small group of leaders at the top, most of them Irish, who made major decisions on such matters as county nominations, job distribution, and assorted public policy issues. Once made, these decisions were not effectively questioned. Those who did not win party endorsement, for example, had virtually no chance of successfully challenging the machine's candidate in a primary election.

The Tyrone County machines, both Democratic and Republican, were fairly typical specimens of the species, neither unusually bad nor outstandingly good. Pursuing their self-interest, the machines' leaders and members had prospered from political office and contracts. Undoubtedly some unnecessary jobs had been created and some public spending was excessive; yet the county organizations also had exemplified some of the virtues of machines. Subordinate ethnic groups had used the machine to advance their collective social position. By the 1960s, the Irish were at the top of the political hierarchy, and Italians were not far behind. The new migrants to the city, blacks and Puerto Ricans, were also beginning to take advantage of the opportunities provided by politics.

In the past, these machines, like others, had provided personal welfare services for local residents and had contributed to a better life for the citizenry. Distinguished men had been advanced to prominent positions in the state, and a basic metropolitan infrastructure of highways and railroads had been built, as well as a magnificent system of county parks. Perhaps it was coincidence, but neighborhoods were safer, more harmonious, and simply more attractive when the neighborhood-based machines were in power.

Raising Funds. The machine raised money in various ways, including sizable contributions from those who did business with the county. Building contractors, automobile dealers, printers, and others who could profit from county government contracts provided many dollars. Government workers who were appointed on a patronage basis constituted another important source of funds. One form of payment was direct assessments on their salaries. As one observer reported, "By the late 1940s there was a great system of kickbacks in terms of your salary. In the old days you gave a certain percentage of your salary to the party. . . . The big thing was when [a party leader] got it knocked down from 5 percent to 2 percent." The system of kickbacks was illegal and was the basis of Kelley's indictment, which charged that he and others committed acts "to create and perpetuate the understanding . . . that annual cash payments . . . of approximately one percent of an employee's salary . . . were a condition of their employment, retention of duty-assignments and other employment-related benefits."

A less crude way of raising money from patronage appointees was through "voluntary contributions." Tickets were sold, usually priced at $100 each, to various party dinners or dances. Since these were technically purchases rather than contributions, the money received did not have to be reported under state election law. Other persons in the office would give cash contributions, also usually about $100, just before election day. The funds would be used for "street money"—compensation to precinct workers for spending election day bringing voters to the polls. The going rate was $120 for a district, comprising a total of 500 voters, of which as few as 20 percent and no more than 50 percent would actually come to the polls. This use of street money continued through Kelley's term of office.

The party eventually changed its approach to fundraising, using more discreet methods. In place of kickbacks, money was raised by contributions from business, tickets to party functions, and election day donations. By the time of Kelley's tenure, donating to the party was an accepted practice, although not a condition of employment. "You didn't have to pay to get a job, but you had to have a political sponsor. The guy who got it was indebted or would feel he was indebted. So these guys would be shoveling tickets [to party functions]." Kelley was given an annual quota of tickets to the county party dinner, amounting to fewer than half the employees of his office. If they could not be sold, "I'd have to eat them," he reported, meaning that he would be expected to pay for them himself. In fact, he never had to test his ability to absorb personal financial loss or digest cardboard.

When the financing system worked as intended, it needed little overt control. There was indeed an "understanding" but it did not require Kelley or anyone else to do more than accept the money. As one of his lawyers argued:

> It was total institutional pressure. The analogy is the United Fund. Take an outfit like Xerox. Everyone in that company has to give to the United Fund or they are in trouble. Everyone knows it. [Similarly, in Tyrone County] you didn't have to black-jack people. The old timers were happy to get off with just $100. They were literally happy. Most

people who got on in terms of benefits, etc., they were really not being leaned on in a sense. It was almost like a peer pressure kind of thing as far as I'm concerned. If everyone else is giving, then you give.

These financing arrangements were one aspect of the effective machine. They provided a secure source of income, whether through kickbacks or systematic contributions. They also provided for the efficient utilization of these funds in face-to-face canvassing on the streets by campaign workers who used their personal friendships to bring voters to the polls. These workers expected individual rewards in return—"street money" at a minimum, a patronage appointment if possible.

Patronage. Employment was the other major aspect of the machine's operation. Under a machine patronage system, public employees would be hired on the basis of their service to the party, and jobs would be distributed so as to induce greater effort on behalf of the party. Once hired, appointees would be expected to work for and contribute to the party. Their rewards on the job, such as promotions and higher salaries or lighter work, would be dependent upon continuing their party work. If their party efforts ceased, they could then expect to be fired. And of course, if the party was defeated in an election, its patronage appointees would lose their jobs, and the newly elected party would bring in its own crop.

The Democratic organization once handled patronage in rough accord with the machine model. Appointments were made with an eye to the party's voting strength. The process was routinized, and a semi-bureaucratic system was established so that:

> you had to go to your senior ward leader and he gave you the application and he brought it down to the headquarters and that's when the job came out. That was done because the ward leader's the guy that wins the election for you and if you don't give him the patronage, if you don't take the people, you're screwed up.

Those gaining the patronage jobs "had to understand that there were certain conditions such as contributions, kissing the ring as they say . . . and there are certain times the party may expect him to do certain things."

Allocating jobs often required considerable negotiation among the political leaders. To take one example:

> P. D. would choose to take [lay claim to] a $6,000 job in the hospital. He would choose to take three of them [rather] than to take a $12,000 job some other place. Then W. H. [said], "These people are his, one is going to the county [prosecutor's] office." And down along the line. [The chairman] would o.k. that and that would be the agenda.

The Machine in Decline

Did the machine work? Was Kelley a good machine operator? Important evidence on the approximately 400 employees who worked under Kelley in the nine years before his retirement in 1979 provides some partial answers. While he kept no discoverable political records, Kelley did remember, in confidential transcripts, the political histories of most of these people—whether they worked for the party or contributed money. These persons' official employment records reveal the specific job titles they held, and the salary increases they did—or did not—receive. Based on these data, we must conclude that, broadly speaking, the machine no longer worked efficiently.

Patronage. A major problem was that the old, semibureaucratic system of allocating jobs had broken down. Instead of a single power center, there now were competing officials. Kelley himself could select individuals for jobs in his office, but he could not get them actually placed on the payroll unless he won approval from the county board. There, he would have to bargain with the minority Republicans as well as with Democrats seeking to bolster their own positions inside—or even outside—the organization.

These competing authorities limited Kelley's own control over hiring. As Kelley lamented:

> A guy would appear at my door from Personnel [and I was told], "this man is interested in working in your department." You looked him over and they come with crutches, they come blind, they come deaf, . . . they come every way and you turn half of them back, but you didn't get one [an appointment within the agency] until you put them on. That was how it worked.

In the patronage system of a model machine, replacement of previous employees with loyal supporters would be expected. But in fact, such changes were infrequent. Civil service regulations (which substituted merit for party loyalty as the chief criterion in government job selections) were one hindrance to Kelley, but they could be partially circumvented. Still, in 1970, when Kelley replaced a Republican in office, there was no significant turnover in personnel. Indeed, 161 employees still working in 1979—virtually half of the total office staff—predated his election. The party, in reality, did not follow the principle that "To the victor belong the spoils," at least not *all* of the spoils.

The most severe application of patronage principles—dismissal of appointees—was quite rare. Most of the older employees had been appointed by Republicans, but none was fired. In fact, Kelley reported dismissing only two employees throughout the 1970s, and both for reasons of poor performance, having nothing to do with partisan considerations. The first "was caught in a go-go joint at 2:30 in the afternoon when he called in that he was on the job," while the second was removed for using his position to compel sexual favors from women.

The actual system of job allocation did not stress winning votes for the party organization. Those officeholders who had a say in appointments often used them to strengthen their personal organizations or to maintain ties of friendship, rather than to allocate jobs to those areas of the county where the party won its votes or in which it hoped to build support. Although nearly a majority of the county's population was nonwhite, and the party drew considerable support from this constituency, blacks had been virtually excluded by an organization dominated by persons of Irish or Italian stock. Kelley did appoint a few blacks, so that by 1978 they comprised about two percent of his agency's total staff. Perhaps this small change might be interpreted as the machine's halting effort to win votes from an emerging constituency. To Kelley, however, the purpose was neither racial equality nor electoral gain. Rather, it was technical—he needed blacks to do the work of his agency in minority areas, because he could not persuade white workers to operate in the ghetto.

Party Resources. Financial deficiencies were evident as well. The data indicate that the party had strayed far from the efficient kickback system of the past. Rather than keeping formal, complete records of contributions, Kelley relied on his impressive memory to keep track of the organization's friends. But contributions were not set on a fixed scale, purchase of tickets to party functions could be substituted for direct payments, and Kelley let many appointees slip through the collections net.

Kelley's recollections of his employees' party services showed considerable laxity with respect to contributions. While 60 percent of the employees under Kelley's jurisdiction made donations to the party, few of them did so regularly. Almost 30 percent did not give at all, and he was unaware of the financial activity of another 10 percent of the employees.

Another form of party service was campaign work. Most of Kelley's employees were in positions that required less than full-time work, providing them with hours of free time potentially available for electioneering. However, these employees were more likely to use that available time on another job than in service to the party: only 20 percent of Kelley's employees definitely performed any campaign work, while 52 percent did not; Kelley did not know the participation record of the remaining 28 percent.

Taken together, these percentages indicate that even minimal party support activities were not performed by all employees. Party "inefficiency" was apparently widespread, since inactivity was about as common among appointees predating Kelley's election as among those named in his term. Pre-Kelley appointees were slightly less active in campaigns and slightly more financially supportive, but both differences might be explained by their older ages. The lax administration of patronage meant the party received less than maximal return for appointments in terms of contributions and campaign work.

Rewards. Appointment (and retention of appointment) is only one aspect of an efficient patronage system. An additional characteristic is an internal reward system in which the behavior of appointees is regulated through the giving, withholding, and retracting of other rewards. In an efficiently operated patronage system we would expect to find contributions and campaign work rewarded with better jobs and/or higher salaries, while nonperformance would be penalized in the same terms, or at least not rewarded.

We can examine the influences on the rewards of job movement and salary increases by comparing them to party contributions and campaigning. In fact, the impact of money contributions was very limited. Whether they gave money or not, nearly two-thirds of the personnel in Kelley's office were likely to stay in the same job. While those who gave were somewhat more likely to be promoted than the nongivers (27 percent compared with 17 percent), they were also more likely to be demoted (10 percent compared with 3 percent). (The data are presented in Table 5-1.) Even among those first appointed in Kelley's term, the relationship is almost negligible,* and the givers were both upwardly and downwardly mobile. In terms of annual salary increases, contributors actually received less benefit (about $50 less) than those appointed by Kelley directly.

Campaign work, while less common than contributions, also had slight impact on the distribution of rewards. Those who worked for the party were somewhat more likely to receive better job titles. Again, the relationship is somewhat stronger among those hired during Kelley's term. Among campaign workers, 39 percent were promoted, compared with 20 percent of the inactive persons in the office. Overall, the campaigners also received slightly better salary increments ($40 annually), but among the Kelley appointees, they were slightly disfavored.

The slight favoritism shown to campaign workers could provide limited evidence that the party was an efficient allocator of rewards. However, this favoritism often was not for the benefit of the party as such, but rather was based on personal friendship between the worker and Kelley. Once a higher salary or better job was secured, the

---

* The statistical measurement used is a coefficient known as Tau. If contributions were perfectly related to job changes, the statistic would equal 1.0. If there were no relationship at all, it would equal 0.0. In this case, it is only .13.

Table 5-1 Patronage Appointee Rewards and Campaign Contributions

Job Changes	All Employees				Pre-Kelley				Kelley			
	Gave	Don't Know	Didn't Give	Total	Gave	Don't Know	Didn't Give	Total	Gave	Don't Know	Didn't Give	Total
	N=207	N=35	N=99	N=341	N=110	N=17	N=34	N=161	N=97	N=18	N=65	N=180
Promoted	27.5%	37.1%	17.2%	25.5%	20.9%	35.3%	17.6%	21.7%	35.1%	38.9%	16.9%	28.9%
Stable	62.8	57.1	79.8	67.2	65.5	52.9	76.5	66.5	59.7	61.1	81.6	67.8
Demoted	9.7	5.8	3.0	7.3	13.6	11.8	5.9	11.8	5.2	—	1.5	3.3
	100.0%	100.0%	100.0%	100.0%	100.0%	100.0%	100.0%	100.0%	100.0%	100.0%	100.0%	100.0%
		Tau = .02				Tau = −.05				Tau = .13		
Annual Increase ($)	1,067	1,229	1,112	1,095	852	1,059	908	908	1,230	1,342	1,241	1,245

campaigner could be quite confident of retaining it. Recall, also, that because only a fraction of the staff worked in campaigns at all, the organization overall did not benefit from the large number of patronage appointees.

In sum, campaign contributions and especially campaign work were not conditions for appointment in Kelley's agency. Nor did performance of these partisan activities consistently lead to promotions or salary raises for the employees. In contrast to the county's patronage operation in the past, the present patronage system is poorly administered and is not operated with an eye toward winning new voters or encouraging the ongoing partisan participation of appointees.

Other research on patronage systems has uncovered similar "inefficiency" in machines. For example, in studying highway workers in Pennsylvania in the mid-1950s, political scientist Frank Sorauf found that they rarely did any work for the political party responsible for their appointments, that almost no dismissals occurred after a change in administration, and that those who held these positions felt little obligation to work for the party.

Sources of Decline

What happened? Why did the once efficient Tyrone County machine become ineffective in operating its patronage system? Some of the causes were external, due to changes in the political and social environment, and some were due to changes in and characteristics of the party organization itself.

External Causes. The major external change was in the structure of government. Constitutional revisions and subsequent court decisions related to reapportionment of electoral districts eliminated the provision that all officials were elected at-large for the entire constituency, requiring instead their election from separate districts. This change undercut the county machine's power to exercise discipline over the entire ticket. Local organizations could now go their own way. Black factions in Bradford, for example, have since been able to run their own candidates for the county board without approval of the previously dominant central leadership.

Another important change was the creation of a single "county executive" to replace the previous collection of separate officials heading each administrative agency. This executive holds the principal appointing and budgetary power for the county. The office was created through a popular referendum promoted by reform-minded activists who correctly saw the constitutional change as a means of overcoming the power of the machine. Inspired by policy goals, voicing "good government" slogans, and using modern advertising techniques, they won voter acceptance of the new system over the opposition of the Democratic machine. Then, in the election for the position of county executive, the reform groups elected Marlene Weisman, a young, glamorous, and articulate state legislator. The machine's candidate, a dull party veteran, was thoroughly outclassed. Defeat in this election meant that the party no longer had access to hundreds of patronage positions and other preferments available to the county government. This loss capped the antimachine trends set in motion by other formal changes, such as the extension of civil service laws to many jobs and detailed regulation of administration, including state laws providing for county purchasing by closed and competitive bidding.

Internal Causes. Even before these governmental changes took effect, the machine was losing its resources. Appointments were no longer made simply for party reasons. Kelley had found it necessary to hire people on the basis of their technical expertise, to give them the highest salaries available, and to refrain from asking them to contribute to or work for the party. The administrative tasks of the agency had now become too complex in many instances to be done by persons whose only qualification was their canvassing ability on election day. In other instances, appointments or promotions were still made on nontechnical grounds, but not on party grounds. Personal friends might be rewarded, or those who contributed to Kelley's—not the party's—campaign might find favor.

A basic problem for the machine—indeed for any organization—is that it deals with real people, not with an abstract model. In theory, persons could be hired or fired, promoted or demoted, depending on their party service. In reality, a widow who had been in the office for twenty years would not be asked for any work or money for the party. Persons kept their jobs because they were friends of the party chairman who had retired to Florida but was still fondly remembered. Demands for a kickback from a clerk making only $6,000 a year would be seen as unfair. Firing long-term appointees just because their districts did not turn out a large Democratic vote would upset personal relationships in the office and were "just not worth the trouble."

These personal matters become more important as an organization ages, particularly if the organization is built on personal loyalty. When the Democrats first took over the county counsel office in 1970, they had few obligations to the persons on that staff, and they still needed to worry about their possible defeat in future elections. As time went on, however, closer networks were established within the office while the outside demands of elections became less pressing. A determined leadership could overcome these tendencies, but few politicians calculate so well.

The machine, if it were thinking only of votes, should have brought large numbers of nonwhites into patronage jobs, as a means of securing the support of these new voting groups. But this action would have disrupted the established ethnic ties within the party, where Irish and Italians had become used to their near-monopoly of positions. A fully efficient party would probably distribute jobs on some accounting principle, such as so many jobs for so many votes. Doing so, however, would mean that established patterns of distributing jobs among the various wards and towns would be upset. It was easier to follow the old political adage, "To get along, go along."

Furthermore, the party was affected by changes in campaigning itself. Increasingly, emphasis was placed on impersonal forms of campaigning such as greater use of the mass media. The street skills and personal contacts of patronage appointees were of little use in this new environment. What was needed was money—and a lot of it—to purchase time and talent for advertising the party. The money could be obtained from business contributions more readily than from the patronage appointees' kickbacks and dinner tickets. In an economic sense, the old machine workers became technologically unemployed, and they could be left alone with their minor jobs and low income.

The machine also became lazy, or spoiled, by its long record of success. As the county became more Democratic due to population changes, frequently leading to countywide sweeps of all races, machine politics was unnecessary. Given the changed demographic base, the party did not need a strong organization. As one commentator said, "The Chairman was no genius. He could have run anyone and win any election with only five guys working." The efficient use of patronage and insistence on regular contributions were not crucial, given the party's electoral strength. It was easier to stay with tradition, keep people in their jobs, and allow the machine to atrophy—until it was too late to make repairs.

By the time of Kelley's tenure, after a period of sustained and barely noticed change, the vaunted discipline of the machine no longer existed. Rather than a strong party exerting control, there was a mythical memory of a disciplined organization. As one politico observed:

> There was no such [expletive deleted] thing as a party.... There were contributions and donating to a nonexisting party.... If an individual wouldn't do it, nothing would happen to him and [the county chairman] no more knew who gave or who didn't give than the Wizard of Oz because it was all an illusion. The party kept winning. As long as [the chairman] was in absolute control, everybody was giving because there was a myth that the party is so powerful you better not buck the party.

As Plato first taught, political myth can also be the basis of political power. The small urban machine we have described, by the 1970s, was no longer based on discipline but, to quote Jimmy Breslin's *How The Good Guys Finally Won*, on

> Illusion. Mirrors and blue smoke, beautiful blue smoke rolling over the surface of highly polished mirrors, first a thin veil of blue smoke, then a thick cloud that suddenly dissolves into wisps of blue smoke, the mirrors catching it all, bouncing it back and forth. If somebody tells you how to look, there can be seen in the smoke great, magnificent shapes, castles and kingdoms, and maybe they can be yours.

The illusion and blue smoke of party control concealed what was, in fact, a withering political machine. The party simply was not able to adapt to changing circumstances and, as new groups emerged on the political scene, power shifted elsewhere.

CHANGE IN THE NATIONAL PARTIES: FOR BETTER? FOR WORSE?

The character of politics evident on the smaller stage of Bradford and Tyrone County is also evident in the larger world of national parties of the United States. In general, party organizations are changing from an emphasis on electoral victory and individual material rewards to an increasing concern with policy issues and the satisfaction of policy preferences as incentives for political activity. As part of this development, the parties are offering their members more opportunities for participation, while their structure is becoming more centralized and bureaucratic. In sum, the parties are coming closer to the model of the policy party as discussed earlier in this study.

Changes in the national parties are especially evident in four specific areas: campaign finance, presidential nominations, election campaigns, and party coalitions. Whether this new form of politics better meets public needs than does the more private-minded organization like that of the Tyrone County machine is open to debate.

Campaign Finance

Until recently, money for elections was raised from donations by party members such as those in Kelley's office, contributions by individuals seeking government favors, and the candidate's family and friends. In a smoothly running organization, all funds would be channeled through a single party treasury. This procedure has the advantage of freeing the individual candidate from any obligation to particular contributors, each of whom has to compete with other financial supporters for the attention of the party leadership.

Today, the major sources of campaign funds are persons and groups who contribute directly to individual politicians. Particularly important are the new political action committees (PACs), which accumulate funds from individuals with similar policy interests (for example, corporation executives or advocates of antiabortion laws) and then provide contributions of up to $5,000 to favored candidates. These groups have become very important since 1974, when abuses revealed in the Watergate scandal led to limits on individual contributions under the Federal Election Campaign Act Amendments of 1974. Although the Supreme Court declared many features of the law unconstitutional in its 1976 *Buckley* v. *Valeo* ruling, it upheld the provisions of the 1974 statute that limited how much political committees could contribute to individual campaigns.*

By the 1980 election, over 2,600 PACs provided four times as much money to congressional nominees as did parties; PACs gave House and Senate candidates $55 million and spent nearly $140 million at all levels.

The rise of PACs is part of a gradual shift to issue-oriented politics that undermined the Tyrone Democratic machine. These donations are not made because of personal friendship with a candidate, or to claim a patronage job, or to obtain an individual favor, such as a building contract. PACs are interested in the broader questions of public policy, and they use their money to advance their interests. Contributions of PACs associated with the oil industry in 1980 provide one example. These various groups provided at least $5,000 to 241 congressional candidates, a potential majority in the House of Representatives. Of course, few, if any, members of Congress would be "bought" by such contributions, but they would at least give a respectful hearing to these generous supporters. Access, rather than direct influence, is the primary objective of PAC contributors.

Does the new system make legislators more responsive to important interests? Or does it make them particularly responsive to interests with money? PACs often represent "single-interest groups" that are concerned only with a legislator's position on a particular issue, such as abortion, or wilderness preservation, or oil taxation. Does this narrow focus promote more direct ties between the policy interests of constituents and the policy decisions of government? Or does it make it more difficult for government to compromise different interests and to seek policies that define and advance the common welfare?

The new system of campaign finance is also structurally different from the old one. In the past, money was raised and spent locally, as exemplified in the study of Tyrone County. In the new system, money is raised nationally and is then given to individual candidates. An interest group, such as a labor union, will raise money from its members

---

* See pp. 97-98 for an interesting example of the influence of PACs on public policy.

nationwide and then use it in those races that seem most critical and most likely to be affected. Understandably, contributors want to target their efforts where they are most needed. They essentially ignored parties in this form of campaign finance in favor of establishing a direct relationship with the candidate.

The same structure is evident in presidential campaigns which, since 1976, have been partially financed by the federal government. Qualifying candidates who accept statutory limits on their spending ($17 million before the party conventions and $30 million in the general election) are given funds both to seek nomination and to campaign. National money, now raised from the taxpayers, is again distributed to individual candidates, while the parties receive money only for the purpose of conducting their conventions. This system has been praised for eliminating some of the abuses in campaign finance revealed in the Watergate investigations. Another effect, however, is to make candidates for the presidential nomination essentially independent of the traditional party organization. Just as the Tyrone County Democratic machine was undermined (and eventually replaced) by individual and factional competition over jobs and nominations, so too, on the larger national scene, the direct funding of candidates allows them to conduct their campaigns independent of (or even against) the existing party. Jimmy Carter's successful nomination drive in 1976 is a classic example of a campaign directed against "the Washington Establishment." After becoming president, however, Carter found it difficult to win the cooperation of that "Establishment," which greatly handicapped his performance in the White House.

When money is funneled through the parties, candidates have to pay more attention to group demands made through and by the party. Candidates may have to compromise their policy positions to gain a place on a "balanced ticket" or to get a share of the joint spending of the party. In seeking the spoils of office, the party may blur its policies, but it may also achieve a coalition among competing groups. If this negotiation is successful, the party may come to stand for a broad policy direction that is recognizably different from the other party, at least in some respects. Thus the party can serve as a meliorating influence, a filter through which the more extreme demands are modified.

On the other hand, providing election support directly to candidates leaves them freer to express their own opinions or those of the groups providing contributions. But it also makes it more difficult for legislators supported by different groups to reconcile their differences and to unite on even a general policy direction. With no party program or record to examine, voters may find it difficult to assess praise or blame for the actions of government.

Another way to finance elections would be through the national parties, which might resolve some of the present problems. A well-organized national party could collect contributions from policy-minded individuals and then distribute these funds to party candidates throughout the nation. The national Republican party has taken many steps in this direction. It annually receives contributions from two million individuals and then uses these funds to provide campaign services such as opinion surveys, advertising, and direct donations to state and federal candidates. This effort, however, requires the creation of a large party bureaucracy at central Republican headquarters.

Presidential Nominations

The grandeur of the president's Oval Office in the White House contrasts sharply with the faded decor of the office of the county counsel in Tyrone County. Yet, in nominating candidates to the two positions, the traditional party used similar criteria: it sought an individual who could both unite the party and help it to gain victory. It decided its choice through negotiation and bargaining, sometimes swapping policy positions or cabinet appointments in the process. Nonetheless, the process often worked well. The nomination of Abraham Lincoln, as reported in Eugene H. Roseboom's *History of Presidential Elections*, bears this out: "Midnight conferences of liquor-stimulated politicians, deals for jobs, local leaders pulling wires to save their state tickets, petty malice, and personal jealousies—a strange compound, and the man of destiny emerges."

Underlying the tawdry aspects of traditional nominations were characteristics that often led to good choices. The politicians making these choices used criteria important in predicting a candidate's later success in office. They were concerned about his standing as a politician: Could he work with others? Could his word be trusted? Was he free of skeletons in his personal closet? A president, no less than a county counsel, could not do his job well unless he possessed certain qualities. Although they lacked the modern techniques of measurement, such as public opinion polls, performance on television, and primary election contests, these old-style politicians estimated the potential candidate's appeal to the voters. They wanted a winner above all.

The older means of nominating presidential (or other) candidates had two procedural aspects worthy of note. First, the nominating process was conducted by experts, professional politicians who were the peers and associates of aspirants to office and who, knowing them well, were unlikely to be deceived by them. Second, it was a deliberative process—not in the sense of a college seminar, but in the sense that decisionmaking took place over a long period of time, involved extensive if sometimes earthy discussion, and allowed a considerable degree of flexibility as new arguments were advanced and new facts came to light.

In the contemporary system of presidential nominations, the party organization has been virtually eliminated, along with both its merits and faults. Now the emphasis is on individual participation and on issue appeals, the hallmarks of the new policy party, as well as on the personality of the candidates. Tens of millions of voters—not only a few thousand politicians—are now directly involved. Processes are open and well publicized through the mass media.

The emphasis on wide participation is evident in the way delegates to the national nominating conventions are chosen. Three-fourths of the persons who formally nominate a president are now selected in direct state primaries—a sharp contrast to the methods used as late as 1968, when only a third of the delegates were selected by the mass electorate. Moreover, almost all of these delegates are pledged to a particular presidential candidate. They are usually chosen in each state by proportional representation, so that Democratic delegates from New York, for example, must precisely mirror the primary voters' preferences for the competing Democratic candidates. The importance of participation is further indicated by new party rules, which either require or urge that delegations reflect demographic characteristics of the population, that is, equal numbers of men and women, and particular percentages of racial minorities and youth.

Presidential nominations now stress a direct appeal to the voters. Deliberation in a "smoke-filled room" among a small number of "kingmakers" is being replaced by decisions of ordinary citizens watching candidates on television and voting in primary elections. As a result, the assessment of the leadership qualities of candidates increasingly depends on their effectiveness as campaigners, as measured by their standing in public opinion polls and their success in primaries. The delegates themselves are no longer a group of professional party leaders and are not free to change their mind as they wish, but are bound to follow the decisions of the electorate voting in the primaries.

The process of selecting a presidential nominee has been fundamentally changed. It is, apparently, more open and more subject to mass influence. But some observers are critical, arguing that the new processes have distorted voter opinion in two ways. First, enormous significance is given to the first selections of delegates—particularly those chosen in snowbound caucuses in Iowa in January and primaries in New Hampshire in February. The candidates who lead in these first (and often unrepresentative) tests are quickly acclaimed as the "front-runners" and gain media attention, financial contributions, and increased standing in the opinion polls. In 1976, for example, Jimmy

Carter became the leader in the Democratic race on the basis of only 28,000 votes in the New Hampshire primary. Four years later, Ronald Reagan's victory in the same state soon led five of his six opponents to drop out of the race before a single primary had been held west of the Atlantic seaboard. Indeed, relative success in the New Hampshire primary has become a measure of a candidate's legitimacy as well as political viability.

Second, the new process may misrepresent the policy preferences of the party rank-and-file. Survey evidence has shown that delegates to the Republican National Convention tend to be considerably more conservative than Republican voters, just as Democratic delegates tend to be considerably more liberal than Democratic voters. For example, Democratic delegates have supported school busing, and Republican delegates in 1980 opposed the Equal Rights Amendment, but their respective party members took the opposite positions. With the decline of party control over delegate selection, policy commitments become a more important incentive for political activity, but the result is not always fully representative.

Other aspects of the present presidential nominating system also facilitate the individual candidate's—rather than the party's—expression of policy preferences. Even with government aid, candidates need money, and they are most likely to get it from contributors and political action committees who want to promote their particular causes. The presidential nominating process now emphasizes differences in policy, which are discussed in news conferences, speeches, and face-to-face debates. Seeking delegates throughout the nation, intense advocates of particular policies may attract vital campaign workers.

We now have a *national* system of nominations. Individual candidates seek their party's leadership, but do so independently of any party structures. They make policy promises rather than factional deals. Mass electorates intervene decisively, particularly in the early primary states, while professional politicians hold little power. The deliberations and negotiations of expert peers have been replaced by the unalterable decisions of individual, isolated voters. Kelley probably could not have been nominated under this system, but even Lincoln might have failed. Has the nation benefited?

Campaigning

In election campaigns in Tyrone County, precinct workers focused on local activities to bring out a vote for the entire party ticket. Their major activity was personal contacting of voters they knew and trusted, and spending was primarily in the form of "street money" to compensate these party workers. Candidates were not presented as individuals, but rather as loyal members of a party ticket. That ticket was often headed by a prominent person whose popularity could aid those running for lesser offices. In an illustrative and legendary account quoted by historian Theodore White, a Democratic local leader in Brooklyn assured a minor candidate that his success was guaranteed by Franklin Roosevelt's position as the ticket leader:

> Listen. Did you ever go down to the wharf to see the Staten Island Ferry come in? You ever watch it, you look down in the water at all those chewing-gum wrappers, and the banana peels and the garbage? When the ferryboat comes into the wharf, automatically it pulls all the garbage in too. The name of your ferryboat is Franklin D. Roosevelt—stop worrying!

Campaigning in the modern party is quite different. It is essentially impersonal, conducted through the mass media rather than on a face-to-face basis. While candidates still conduct walking tours to greet the voters, or hold large rallies, the purpose of these events is not to contact the electorate directly, but to provide a colorful background for a newsclip on the evening's television broadcast. Thus, presidential rallies will often be held early in the afternoon or at an airport—not because these are the best scenes for the voters, but because they best meet the time schedules of the news media and because they allow the candidate to appear in several "media markets" in a single day.

Because it is impersonal, modern campaigning is also likely to be more oriented toward technical efficiency. Voters are no longer the relatives and neighbors of local canvassers, but a "market" which has to be "sold" a "product," in this case a political candidate. Advertisers, and the devices of advertising, have become highly significant in contemporary politics. A "product line" is developed—which of the candidate's features or views will be emphasized? A "marketing strategy" is laid out—which groups will be specifically targeted? The same market research firms that periodically survey the public's preferences among detergents are hired to determine its political preferences. The techniques of buying newspaper advertisements and television spots, initially developed commercially to warn of the dangers of body odor, are now used politically to warn of the perils of socialized medicine.

The concept of the electorate as an impersonal market has inevitably stimulated the growth of expert marketeers, persons who claim special skills in the winning of elections. There are now more than 300 nationally recognized firms in this business, as well as many more local groups. In major contests, these firms have totally displaced traditional party organizations in the function of campaign management. Indeed, a candidate's chances for the presidency may be judged more by the quality of his or her consultants than by party support. It is becoming more important to be "endorsed" by a well-known consultant than to win the backing of a group such as the Tyrone County Democratic party. The new methods of campaign financing—combined with presidential nominating procedures—have created a new "industry" of political consulting, an industry whose effect is felt at the state and local levels as well as nationally.

Campaigning has become far more individualistic. Rather than promoting the cause of the "party team," each candidate promotes his or her own cause. Political scientist Richard Fenno quoted one U.S. representative who caustically commented:

> The party is no damn good. . . . They can't organize and they can't raise money. . . . I don't have anything to do with the party organization. . . . They have their function. They give you a vehicle to run on. The real function of the party is to have someone to meet the candidate for Congress when he comes into a strange town.

Running on their own, even though under a party label, candidates must operate as individual entrepreneurs in an electoral market. They can no longer rely on a powerful "ferryboat" to bring them safely to port. They must raise their own money, argue their own policy positions, and receive the judgment of the voters on their isolated candidacies. The new campaigning has certainly affected the way the electorate reacts. Party loyalty influences voter behavior far less than in the past, and assessments of the candidates as individuals and judgments about their programs are more important. Balloting is also much less coherent or stable. Frequently, the voters will "split tickets"—choosing a president of one party and a member of Congress of another. Similarly, they may change their opinions over a short period of time, as illustrated by Jimmy Carter's presidential campaigns, where he went from a narrow victory in 1976 to a landslide defeat in 1980.

The new campaigning raises two important questions for discussion. First, is it really different? Is the new campaigning just a more efficient means of doing what politicians have always done? Is the scientific public opinion poll used today, although far more accurate, any different in kind from the traditional politician's attempt to "keep his ear to the ground"? Is the effort to develop a good "television image" essentially different from previous politicians' attempts to "look good"? Perhaps recent developments are merely refinements of older patterns, not fundamental changes.

A second question concerns the larger effects of these changes. Does the new campaigning allow voters to make judgments on the individual characteristics and policy positions of candidates? Is it easier to make these judgments now, than in times when candidates campaigned as members of a party ticket? Can the voters judge an individual's record in office better than the record of a collective group, the party in power? In short, which system of campaigning better promotes democratic control over government?

Party Coalitions

The decline of machines, and other private-minded local organizations, permits the development of a different national party structure. The dominance of the Tyrone County party machine came from its deep local roots: it was run by people who had lived in the area all of their lives and were intimately familiar with its traditions, people, likes, and dislikes. Kelley kept no written records of contributions not only to avoid the disclosure of possibly incriminating evidence, but also because he personally knew and remembered what "Johnny" had done for the party or how much "the O'Leary widow" could afford to contribute. This localism was also a long-term cause of the machine's inner decay. As neighborhoods changed their character, or were wiped away by housing projects and suburbanization, political loyalties were buried with the rubble of bricks.

To the machine, the national party was vague and remote—a source of limited benefits in the patronage it might provide, a potential source of trouble in the investigations of a zealous federal prosecutor. A state party leader might have more of an impact, but still could be treated like a weak feudal king. The barons of the counties would create alliances that left each of them in control of his own estate, while the king's power was restricted to maintaining these shifting balances of power. Cohesive, hierarchical power existed only at the local level—the county, city, or ward. Kelley himself was a typical machine politician having little concern with national events and only occasional contact even with the state's governor, also a Democrat. He saw the state's chief executive at the county party's annual dinner, and he was present when the governor came to his office, reminded officials that "it was that time of year again," and walked outside while contributions were collected discreetly. Otherwise, Kelley's political world was confined within the boundaries of Tyrone County.

The new policy party is quite different. Its interest is in programs that are primarily national in character. The incentives for participation are not patronage jobs on the county payroll, or personal ties to a fellow Italian or Irishman, but the apparent opportunity to further the cause of civil rights, tax reduction, nuclear arms reduction, or some other national policy. The victory of the national party—as the advocate of appropriate policies and nominator of ideologically suitable candidates—becomes the major purpose of party membership and activity. The local party sees itself less as a *club* for its loyalists and more as a *branch* of a larger entity composed of kindred policy advocates around the nation.

Reflecting these trends, the national party organizations have changed considerably. Among the most active partisans, there is more ideological cohesion than in the past. Previously, given its local base, each party tended to include a wide diversity of opinions, even among its most active adherents, such as delegates to the national conventions. There remains a great deal of diversity among ordinary voters who call themselves Republicans or Democrats. Among the activists, however, there is far more ideological solidarity. Ideology may even be so important to activists that they take public positions different from the voters in their own party, as in the case of convention delegates. A policy party, despite its insistence on internal democratic participation, actually may not represent its voters well.

The national parties are now more centralized—or more accurately, nationalized—than has traditionally been the case in the United States. At one time, political science textbooks frequently cited a common cliché that there were "not two parties in the country, but 100—two in every state." Now, far more power is concentrated at the center and in the parties' national committees. The Democrats have required changes in state party procedures, have completely transformed the system of choosing convention delegates, and have compelled more open access for such groups as women, racial minorities, and youth. The Republicans have taken a different approach, increasing the electoral capabilities of the central organization. The national party now employs over 300 persons, has an annual operating budget of more than $20 million, and publishes its own policy journal.

Although both parties have used very different practices, there is a similar effort to build direct ties between the individual member and the national party. That party is no longer a confederation of autonomous local and state units, such as county machines, but rather a mass membership organization. This organization offers its members agreeable (or at least less disagreeable) policy choices, the advancement of the party's program, and participatory rewards, either through involvement in decisions such as the presidential nomination or the opportunity to contribute dollars to the cause.

The attention given to national policy is also likely to promote a central party bureaucracy, as is already evident in the Republican party. To ensure cohesion on policy questions and efficiency in campaigning, centralized power is needed. Managing a party of this kind becomes a complex task. It requires developing policy positions, ensuring ideological loyalty of candidates, and elaborating campaign techniques appropriate to mass electioneering. Parties are developing their own in-house expertise, including organizers, pollsters, media consultants, and electoral strategists.

With centralization, new questions about parties are raised: Does the new bureaucracy run counter to the emphasis on mass participation? Or have PACs contributed to party *de*centralization by diverting decisions on candidacies to numerous interest groups rather than to the party organizations? Can policy differences between party activists and the rank-and-file members be explained, or justified? More generally, is the policy party preferable? Does its focus on ideology make it more difficult to reconcile conflicting interests within or between the parties?

CONCLUDING OBSERVATIONS

As American political parties change and undergo "reform," Americans remain unhappy. Like Dorothy approaching the Emerald City in the "Wizard of Oz," they may simply desire to go home. To paraphrase George Bernard Shaw, Americans may find that the only tragedy worse than not getting their heart's desire is to achieve it.

The urban political machine has virtually disappeared, thus realizing the goal sought by decades of reformers. In Tyrone County, Kelley passes his last days in office, knowing that he cannot win a new nomination from a weakened organization or win the next election from a suspicious electorate. The party that sustained his career dissolves into contending factions and futilely seeks disciplined canvassers and regular contributions. It watches its control over the county supplanted by a reform administration, curtailed by state supervision, and investigated by federal authorities.

Nationally, too, the private-minded party has declined, its place largely assumed by the new policy party. Elections are no longer financed by individual favor-seekers or by payments of patronage appointees, but by open, well-reported contributions of interest groups or by public funds carefully administered by the national government. Presidential nominators have left the stale air of the smoke-filled room for the clean country air of Iowa and the cool mountain breezes of New Hampshire. Campaigns are no longer conducted on a parochial basis for a ticket that includes the party's "garbage," but have become rationalized, efficient means of presenting the qualities and programs of individual candidates. The decentralized network of state and local parties in America has been replaced by more structured, more ideological, and more efficient national organizations.

Who can complain? Yet, there are complaints. Marlene Weisman, the new reform-minded chief executive of Tyrone County, finds it difficult to get her programs enacted and has been overheard yearning for some patronage to distribute to recalcitrant legislators. Racial

minorities in cities find their advancement in government unintentionally blocked by civil service rules, and the urban poor find their welfare
services strangled in bureaucratic procedures. Members of Congress
complain about the policy demands of the single-interest groups that
now fill their campaign coffers. The Democratic party seeks ways to
reverse the effects of 15 years of changes in its nominating procedures,
in order to bring back the expert judgments of party leaders. Isolated
candidates long for the security of a party organization, as isolated
elected officials wish for party ties to hold together a governing
coalition. Voters, treated as consumers of national political products,
perceive no immediate, personal relevance to politics and vote less often
and less enthusiastically.

The machine avoided some of these problems. To be sure, the
machine deserves little moral credit. It was essentially immoral, based
on an ignoble conception of personal greed as the sole basis of political
action. Its financial costs were great, and eventually were paid largely by
the poor themselves, in the form of inadequate services, municipal taxes
and debt, and the absence of broad-scale social change. Thanksgiving
turkeys ultimately were paltry compensation for poverty unrelieved by
governmental programs to limit hunger and inequity.

Even with these defects, the machine particularly, and the private-
minded party more generally, demonstrate some features that remain
desirable in any political party. The machine cared about individual
voters, it had strong local roots, it reached across class and ethnic
barriers to bring diverse groups into active citizenship, and it recognized
that politics must be based on emotions and personal loyalties and not
only on abstract, intellectual arguments. If the policy party—or any
other—is to endure, it would do well to remember these strengths of the
old urban machines.

SOME QUESTIONS TO EXPLORE

In reviewing the questions already raised in this study, also
consider the following:

How important is money to the success of a political party? What
are the different effects, advantages, and disadvantages of financing
politics through contributions to local parties, through political action
committees, and through the national parties?

How does political financing affect party organization—Is it always
true that "he who pays the piper calls the tune"?

Are there likely to be differences between presidential candidates
selected by party professionals and those chosen in the newer system of
mass participation and primaries? Can and should the smoke-filled
room be revived?

Is the present system of presidential nominations as democratic as is claimed? What are some of the costs of greater participation in party decisionmaking?

What has been the influence of modern technology on campaigning? Are television and advertising techniques the causes of the decline of party organizations or only their effect?

What is the effect of new campaigning strategies on the role of party loyalty in voting and party action within government? Is that effect overstated?

Are ideological and bureaucratic parties better expressions of democratic purpose than local political machines? Will such parties inevitably become distant from the party rank-and-file?

Do policy incentives work? Although the policy party prides itself as internally democratic, how does this claim fit with the observed differences in views between party activists and the voters?

Beyond these particular questions, there is the more general and basic issue posed at the outset of the study: *What is the most feasible (if not necessarily the ideal) way to organize politics?* Like many questions about politics, this one depends first on a view of human nature. Can people generally be expected to act altruistically, to participate in politics to advance the "common good," and to focus on general issues of public policy? If so, a policy party is feasible. Consider the alternative view. Can people generally be expected to act individualistically, to participate in politics principally to advance their particular interests, and to focus on more self-serving issues of public policy? In this case, the private-minded party is more feasible. Because these two parties are ideal types, neither exists in reality. Political analysts from the Founders forward have recognized that effective political institutions must take both public and private interest into account.

Beyond this philosophical question, there is another issue of feasibility, which relates to the specific characteristics of American government. Political parties do not exist in isolation, but are in part creatures of their political and social environment. The possibility of creating either a private-minded or a policy party may be increased or decreased by that environment.

Three features of our governmental institutions—and the social environment they reflect—are particularly relevant here:

(1) Federalism—the division of power between national and state authorities—complicates policymaking. A desired policy often cannot be accomplished by a single national law, but instead requires separate action at the different levels of government.

(2) At the national level, policymaking is further complicated by the division of power between Congress and the president, the further division of Congress into the House and Senate, and the independent

authority of the Supreme Court. Achieving unified action in the face of these well-known "checks and balances" is a formidable task. These difficulties are not critical for the private-minded party, which is not primarily concerned with achieving programmatic goals. They are very great problems, by contrast, for the policy party.

(3) Elections in the United States are held at fixed intervals and for specific offices, regardless of the timetable for policy actions. There is no way in which an election can be called on just one issue, while there may be elections scheduled when there are no obvious issues to be resolved. This rigidity of our electoral calendar adds to the problems of a policy party, which seeks to turn elections into "mandates" in support of its favorite programs.

These facts about American political institutions are too well established in the Constitution and in American beliefs to be changed. In this light, how feasible is the achievement of a policy party? What limits, if any, do these characteristics create for further changes in political finance, presidential nominations, campaign techniques, and national party organizations? Is the private-minded party the only kind of political organization that can succeed in this environment?

Feasibility has another aspect. Even if it is desirable and possible to structure parties in a particular fashion, we must consider the eventual results. One of the few enduring truths of social science is that there are always unintended consequences which result from any social action. The machine provided an enduring example: these parties only *intended* to win political power, but their *effect* was to promote social welfare. Reform of the presidential nominating process offers another example. The stated *intention* of the reformers was to strengthen the party organizations; the *effect*, they now agree, has been precisely the opposite.

In considering parties, then, we need to keep in mind the effects of present structures and the possible results of any changes. The advantages and defects of a private-minded party have to be measured against the advantages and defects of a policy party. If we eliminate the personal favoritism of the machine, must we also eliminate its neighborly closeness? If we adopt the national coherence of the policy party must we also accept its reliance on slick campaign techniques? Are campaign contributions by patronage employees any more corrupting than contributions by political action committees? Opening the presidential nominating process allows for broader participation, but is this democratic achievement also a public loss if it means that less expert judgments are made?

There are no "correct" answers to these questions. Reflecting life, politics always involves conflicts, uncertainty, and compromise. The profession of politics, as sociologist Max Weber wrote, is "a strong and slow boring of hard boards." The study of politics requires the same determination.

SOURCES AND READINGS

Data collected for this study came from official employment records of county job holders and from lengthy transcripts of interviews with Kelley (a Democrat first elected in 1970) and other knowledgeable "old timers" in which the workings of the party organization—both past and present—were discussed. Because these interviews were conducted as part of a confidential and serious legal investigation, the authors have reason to accept the statements as fully honest.

In addition to these data, several published studies are valuable to an understanding of political parties. There is a long tradition of general theories about political parties. Among the first was Robert Michels's study of the Social Democratic Party in Germany, published in 1911, *Political Parties* (New York: Dover Books, 1959), which analyzed the continuing problem of the relationship between democratic participation and oligarchical leadership, particularly in a political party devoted to policy objectives. Very different is Anthony Downs, *An Economic Theory of Democracy* (New York: Harper & Row, 1957), where the party's focus on private ends, particularly electoral victory, is the premise for a deductive theory of party and voter behavior. For background in theories of political participation, no student can neglect Max Weber's insightful essay published in 1920, *Politics as a Vocation* (Philadelphia: Fortress Press, 1965).

The place of political parties in American political thought during the early years of the republic has been traced by Richard Hofstadter in *The Idea of a Party System* (Berkeley: University of California Press, 1969), and through the contemporary period by Austin Ranney in *Curing the Mischiefs of Faction* (Berkeley: University of California Press, 1975). To fully understand this debate, it is helpful to return to the arguments of two prominent American politicians—James Madison's attack on "factions" in *The Federalist* No. 10, first published in 1787 (New York: Modern Library, 1941), and Martin Van Buren's defense of parties, analyzed in an exceptional biography by Robert Remini, *Martin Van Buren and the Making of the Democratic Party* (New York: Columbia University Press, 1959).

Empirical studies of American parties fill library shelves. The best introduction to the classic machine is George Washington Plunkitt's colorful first-hand account, recorded in W. L. Riordan, *Plunkitt of Tammany Hall* (New York: E. P. Dutton, 1963). Among many scholarly studies are Dayton D. McKean, *The Boss* (New York: Russell, 1940) on Frank Hague of Jersey City; Harold Gosnell, *Machine Politics: Chicago*

Model, 2d ed. (Chicago: University of Chicago Press, 1968) on the Windy City in the 1930s; and Milton Rakove, *Don't Make No Waves, Don't Back No Losers* (Bloomington: Indiana University Press, 1975), on the same organization in contemporary times. The machine's positive features are discussed in a classic essay by Robert Merton in *Social Theory and Social Structure* (Glencoe, Ill.: The Free Press, 1957), pp. 71-82. Journalist-reformer Lincoln Steffens provides a balanced but negative evaluation of the machine in action in his *Autobiography* first published in 1931 (New York: Harcourt Brace Jovanovich, 1968).

A landmark work in political science, *Toward a More Responsible Two-Party System* (Washington, D. C.: American Political Science Association, 1950) offers several recommendations for modern parties in the United States. James Q. Wilson examines and criticizes "reform" politics in three cities in *The Amateur Democrat* (Chicago: University of Chicago Press, 1962). Further criticisms are raised in Jeane Kirkpatrick's *Dismantling the Parties* (Washington, D.C.: American Enterprise Institute, 1978). The history of Democratic party reform and new forms of national party organization are described by William Crotty in *Decision for the Democrats* (Baltimore: Johns Hopkins University Press, 1978). Current changes in American party politics are examined and deplored by David S. Broder in *The Party's Over* (New York: Harper & Row, 1977), but looked on more complacently by Cornelius Cotter and John Bibby in "Institutional Development of Parties and the Thesis of Party Decline," *Political Science Quarterly* 95 (Spring 1980): 1-27.

The first comprehensive study of political consultants and campaign experts is provided by Larry J. Sabato, *The Rise of Political Consultants* (New York: Basic Books, 1981). Herbert Alexander's *Financing Politics*, 2d ed. (Washington, D.C.: CQ Press, 1980) outlines the role of party money, and Thomas Patterson examines the effect of the mass media on voters and voting in a careful study of the 1976 election, *The Mass Media Election* (New York: Praeger, 1980). Changes in the presidential nominating system are carefully analyzed by John Aldrich, *Before the Convention* (Chicago: University of Chicago Press, 1980) and Thomas Marshall, *Presidential Nominations in a Reform Age* (New York: Praeger, 1981).

The subject of party change generally is well considered in a group of essays edited by Robert Goldwin, *Political Parties in the Eighties* (Washington, D.C.: American Enterprise Institute, 1980). The views of several scholars, elected officials, and journalists on the current status of American parties are presented in *Party Coalitions in the 1980s*, edited by Seymour Martin Lipset (San Francisco: Institute for Contemporary Studies, 1981).

6

Domestic Policy

Resolving the Oil Pricing Issue: A Key to National Energy Policy

Bruce I. Oppenheimer

On January 28, 1981, eight days after taking office, President Ronald Reagan issued an executive order ending price controls on domestic oil. This action concluded a policy struggle that had lasted at least since the October 1973 Arab oil embargo and that involved four different presidential administrations and five Congresses. All tried to resolve the oil pricing issue, which lay at the heart of the establishment of a national energy policy. Without its resolution key public and private decisions about energy exploration, use, and conservation could only be made in an environment of great uncertainty, if at all. During this eight-year period, world oil prices rose from slightly over $5 per barrel to about $35 per barrel. Yet rising oil prices did not bring the issue any closer to resolution. And building the presidential-congressional coalitions needed to develop a solution proved nearly impossible.

Prior to Reagan's executive order, four major efforts to establish oil pricing policy had been undertaken. The first produced congressional passage of the Emergency Energy Act of 1974, which called for a rollback in domestic oil prices and extended price controls to oil not previously under controls. President Richard Nixon vetoed the bill because he preferred to decontrol oil prices and to impose a windfall profits tax on the oil companies; the Senate sustained his veto. Then, in 1975, President Gerald R. Ford struggled with the Democratic 94th

Congress for an entire year over the oil pricing issue. Ultimately, he extended a new system of oil price controls until June 1979 rather than face the adverse economic and electoral consequences that a sudden soar in oil prices might cause. In 1977 President Jimmy Carter unveiled his energy policy package. A key ingredient was the crude oil equalization tax (COET), a mechanism designed to raise controlled domestic oil prices to the world price level. The COET survived the House but was jettisoned in the Senate when priority was assigned to the natural gas pricing section of the package. The final major effort to establish oil pricing policy was Carter's decision in 1979 to link oil price decontrol and a windfall profits tax. Ironically, this proposal, made as requirements for oil price controls were about to expire, did not differ significantly from President Nixon's approach in 1974 and President Ford's in 1975.

This case study focuses on these four efforts to formulate oil pricing policy and to mobilize the political support to enact it. The objective is not only to provide information about an extremely important issue area, but also to illustrate significant questions about how American policymaking works.

THE CONTEXT

Why were price controls placed on domestic oil production in the first place? And what were the general terms of the public debate over oil pricing? To understand the context of the struggle, we must first address these two questions.

The Origins of Oil Price Controls

Prior to the 1970s there were government policies affecting oil pricing, but none placed price controls on oil. Many of the early policies were designed at first to protect domestic producers from the problems created by an oversupply of oil and later to insulate the domestic oil firms from a glut of cheap foreign oil. In the 1920s and 1930s oil-producing states established regulatory bodies to set and allocate production quotas. Without such regulations prices on oil had dropped as low as 10¢ per barrel during the Great Depression. Eventually control over excess production was transferred to the federal government and also was regulated by interstate agreements. These policies stabilized oil prices and production until after World War II when inexpensive foreign oil threatened domestic producers. In the 1950s President Dwight Eisenhower first established voluntary and then mandatory quotas on oil imports into the United States to deal with the problem. An import quota system remained in effect until 1973. Despite tax policies that subsidized the exploration and production of domestic oil, the price of imported oil remained lower than domestic oil until the early 1970s.

Two factors altered this situation. First, U.S. energy demand grew tremendously. Oil consumption rose from less than 10 million barrels per day in 1961 to 17 million barrels per day in 1973. Because domestic production could not keep pace with this growth in demand, the United States increasingly relied upon imported oil to meet consumption levels. By 1973 imported oil accounted for more than 35 percent of U.S. consumption, nearly double what it had been in 1961. Second, the Organization of Petroleum Exporting Countries (OPEC), created in 1960, had developed into an effectively organized cartel by the early 1970s. Recognizing the growing demand for oil, OPEC had begun to ask for and get price increases even prior to the 1973 embargo.

It was in this environment of a new economic order for oil that price controls on domestic oil production were first imposed. However, the reasons for the start of price controls on oil resulted from the need for the Nixon administration to respond generally to the problem of inflation, not from actions by OPEC. Under the 1970 Economic Stabilization Act, Congress gave the president the power to implement wage and price controls. Using this authority, President Nixon's Cost of Living Council established wage and price guidelines for various industries.

In the last phase of the Nixon program, the Council established two oil price categories—"old" oil and "new" oil. Old oil (produced from wells existing prior to 1973) was put under price controls, whereas new oil (produced from new wells or in excess of previous-year production from old wells) was not. At first, the consequences of this two-tiered system were slight because the prices for new and old oil were relatively close—$4.25 per barrel for old oil and slightly over $5 for new oil. But after the 1973 Arab-Israeli war and the accompanying Arab oil embargo against the United States and some European nations, the price of uncontrolled oil doubled while that of old oil was allowed to rise only a dollar a barrel.

In reaction to the embargo, Congress quickly enacted the Emergency Petroleum Allocation Act (EPAA), which gave President Nixon added authority over the allocation and pricing of oil. Because of fuel shortages in the spring of 1973, the EPAA had been in the legislative pipeline well before the embargo. Indeed, at the time of the embargo in October the House was considering the allocation bill on the floor, and the Senate already had acted on it in June 1973. The House and the conference committee, composed of House and Senate members working with unusual speed, completed action on the bill within a month of the onset of the embargo. EPAA placed price controls on oil under separate authority from broader wage and price controls; the latter were due to expire in April 1974, whereas EPAA authority was to continue until March 1975. However, EPAA was understood to be only a stopgap response to shortages created by the embargo. Congress and the Nixon administration both recognized that what was really needed was a long-term policy on the oil pricing issue.

Two Opposing Approaches

The public debate on this long-term policy revealed two conflicting approaches to the problem. The first—the production approach—contended that the way to solve the energy crisis was to encourage exploration and development of new domestic energy sources. Price control, especially if extended to "new" oil, would discourage the search for new domestic supplies and thus make America even more dependent on foreign sources. Proponents of the production approach included individuals from oil-producing areas of the country, oil industry officials, and those who believed in market, rather than government, solutions.

The alternate position reflected a conservation-consumer approach. Its adherents believed that the price of controlled oil was high enough to stimulate added production. They argued, therefore, that allowing it to rise to the OPEC cartel price either would not bring forth significant additional domestic supply of oil or would bring it forth at excessive economic cost to the consumer. The sole beneficiaries of decontrol, they contended, would be the oil companies. The solution the conservation-consumer camp advanced was to cut the demand for oil by providing incentives to conserve and disincentives to consume. Hence they not only opposed efforts to decontrol oil prices, but generally desired to extend price controls. Those from energy-consuming areas, many environmentalists, and those holding more liberal political philosophies tended to favor conservation-consumer approaches.

Because neither side was able to muster political majorities during the eight-year struggle, although each came close at some point, it became largely the task of individuals not aligned with either group to seek some compromise solution. They knew that Americans had grown accustomed to artificially cheap energy. Even before the embargo Americans were paying far lower energy prices than were their western allies. Regular gasoline which sold for 40¢ a gallon in the U.S. in 1973 was $1.14 in France, 80¢ in Italy, 67¢ in Britain, and $1.50 in West Germany. With America's comparatively low gasoline tax, its price controls, and its federal tax policy which, in effect, continued to subsidize oil companies, these gasoline price differences grew even larger after the embargo.

Those in this nonaligned middle group realized that significant conservation would not be achieved if controls kept domestic oil prices well below world market prices. (And they proved to be correct. Between 1973 and 1978 American oil consumption rose from 16.97 million barrels per day to 18.27 million while in Europe it declined from 15.15 million to 13.92 million.) Yet they wished to avoid the sudden economic shock immediate decontrol would have on the American economy. They recognized that as long as price controls existed some production would be held back and some new sources would go untapped, yet they did not want the energy companies to reap windfall profits because of pricing and production decisions made by the OPEC cartel.

At various points during their administrations, Presidents Nixon, Ford, and Carter fell in this nonaligned group, as did a small minority in the Congress. Their problem was to formulate a policy around which they could rally House and Senate support and then build the majorities to enact it. Thus, they had to address questions of policy and of bargaining. How could oil price decontrol be achieved so as to stimulate domestic production and yet not place an undue strain on an already inflationary economy? How could conservation be achieved without having a disastrous impact on lower-income Americans? What should be done with the enormous profits on revenues that would accrue from bringing domestic oil prices up to the world price? And could any policy be formulated around which a majority consensus could be built and still be "good" public policy?

THE EMERGENCY ENERGY ACT: A COMPROMISE SCRAPPED AND AN EXTREME MEASURE VETOED (1973-1974)

On November 7, 1973, President Nixon asked Congress to take certain short- and long-term actions in response to the Arab oil embargo. Congress acted rapidly. Senator Henry M. "Scoop" Jackson, D-Wash., already had introduced an energy bill (S 2589), and the Interior and Insular Affairs Committee, which he chaired, held hearings on it the day after Nixon's request. By November 13, the committee reported out a bill giving the President many of the powers he had requested. Although the bill included sections on allocation authority, relaxation of environmental standards, development of contingency rationing plans, and conservation requirements, it left the price control issue untouched. On the Senate floor that issue arose when Senator James Buckley, Cons./R-N.Y., tried unsuccessfully to remove oil price controls established under the authority of the Economic Stabilization

Act. Few major changes were made in the committee's bill, and it passed easily on November 19 by a 78-6 vote.

In the House, the Committee on Interstate and Foreign Commerce reported a different and more controversial energy bill than the Senate's. The House bill granted the president less authority than the Senate had; it required that presidential energy conservation proposals be approved by the Congress, and it also called for the regulation of windfall profits. The House bill was reported out by the Commerce Committee on December 7 by a highly partisan vote of 24-13. Not surprisingly, the windfall profits section was highly controversial. It provided that the president specify prices for the sale of oil to "avoid windfall profits by sellers." Moreover, it permitted individuals who believed that the prices they were being charged for oil allowed for windfall profits to ask the Renegotiation Board to rule whether excess profits were being taken.

On the House floor several efforts were made at amending this section. The key amendment was offered by James Broyhill of North Carolina, a Commerce Committee Republican, and Democrat Joe Waggonner of Louisiana, the leader of the conservative southern Democrats and a strong oil industry supporter. Their amendment deleted the provision allowing the Renegotiation Board to review claims of windfall profits and instead gave the president authority to develop a plan to deal with unreasonable profits. Waggonner argued that whereas the review authority effectively gave the Renegotiation Board the power to tax profits, the determination of a windfall profits tax properly rested with the tax-writing committee of the House, Ways and Means (of which Waggonner was, incidentally, a member). The Broyhill-Waggonner amendment was defeated by a 188-213 vote, with support for it coming primarily from Republicans and oil-state Democrats. This alignment was a common one on energy issues in the 1970s although there were variations which prevented either the production or consumer-conservation side from winning consistently. In this case, given the importance and closeness of the vote, it is surprising that the Nixon administration did not take a position on the amendment.

Other amendments were offered to the House bill including several to exempt independent oil producers from full coverage by the windfall profits section. This was a common practice on energy legislation as either the means of attracting the support of members of Congress from districts with strong small-producer interests or as the price these members tried to exact for their support. In this case their support was not needed, and the amendments were defeated. It was clear that in the face of an oil embargo House members would be reluctant to vote against an emergency energy bill even if it were not exactly to their liking. On December 14, 1973, following defeat of a motion to recommit the bill to the Commerce Committee, the House passed the bill by an overwhelming 265-112 vote. The House bill then went to a conference committee to iron out the many differences between the two versions.

Conference Committee Compromise

Often it takes months for a conference committee to settle House-Senate differences on controversial legislation. But in this case the public's frustrations with energy shortages and gasoline lines spurred Congress to move quickly. Within a week the conferees came to an agreement and reported back to their respective bodies. Their report incorporated the windfall profits section of the House bill with modest modifications. The president could set prices to avoid windfall profits, and parties who believed that the prices produced windfall profits could still appeal to the Renegotiation Board. Enforcement of this provision was, however, not to begin until January 1, 1975.

This compromise reflected the conferees' recognition that the House provision calling for the Renegotiation Board to review charges of windfall profits was probably unworkable and yet there was a need, in the face of rapidly rising oil prices, to take some action. Democratic Senator Edmund Muskie of Maine spoke to this problem during Senate debate on the conference report:

> The provision can be considered an incentive for the appropriate committees of the Congress to begin their deliberations on this issue early next year.
> This serves notice that price gouging and windfall profits will not be allowed, but gives Congress, and the appropriate tax committees in Congress, time to formulate the best possible approach. If they devise no better language then the provision in this bill will automatically take effect.

Despite the compromise no final agreement on the bill was reached before the session ended. Senators Russell Long, D-La., and Paul Fannin, R-Ariz., the respective party leaders on the Senate Finance Committee, filibustered the conference report until Jackson agreed to drop the windfall profits section. The Senate then attached the revised bill as a rider to a minor piece of legislation and sent it to the House. The House responded, and in a series of votes reiterated its commitment to the windfall profits section and rejected the new Senate compromise. The first session of the 93rd Congress adjourned December 22, 1973, without resolving the oil pricing (and profits) issue.

Recommittal and a Second Conference Report

The situation did not improve much in the second session. In a special energy message to the Congress on January 23, 1974, President Nixon asked Congress to enact a windfall profits tax. He emphasized:

"We must not permit private profiteering at the expense of public sacrifice," and urged Congress to "[prevent] major domestic energy producers from making unconscionable profits as a result of the energy crisis." Nixon's windfall profits proposal was in the form of a tax on the excess profits of oil companies. Congress's immediate response, however, was to continue the stalemate. Because the start of a new session diminished the effectiveness of a filibuster, the conference report on S 2589 was again brought to the Senate floor in late January. But Long and Fannin found new allies in their fight against the windfall profits provision. Some liberal Democrats led by Senator Gaylord Nelson of Wisconsin also attacked it. Nelson, a member of the Finance Committee and friend of Chairman Long despite their policy differences, argued that the windfall provision "is quite clearly unworkable, unenforceable and almost certainly unconstitutional." Despite pleas from Jackson and Republican Howard Baker of Tennessee to use the bill to push Congress to act on the oil pricing issue, a majority of the Senate voted to recommit the bill to the conference committee.

This proved to be a strategic error on the part of oil industry supporters. The reconvened conference committee decided to avoid conflict with the tax-writing committees by dropping the windfall profits approach to the oil pricing issue and shifting instead to price rollbacks and controls. This change was led by Scoop Jackson, who as a potential presidential candidate desired to demonstrate leadership on energy issues. The new provision was in neither the original Senate nor House bill. It set an average price of $5.25 per barrel on all domestic crude oil, which was the price ceiling already in effect for old oil. The effect of this, however, was to extend price controls to new oil which at the time was selling for $10.35 per barrel. Thus, the price on new oil would have to be rolled back to $5.25 per barrel or offset by pricing old oil for less than $5.25 per barrel in such a way as to produce an overall average of $5.25 per barrel for all oil. The provision did, however, allow the president to raise prices on oil up to $7.09 per barrel to encourage the production of costly oil sources.

Notwithstanding opposition on both the Senate and House floors and from the Nixon administration, the new conference report was adopted. In the Senate, Fannin complained: "The most recent version of S 2589 contains all of the infirmities of the older conference report plus additional infirmities." Jackson claimed that the rollback was the only way to deal with "unreasonable windfall profits." When Fannin tried to recommit the second conference report many of the supporters of the first recommittal switched. Those who shifted included liberals who had opposed other provisions in the first conference report and some southern Democrats for whom "sweeteners" had been added to the bill.

In the House, Republicans Clarence Brown of Ohio and John Anderson of Illinois claimed the price control provision would raise the price of old oil to $7.09, which was too high, and discourage new exploration for oil for which the $7.09 price was not sufficient. Defenders of the provision argued that these were average prices and that since the $7.09 per barrel price was nearly twice as high as a year earlier, it offered sufficient incentive for exploration. With waiting lines still long at gasoline stations and almost daily reports of record earnings from the major oil companies, it is hardly surprising that the House handily defeated the effort to remove the price rollback provision.

Thus S 2589 was finally cleared and sent to the President on February 27, 1974, for his signature. But on March 6, Nixon vetoed the bill. The price rollback, he claimed, "would set domestic crude oil prices at such low levels that the oil industry would be unable to sustain its present production of petroleum products, including gasoline." Although a majority of the Senate voted to override the veto, the 58-40 vote fell short of the two-thirds needed for passage. The veto was sustained because several conservative Democrats, who had first voted to recommit the bill and then voted for it on final passage, joined with Republicans on the override vote.

At this point, S 2589, as well as other attempts to resolve the oil pricing issue, were for all practical purposes dead. The urgency of the issue soon faded. Thus, Congress and the administration could tolerate the continued stalemate. Moreover, the provisions of EPAA kept price controls on old oil, which at that time comprised about 70 percent of domestic production. Congress was able in other legislation to establish a new Federal Energy Administration to administer oil price controls and to extend the EPAA until August 31, 1975. But the oil pricing issue remained unresolved as other issues—particularly the impeachment proceedings against President Nixon—displaced it in the attention of policymakers and the public.

The oil pricing issue was not settled in 1973-1974 because those holding extreme positions on the issue combined to defeat a compromise developed by those in the middle. The coalition that formed in the Senate to recommit the first conference report on the emergency energy bill was composed of production-oriented senators who opposed the windfall profits provision and some conservation-oriented senators who viewed the windfall profits section as weak and unworkable. Combined, these extremes had enough votes to reject the compromise. The conservation-consumer side next offered the more extreme price rollback solution, which then proved unacceptable to President Nixon and to production-oriented senators willing to sustain his veto. The conservation-consumerists could afford not to compromise. They knew that public sentiment would prevent the production advocates from building the legislative majorities necessary for price decontrol and that, consequently, price controls would continue on old oil under EPAA authority. A final decision on oil pricing could, therefore, simply be postponed.

THE FORD ADMINISTRATION AND THE DEMOCRATIC HOUSE BID FOR A MAJORITY (1975)

With President Nixon's resignation August 9, 1974, the nation's preoccupation with Watergate began to subside, and Congress and the White House could again start to focus on pressing policy problems. The new president, Gerald R. Ford, knew he would have only two years to build a record on which to seek election, and in doing so he would have to address the energy policy question. When the 94th Congress convened on January 14, 1975, the Democrats held a two-to-one majority in the House and a 62-38 margin in the Senate. These large party advantages promised legislative results on the energy pricing issue and a capacity to bargain with a Republican administration. In addition, energy policies developed by a Democratic Congress could serve as a base for a Democratic presidential nominee in 1976. Finally, a series of congressional reforms designed to improve the policymaking capabilities of the Congress were at last in place. Begun in the late 1960s, the reforms were intended to improve congressional staff and technical resources and to curb the power of committee chairmen who in the past, at times, had blocked key legislation. Legislative agencies such as the Office of Technology Assessment (OTA) would bring their expertise to bear on energy issues. Thus, there was great optimism as 1975 began that an integrated national energy policy could finally be developed.

In a nationwide television address on January 13, President Ford broadly outlined his proposals on energy and the economy which, when later presented formally to the Congress, included the decontrol of oil prices and a tax on windfall profits. That same day the House Democratic leadership presented a range of energy policy options that had been prepared by a task force of the House Democratic Steering and Policy Committee chaired by Jim Wright, a Texas moderate. The leadership's plan emphasized methods of discouraging energy consumption and of encouraging conservation, although it left the details to be developed by the various congressional committees with jurisdiction over energy legislation. By contrast, the Ford statement stressed increased domestic production as the key to less dependence on foreign energy sources. The two approaches, however, did share a common theme: energy prices must increase.

Efforts to Construct a Compromise

Movement toward a compromise seemed to be developing in late February when the Wright task force, together with its Senate Democratic counterpart, endorsed a more liberal price for "new" oil and an excess profits tax on the major oil companies. They continued to oppose, however, the Ford administration's recommendation for removing price controls on "old" oil. Less than a week later energy policy hearings by the House Committee on Ways and Means unveiled a series of reports prepared by the committee's Democratic members. Among the proposals included in the summary of the reports, as presented by Chairman Al Ullman, D-Ore., was "a windfall profits tax based on the assumption of gradual deregulation of oil...." Ullman indicated that he had "discussed both the timing and substantive aspects of price regulation, energy conservation and allocation with Congressman John Dingell, Energy and Power Subcommittee Chairman, House Interstate and Foreign Commerce Committee." He thus recognized that decontrol and the windfall profits tax were linked, and that jurisdiction over the tax belonged to Ways and Means while Commerce held jurisdiction over price control legislation.

Thus, when the first witness, Secretary of the Treasury William Simon, reiterated the Ford administration's proposal for decontrol of crude oil prices and a windfall profits tax, there appeared to be agreement on the broad issue of oil pricing. But many other questions remained unresolved. How quickly should prices be decontrolled and on what kinds of oil? What structure should a windfall profits tax take? And should companies be allowed a credit against a windfall tax if they invested the profits in exploration for new sources of oil (known as a "plowback")? These were the issues under discussion as the Ways and Means Committee hearings progressed.

On the second day a panel of leading economists representing different schools of thought supported a policy of decontrol. They agreed, moreover, that decontrol by quantity (a certain percentage of oil being removed from price controls at a time) was preferable to decontrol by price (allowing the controlled price to increase gradually until it reached the market price). Decontrol by price, they argued, would give producers an incentive to withhold oil production until the decontrol process was completed.

President Ford, observing the movement toward consensus, announced delay of his decision to decontrol oil prices until May 1 to give Congress time to pass an energy tax bill. By the end of March the Ways and Means Committee began to mark up the draft energy tax bill introduced by Ullman which provided for a windfall profits tax if price decontrol occurred. The proposed tax had no plowback provision and was scheduled to be phased out over 16 years (by 1990).

Soon thereafter, however, the momentum switched to the opponents of the compromise, who were organizing to pull apart the delicate coalition. Senator Jackson skillfully and successfully moved a Standby Energy Authorities Act (S 622) through the Senate. His bill continued price controls on "old" oil at $5.25 a barrel (except when produced through expensive recovery processes) and also required the president to set a ceiling price on "new" oil. During floor consideration of the bill Senator Henry Bellmon, R-Okla., offered an amendment to decontrol oil prices by 1977, but it was overwhelmingly defeated. Thus, despite the House's apparent readiness to compromise on oil pricing with the Ford administration, the Senate followed Jackson's lead and established a more extreme position from which to bargain. President Ford countered the Senate action with a new proposal to end price controls on "old" oil over a two-year period but delayed formalizing it to give the House time to act.

However, two sets of opponents to the compromise also began to organize in the House. Liberal Democrats on the Ways and Means Committee who favored energy conservation realized that the enactment of a windfall profits tax would make passage of oil price decontrol possible. To defeat decontrol, they withdrew their support for a windfall profits tax. They were joined in their opposition to the tax by production-oriented Ways and Means members from energy producing districts who were for decontrol but opposed a windfall tax, especially one without a plowback provision.

Faced with this two-pronged attack, Ullman was forced to retreat in an effort to save other parts of his energy tax bill. Retention of the windfall profits tax would cause the loss of support for the entire bill of four oil-state Democrats and several liberals on his committee. This would be more than sufficient to deprive Ullman of majority support on Ways and Means. So the windfall profits section gradually slipped away during the markup of the bill, culminating in a formal vote of 27-8 by Ways and Means on May 12 to hold off action on a windfall tax until the Commerce Committee acted. Although Barber B. Conable, Jr., of New York, a leading Ways and Means Republican, charged that Democrats "have not had any intention of having a windfall profits tax for a long time," opposition to it also came from oil-state and extreme conservative Republicans. Thus, the energy tax bill (HR 6860), as reported by the Ways and Means Committee, was missing perhaps its most crucial component.

The House leadership still hoped to salvage the oil price decontrol-windfall profits tax compromise by making use of the Commerce Committee's energy conservation bill. Under this strategy, the Rules Committee would provide the procedure for joint consideration of the Ways and Means and Commerce energy bills on the House floor and would make in order an amendment connecting oil price decontrol with a windfall profits tax. Thus a possibility of saving the compromise still existed. But opponents of the compromise undercut this strategy by slowing the Commerce Committee's progress on the bill.

Meanwhile, the Democratic House leadership was being pressed by Chairman Ullman not to wait for the Commerce bill and to bring his energy tax bill to the House floor before the Memorial Day recess. President Ford intensified the pressure. In a televised speech he dramatized Congress's failure to act on his energy proposals by ripping pages off a calendar to indicate the time that had elapsed without action. House leaders felt they could no longer delay the energy tax bill and, immediately following the recess, the Rules Committee reported the bill. The chance for merger of the two bills thus was lost, and an energy tax bill stripped of most of its significant provisions passed the House on June 19 by a 291-130 vote that primarily reflected party lines.

The Commerce Bill Offers Another Opportunity

The House Commerce Committee finally reported its energy bill (HR 7014) five days after the House completed action on the energy tax bill. Initially, the Commerce bill had given proponents of a decontrol-windfall tax compromise another chance because at the subcommittee stage it provided for the decontrol of oil prices over a four-year period *on the condition* that a windfall profits tax was in place. The proposal was advocated by Robert Krueger, D-Texas, and Clarence Brown, R-Ohio, both members of the Commerce Committee's Energy and Power Subcommittee. Krueger, an ambitious freshman who aspired to a Senate seat, was relatively moderate on the oil pricing issue, especially for a Texan. He was willing to accept a windfall tax if decontrol would be achieved, especially if he were credited with developing the compromise. Brown, a skilled and more experienced member, also favored decontrol but knew that Democratic support for that position was necessary, given the party's two-to-one majority in the House. Realizing that Krueger would have a better chance of persuading Democrats, especially those among the large freshman class, than he would, Brown permitted the proposal to become identified with Krueger rather than with himself.

In the full committee, however, Krueger's decontrol provision was removed from the bill by a margin of one vote. It was replaced by a new price control title favored by the conservation-consumer side. The new title, prepared by Democrats Harley Staggers of West Virginia and Bob Eckhardt of Texas, kept controls on "old" oil and placed a $7.50 per barrel ceiling on new oil. Krueger obtained permission from the Rules Committee to offer his decontrol proposal as an amendment on the

House floor. It was clear that Krueger would have the support of many production-oriented members who by now were willing to accept a windfall tax rather than the further extension of price controls. He had to win the support of those in the middle, however, to achieve a majority.

With price control authority under EPAA scheduled to expire August 31, 1975, and with Congress set to recess in 10 days for the month of August, the House took up the Commerce bill, HR 7014. Utter confusion reigned as the competing sides bid for majority support in the manner of a free-wheeling auction. Five key votes on the oil pricing issue were taken on the House floor, three directly concerned with the pricing title of the Commerce Committee's bill and the two others with a resolution to disapprove presidential proposals for gradual decontrol of oil prices. (The president had the authority to decontrol under EPAA, but it was subject to congressional veto.)

On July 23 the House passed a resolution disapproving by a 262-167 vote an administration proposal to decontrol the price of "old" oil over a 30-month period and to place a ceiling price of $13.50 per barrel on "new" oil. Those opposed to decontrol and those wanting to give Congress an opportunity to resolve the oil pricing issue joined forces in support of the disapproval resolution.

On that same day the House also considered the Krueger amendment (linking gradual price decontrol with a windfall profits tax) to HR 7014, with debate on it primarily focused on a jurisdictional argument. Opponents of decontrol contended that its provisions on a windfall profits tax were properly within the jurisdiction of the Ways and Means Committee, not the Commerce Committee. This argument forced Al Ullman, who had originally favored the linking of decontrol and windfall profits tax, to take the floor as chair of Ways and Means and defend his committee's jurisdiction over tax matters, even though the committee had never gotten around to designating a windfall profits tax. To defuse this quarrel which meant certain defeat for the Krueger amendment, Jim Wright amended Krueger's proposal to make the windfall profits section acceptable to Ullman. But in doing so Wright also had to weaken the linkage between decontrol and a windfall profits tax. This in turn eroded support among House members who were willing to back decontrol only if assured of a strong windfall profits tax. As a result, the Krueger amendment was narrowly defeated, 202-220.

Immediately following the vote, moderate Democrat Charles Wilson of Texas made a motion to strike from the bill the pricing language (the Staggers-Eckhardt provision that would continue controls on old oil and extend them to new oil). Some of those who had just voted against the amended Krueger provision also were unwilling to accept the relatively strict two-tiered pricing in the bill. Wilson's motion carried 215-199, and HR 7014 was at least temporarily without any language on pricing.

At this stage it was crucial for President Ford to try anew to construct a majority. Of course, he could have let price controls cease when the EPAA expired, but at the risk of being held publicly accountable for the sudden energy price increases that would inevitably result. However, that was not a feasible strategy for an administration already faced with inflation and unemployment figures in the double-digits little more than a year before a presidential election. Instead, Ford adjusted his bid for congressional support with a new price decontrol plan. The phase-out period for controls on "old" oil was changed from 30 to 39 months and the ceiling price on "new" oil was lowered from $13.50 to $11.50. Meanwhile, Staggers and Eckhardt also put forward an adjusted price control proposal. To their $5.25 and $7.50 prices for "old" and "new" oil respectively, they added a new category to cover high-cost oil produced above the Arctic Circle, beyond the Outer Continental Shelf, or through expensive recovery processes, and set a $10 per barrel price for it.

When the House returned to consideration of HR 7014 on July 30, the new Staggers-Eckhardt proposal won out over a revised decontrol amendment offered by Krueger, which essentially provided for the new Ford decontrol plan contingent on enactment of a windfall profits tax. The three-tiered Staggers-Eckhardt pricing scheme prevailed because it attracted the support of members from energy-producing areas in Colorado, Kentucky, Pennsylvania, and West Virginia who had opposed the first Staggers-Eckhardt proposal and whose districts would benefit from the new oil price category. Following adoption of the Staggers-Eckhardt amendment, the House passed a resolution disapproving the new Ford decontrol plan by a 228-189 vote, with support for the President coming exclusively from Republicans and oil-state Democrats.

In their final form the pricing provisions produced in the conference committee differed substantially from either the two-tiered system in the Senate bill (S 622) or the three-tiered system in HR 7014. Congress only specified a single average price of $7.66 per barrel for domestic oil and left to the president and his energy advisors the task of setting prices to arrive at that average. The $7.66 average was more than a dollar a barrel less than the price of oil at the time, and hence the presidential rollback of some oil prices would be necessary. Furthermore, the legislation continued price controls for a 39-month period (until June 1, 1979), and after that permitted them by presidential discretion through the end of September 1981.

President Ford chose to sign the legislation despite three counts against it: no Republican conferee endorsed the conference report;

Republicans in both houses tried unsuccessfully to gut the pricing provisions; and he himself had opposed price rollbacks and the continuation of controls. The legislation did, however, give the president added emergency powers for dealing with the energy administration. Overall, Ford's decision is most understandable in terms of practical politics. The following year, 1976, was an election year, and he could not expect Congress to be any more willing then to decontrol oil prices than it had been in 1975. Decontrol—whether or not coupled with a windfall profits tax—would mean even higher energy prices to consumers in the short term. Hence it posed a political risk that few elected officeholders cared to chance at that time.

Explaining the 1975 Outcome

Given the optimism early in 1975, why was the long-term resolution to the oil pricing issue again discarded in favor of a short-term continuation of price controls? The basic explanation is that the majorities in Congress necessary to produce the long-term resolution did not exist. Policies increasing energy prices would not be popular at any time, but they were especially vulnerable to public backlash when inflation and unemployment were high. Moreover, members of Congress from consuming areas could not support a boost in energy prices unless a significant windfall profits tax was in place. However, the conservation-consumer advocates who favored continued price controls prevented the House from ever considering a fully elaborated windfall profits tax in combination with a decontrol proposal.

As a result of these political conflicts, the compromise seemingly reached in March 1975 between the Ford administration and two key chairs, Al Ullman of Ways and Means and John Dingell of the Energy and Power Subcommittee, began unraveling. Once this became apparent, President Ford was forced to try to salvage the production-side approach by a series of proposals for gradual decontrol which diffused the economic impact of higher oil prices. House Democrats in the conservation-consumer camp, in response, returned to proposals extending price controls. In the end, President Ford was outbid by Staggers and Eckhardt, price controls were continued, and a final decision on oil pricing was again postponed.

THE CRUDE OIL EQUALIZATION TAX: A NEW APPROACH TO THE OIL PRICING ISSUE (1977-1978)

No serious effort to resurrect the oil pricing issue took place in 1976 because the Democratic Congress and the Ford administration reached a stalemate on a range of far less difficult issues than oil pricing. Those favoring the conservation position on energy questions at least were satisfied that price controls continued. They also had hopes that with the election of a Democratic president in November their position would receive a more favorable reception in the executive branch. After all, in advocating oil price decontrol even with a windfall profits tax, Ford appeared to side with those favoring production solutions to the energy problem.

During the early months of the Carter administration, the opportunity to develop an integrated energy policy appeared better than at any time since the 1973 embargo. The new Democratic president gave a national energy policy top priority, and he enjoyed sizable Democratic majorities in both the House and Senate to back him up. Moreover, in anticipation of receiving Carter's energy proposals, the House had created an ad hoc Select Committee on Energy with secondary jurisdiction over each component of energy policy after it had first been considered by the particular standing committee and subcommittee with original jurisdiction over that policy area (for example, Ways and Means, Science and Technology, Commerce, Public Works, etc.). Hence the ad hoc committee would be able to prevent delay in the standing committees, to settle any policy disputes among them, to integrate the policy pieces into a package, and to bring energy policy to the floor of the House as a coherent entity.

Thus, when President Carter on April 18, 1977, presented his energy proposals to the public and two days later outlined the specifics in a speech to a joint session of the Congress, the mechanism for holding the package intact through the maze of committees and subcommittees already was conceived. On April 21 the House formally adopted the resolution (H 509) establishing the ad hoc committee.

The Carter package heavily favored the conservation-consumer approach to energy issues. It included proposals for tax incentives to encourage energy-saving measures in buildings, utility rate restructuring, coal conversion by utilities and other industrial energy users, "gas guzzler taxes" on cars not meeting federal mileage standards, and the development of new renewable energy sources. In addition, Carter called for continuing existing price controls on natural gas and extending those controls to cover intrastate as well as interstate natural gas. The President's solution to the energy crisis was to get Americans to use energy more wisely and to switch consumption from oil and gas to more plentiful or renewable energy sources. In his view, oil and natural gas prices were already high enough to encourage new exploration and discovery. Decontrol of those prices, therefore, would only give oil and gas companies windfall profits without significantly increasing production.

On the pricing of oil, Carter's proposal was a hybrid that fit snugly with neither the producer nor consumer side of the issue. It shared with the Nixon and Ford proposals the idea that domestic oil prices should be brought up to the world price; otherwise, the consumption of domestic oil would be subsidized. Conservation would be encouraged only if oil prices reflected replacement costs in terms of world prices. However, Ford and Nixon proposed to raise domestic oil prices to the world price through decontrol, whereas Carter chose to reach that objective through a tax on crude oil on delivery at the refinery, to be implemented in stages over a three-year period. A system of price controls would remain in effect although the price of "new" oil would be allowed to rise to the 1977 world market price and producers could increase prices to reflect general inflation. Thus, when fully in place the tax proposed by Carter would be equal to the difference between these new controlled prices and the world market price for oil. It was appropriately named the Crude Oil Equalization Tax (COET). The COET was designed to prevent producers from receiving windfall profits and yet achieve oil conservation by gradually raising the price consumers paid for oil to the world price. Carter further proposed that the revenues from the COET be fully rebated to consumers to help offset the economic impact of higher energy prices.

Carter Victory: COET Survives in the House

Not surprisingly, the COET proposal provoked opposition. Together with the other tax proposals in the Carter energy program, it was referred to the House Ways and Means Committee, which held extensive hearings on it in late May and early June of 1977. At those hearings representatives of oil industry groups, labor unions, and consumer organizations expressed dissatisfaction with COET, albeit for different reasons.

Lee White of the Consumer Federation of America adamantly opposed COET:

> ... This is really very disturbing. We have for a long time supported price controls on oil and on natural gas as a far more effective and useful mechanism than to take, as the Carter administration does, the world price as a standard. To make up any difference between domestic oil and the world oil price by a tax just to make sure we are following the OPEC level is incomprehensible to us.

White called instead for the continuation of price controls, a position supported by Andrew J. Biemiller, the chief lobbyist for the AFL-CIO. The labor organization, however, was willing to support most of the Carter package and its general objectives.

Those taking the production approach to the energy issue opposed COET just as vigorously. Testifying for the American Petroleum

Institute, Harold D. Hoopman declared: "We are convinced it would be far more effective both for the economy and for the energy situation to remove wellhead price controls and allow the market to operate." Realizing that this advice would not be heeded, Hoopman proposed an alternate COET, one that would be "only transitional and phased out over a 3-or-4-year period to provide the funds necessary to meet increased energy requirements." A. V. Jones, Jr., president of the Independent Petroleum Association of America, an organization of smaller producers, was even more vehement in his opposition to Carter's conservation-oriented approach:

> The unfounded premises of the administration may be summarized as follows: (1) the domestic oil industry cannot make any significant additions to our domestic oil and gas reserves and producing capacity; (2) even if it had a vast potential, the industry does not have and cannot obtain the drilling rigs and other supplies and materials adequate to do its job; and (3) there is, therefore, no need to provide additional incentives by permitting the industry to generate increased capital resources for exploration, development and production.
>
> Nothing in our experience or in the history of our industry justifies these keystone conclusions. Independent producers are dismayed with the administration's defeatist approach to the energy supply policy.

Opposition to COET thus came from both producer and consumer groups, as it had earlier on the proposal for linking oil price decontrol to a windfall profits tax. In 1975, however, the conservation-consumer side had been more strongly opposed than the production side; but with COET the reverse was true. Support for each of these proposals came largely from the particular administration which had formulated them, its party's members in Congress, and some of those seeking a middle position between the extremes.

Compared with Presidents Nixon and Ford, however, Jimmy Carter had a definite advantage in dealing with Congress. His party possessed a two-to-one majority in the House and a 62-38 margin in the Senate. Ford and Nixon needed to build majorities for their programs through coalitions and bargaining with Democrats in Congress, whereas Carter, in terms of partisan numbers, had only to keep Democratic opposition or defection within tolerable limits. The President also was aided by the reluctance of Democratic House members to oppose the first major policy initiatives of a newly elected president of their own party. During this "honeymoon" period, congressional Democrats might even support proposals, such as COET, which faced strong interest group opposition.

Ways and Means thus reported COET favorably, 21-16, with only 4 of 25 Democrats joining the 12 Republicans to oppose it. Ways and Means did make one significant modification of COET, adding a new oil category, the price of which would be uncontrolled and therefore not subject to COET. Oil-state Democrat Jim Jones of Oklahoma proposed the amendment exempting this so-called "new new oil," that is, oil from properties not in production 90 days prior to Carter's mid-April announcement of his energy plan. While this provided an added production incentive, the committee balked at a Republican amendment to return some of the revenues from COET to the oil producers if they drilled more wells. Importantly, Ways and Means also scheduled COET to expire in four years (by September 30, 1981) by which time oil prices might be decontrolled. This was a clear response by the committee to the oil industry's request to limit the duration of COET or, at least, not make it permanent.

The Ways and Means action on the tax part of the energy program was forwarded to the ad hoc Committee on Energy to which the other pieces of the package were also sent. Speaker Thomas P. "Tip" O'Neill, Jr., D-Mass., had selected the Democratic members of the committee with great care. They were broadly representative of Democratic House members in the range of their energy views, but those holding strong production or conservation-consumer positions tended to be individuals with whom the leadership could negotiate. To ensure a unified party position, the Democratic members of the committee caucused to resolve their differences before meeting with the Republicans. Although many items—especially natural gas price regulation, a gasoline tax increase, and coal conversion—were the focus of controversy for the ad hoc Energy Committee, COET was not among them. Instead, it would be tested on the House floor.

And tested it was. Although the House Rules Committee had limited the number of amendments that could be offered to the energy package, several were directed at COET. The prime one was a revamped version of a "plowback" amendment earlier defeated in the Ways and Means Committee, offered by Democrats Jim Jones of Oklahoma and Patricia Schroeder of Colorado. An outspoken junior House member with strong credentials among liberal Democrats, Schroeder gave credibility to the amendment as being something other than a proindustry loophole. When she found herself under attack for sponsoring it, Schroeder took the floor to defend the need of small producers for production incentives:

> What we are trying to say is we need some incentives for these people to keep gambling. They are gambling to kingdom come. The majors have done a very brilliant thing. They are drilling abroad because it is cheaper to drill abroad. They are much more apt to hit a flowing hole abroad. ... Why do we not have the same kind of equity for domestic drillers?

But the complex amendment was hard to understand and created uncertainty about who would benefit from a plowback of 3 percent of COET to drillers who qualified. It was defeated narrowly, 198-223, because few other northern Democrats were willing to side with Schroeder on the matter.

Other attempts to modify COET also were unsuccessful. In every case but one, the Democratic leadership was able to hold enough party members to produce a majority. The critical House test for COET came on a motion to recommit the legislation to the ad hoc committee with the instruction that it delete COET. Wisconsin Republican William Steiger, a Ways and Means member who offered the recommittal motion, contended that COET was not an effective conservation instrument and would not reduce imports. It was really a disguise, he maintained, for a revenue raising measure. "The rebates are more an illusion than the reality promised in the President's address to this chamber." Chairman Ullman responded that Steiger's motion "effectively guts the bill. The equalization tax is the centerpiece of our energy policy." The Democratic House majority prevailed (203-219) even though all but three Republicans supported Steiger's motion. An anticlimactic final passage vote followed, giving the Carter administration a major legislative victory. The House had completed work on Carter's energy package on schedule and most of the package, including COET, had survived intact.

COET Defeat in the Senate

The administration's celebration was brief because its energy program, especially the COET, had rougher going in the Senate. For one thing, the Democratic margin in the Senate was not quite as favorable as in the House, and Carter's victories in the House had been relatively narrow. In addition, there was no Senate counterpart to the House ad hoc committee which the Democratic leadership could use to construct its compromise. The energy package had to be taken up in a series of separate bills. Then, too, whatever "honeymoon" advantage Carter enjoyed in the House no longer existed by September when the Senate considered the administration's energy package. Finally, the Senate Finance Committee, which had jurisdiction over COET, and particularly its chair, Louisiana Democrat Russell Long, had a reputation for designing tax policies favorable to the oil and gas industry.

As the Finance Committee began hearings on COET in mid-September, discussion immediately centered on what to do with the revenues from COET (estimated at $39 billion through September 1981). Long favored using the proceeds to help develop new energy sources, and Majority Leader Robert Byrd, D-W.Va., whose job it was to steer the Carter program through the Senate, offered testimony to the committee in support of a similar position. But opposition to COET continued to grow. By the time the Finance Committee took a vote on the tax on September 26, a 10-6 majority favored killing it. The 10 votes against COET were cast by two proconsumer Democrats, the seven Republicans on the committee, and conservative independent Harry F. Byrd, Jr. of Virginia.

Ironically, Long now seemed willing to support COET if the revenues would be used to finance new exploration, but his efforts to resurrect the proposal resulted in more frustration. With Finance Committee Democrats split on COET, and Republicans united against it in any form, the committee finally decided not to include COET in the energy tax proposals it sent to the floor. COET could still be saved in the conference committee, where Russell Long would play a key role, but Senate floor action nearly eliminated that option. Senator William Roth, R-Del., offered a sense of the Senate amendment that the Senate conferees on the energy tax bill reject any efforts to levy a crude oil tax. Although this nonbinding amendment was defeated, the Senate clearly indicated that it could not be relied on to support COET if it survived the energy tax conference.

COET: A Dead Horse

When the energy tax conferees met in the second session of the 95th Congress, COET was no longer the centerpiece of the Carter energy program. Russell Long, who had become displeased with other facets of the energy package, claimed in March 1978 that COET was a "dead horse," and he was unwilling to use his influence with other Senate conferees even to negotiate with the House conferees on a compromise on COET. Meanwhile, the Carter administration was preoccupied with putting together a difficult compromise of the natural gas pricing component of the energy package. (Some proadministration participants in the struggle over the Carter package later claimed that Carter officials always had considered COET an expendable part of the package and that resolution of the gas pricing issue was their paramount concern.)

By May, Speaker O'Neill announced that he was considering separating the tax portion from the rest of the energy package in an effort to win over an additional conferee for the natural gas compromise. This action would kill COET because by that time it was clear that COET could get to the President's desk only if it were part of an entire conference agreement package. It could not be exposed to a separate up-or-down vote in either the House or Senate and survive. Although the tax bill was not split off, the COET was for all practical purposes dropped. Long simply attached the Senate energy tax bill as an amendment to a minor tax bill. Next, he requested a conference on this minor bill with the House. Hence COET was not a subject for conference negotiations because it was not a part of either the Senate or House bill in the conference. Once again, presidential efforts to resolve the oil pricing issue failed because developing majorities in favor of higher oil prices proved too difficult. Nixon and Ford had inadequate Republican support in Congress to secure even gradual price decontrol, and Carter suffered the defections of too many producer- and consumer-oriented Democrats, even with his party's majorities in both chambers. Moreover, as both Carter and Ford discovered, even loyal supporters in Congress became increasingly unwilling to embrace unpopular policies during an election year.

The Carter administration's national energy package met with some success during the 95th Congress (1977-1979). Many of the component parts were in place by the end of 1978, including a natural gas pricing compromise. But the oil pricing issue remained the one major unresolved piece of this energy puzzle. Without it, the United States still lacked a truly broad-range approach to energy policy. When OPEC announced a new round of oil price increases in December 1978, the difference between domestic and world oil prices again widened. The oil pricing issue took on renewed urgency and quickly returned to center stage.

RETURN TO GO: DECONTROL AND A WINDFALL PROFITS TAX (1979-1980)

Changed circumstances constrained the President's energy policy choices more than ever. Mandatory oil price controls set by EPAA were due to end on June 1, 1979; from then through the expiration of EPAA itself on September 30, 1981, price controls could be maintained by presidential action. If not renewed by the latter date, however, price controls would be lifted. Hence, unlike the situation in the past, a continued failure to resolve the oil pricing controversy would result in price decontrol, not in the continuance of price controls. But because of the erosion of Carter's political support, he could not expect to gain congressional concurrence in a reauthorization of price controls. Public opinion polls showed that his own popularity had slipped considerably. In addition, Republicans had picked up some seats from Democrats in both chambers in the 1978 mid-term elections. Combined with production-oriented Democrats, they comprised a majority to block further extension of oil price controls.

On the one side, then, Carter did not have the votes to gain adoption of a modified COET proposal or an extension of the EPAA. Yet on the other side he could no better tolerate the political and economic consequences of immediate price decontrol than the Ford administration could back in 1975. A compromise solution was needed. It emerged in early 1979 when the administration returned to an old formulation in modified form—gradual price decontrol linked to a windfall profits tax.

On April 5, President Carter described decontrol as "a painful step. . . . Each one of us will have to use less oil and pay more for it." He argued that decontrol was necessary "to stop encouraging waste by holding the price of American oil down far below its replacement or true value." He also asked Congress to enact a windfall profits tax and urged the American people to use their influence to stop the oil companies from defeating it. Carter called for the revenues from the windfall profits tax to be used to establish an Energy Security Fund for future energy research and development and to assist low-income families in paying for increased energy costs.

The formal Carter proposals were very complex. Regarding decontrol, the President indicated that beginning June 1, 1979, he would use his EPAA authority to raise gradually the amount of oil that would initially qualify for high-price categories and later for removal of all price controls. This would occur in monthly changes and all residual oil price control would be lifted by October 1, 1981. This decontrol-by-quantity formulation was in keeping with the recommendations that economists had made during the 1975 Ways and Means Committee hearings and was designed to keep producers from withholding production. In addition, some types of oil would be reclassified to allow them to qualify immediately for higher prices. The windfall profits tax proposal called for a 50 percent tax on the price increase, measured against specified base prices, which would result from decontrol. Some oil that could be produced only at very high costs would be exempted from windfall profits taxes. In addition, a windfall profits tax of 50 percent also would apply to any domestic increases resulting from future OPEC price rises and to newly discovered oil.

Under powers granted by the EPAA, the President could handle price decontrol on his own; after June 1, 1979, Congress no longer had authority (as it had in 1975) to disapprove decontrol proposals. However, the windfall profits tax was new legislation; hence it required congressional enactment. This key difference in the two basic components of the Carter proposal shifted the political advantage in the energy pricing struggle from the conservation-consumer side to those favoring production interests. Price decontrol would be well under way before passage of a windfall profits tax.

Opposition to Carter's compromise policy came from both extremes. Consumer-conservation advocates deplored the phasing out of price controls and the production camp criticized the windfall profits tax as unnecessary and its rates as too steep. Some House Commerce

Committee liberals led by Toby Moffett, D-Conn., attempted to extend price control by tacking such a provision onto a Department of Energy authorization bill. In May they lost an unexpectedly close vote in the Commerce Committee, as its members responded to public dissatisfaction with a new round of rapid gasoline price increases and with long lines at gasoline stations. To prevent the possible adoption of Moffett's amendment by the House, the leadership delayed scheduling the legislation for floor consideration until October. By that time the gasoline lines had disappeared, and the House already had passed a stiff windfall profits bill. Moffett's amendment was rejected handily, 135-297; its support came mostly from Northeast and big-city Democrats. For all practical purposes the defeat of this amendment signaled that the fight against gradual decontrol was over.

Not to be outdone, some production advocates sought to modify the other half of Carter's plan, the windfall profits tax. However, they recognized that the political price for decontrol would be some type of windfall profits tax. Hence they concentrated on altering the tax proposal rather than on trying to defeat it outright. The struggle focused, therefore, on specific details of the windfall profits tax: the tax rates; to what kinds of oil the rates would apply; what, if any, production would be exempt from the tax; how long the tax would last; and what to do with the revenues from it.

The Ways and Means Committee, which was the initial decisionmaking point, established one benchmark for the upcoming struggle. Composed of 25 Democrats (only 2 of whom came from strong production-oriented constituencies) and 12 Republicans, Ways and Means was more intensely in favor of the tax than the House or the Senate as a whole. Anticipating that the measure it reported was likely to be weakened at some later stage in the legislative process, the committee followed a strategy of producing a tougher tax than the Carter administration had requested.

The committee bill raised the tax from the 50 percent level requested by the President to 70 percent, tightened its coverage of old oil, and continued the tax on certain classes of oil beyond the 1990 phase-out date recommended by Carter. The committee's only significant concession to the opposition was on the category of newly discovered oil, and even then the concession was limited. Whereas oil interests wanted to eliminate the tax entirely on that class of oil, they had to settle in the committee for a compromise that allowed for annual increases in the base price above which the windfall profits tax would apply.

On the House floor, however, the balance of contending forces was less favorable to those pushing for a strong windfall profits tax, and the result was a weakening of the Ways and Means bill (HR 3919). The key vote came on an amendment offered by Jim Jones and oil-state

Republican Henson Moore of Louisiana, both members of Ways and Means. The amendment sought to limit the tax rate to 60 percent and to end the tax by 1990. In the Ways and Means Committee Jones and Moore had been unsuccessful with their proposal, but now, on the House floor, they won easily by a 236-186 vote. Nearly all the Republicans and one-third of the Democrats (many from oil-producing districts) supported their amendment. On the other hand, a Democratic majority was able to defeat a Republican attempt to recommit the bill with the instruction that the Ways and Means Committee add a plowback provision. The House proceeded to pass the bill by voice vote.

Compared with the 50 percent tax rate the President had requested, the measure approved by the House provided for a higher tax rate (60 percent) for most categories of oil, but treated newly discovered oil more leniently (30 percent); on balance, it would yield somewhat more revenue. In line with the expectations of Ways and Means, the House bill had weakened the committee's product. Further pressure to soften the legislation could be anticipated in the Senate, but Ways and Means still had an extra card with which to bargain. The question of how to spend the revenues from the new tax deliberately had not been included in the House bill, giving the House some leverage and elbow room in any subsequent dealings with the Senate on compromising their differences.

The Bill Moves to the Senate

As the Senate Finance Committee began hearings in July on the windfall profits tax, the administration knew that it had to keep enough of its proposals in the committee's bill to have a good chance of an acceptable final bill from the House-Senate conference committee. But it soon became clear that Finance Committee members had other ideas. Republicans again tried to add a plowback provision. Other members wanted to ease the tax as it applied to independent oil producers and to eliminate the tax on Alaskan oil. Chairman Russell Long was again concerned that production incentives not be ignored. In contrast to these efforts, the focus of the administration, beyond preserving much of the House bill, was to tighten the tax on newly discovered oil.

Two related events of mid-1979 strengthened the Carter administration's position. First, in late June OPEC announced the second major price rise of the year for crude oil, increasing it from $14.55 a barrel to $18-$23.50 a barrel (varying by country). This meant that American oil companies would have even larger windfall profits from price decontrol. Second, when the major oil firms announced their quarterly earnings, it was clear to all that their profits were already at record levels. Seeking to exploit these events, President Carter opened his July 25 news conference by urging the public to support a tough windfall profits tax:

Now it is the turn of the United States Senate to act, and there will be a massive struggle to gut the windfall profits tax bill. If this happens, then we cannot reach our energy goals.

I want to serve notice tonight that I will do everything in my power as President to see that the windfall profits tax is passed because I consider it to be crucial to our Nation's future.

But the Senate Finance Committee and Chairman Long effectively countered by defusing the sense of urgency set in motion by the President. The committee dragged out its consideration of the energy bill by holding lengthy hearings and by requesting ever more detailed estimates on particular items from its staff economists. Much of its time was spent discussing proposals for spending the windfall profits tax revenues in the form of tax credits for business and residential expenditures on energy conservation equipment. After all, since price decontrol had already begun, proproduction senators had little incentive to expedite the passage of a tax on the profits derived from decontrol. It was not until October 25th, nearly four months after the House had passed HR 3919, that the committee reported the bill.

In almost every respect, the Senate Finance Committee bill was weaker than the House-passed version. It exempted newly discovered oil from the windfall profits tax, phased out the tax earlier, and raised about half as much revenue. Thus, just as House Ways and Means gave Carter more than he had asked for, Senate Finance gave him less. And just as producer interests worked to persuade a House majority to weaken the Ways and Means bill, so Carter officials would have to work with the conservation-consumer side to persuade the Senate to strengthen the Finance Committee's bill.

The Senate Makes Adjustments

Of the many amendments to the Finance Committee's bill that the Senate considered, three received primary attention. The first, offered by Texas Democrat Lloyd Bentsen, exempted from the windfall profits tax the first 1,000 barrels a day of production by independents exclusively involved in exploration and production of oil. The independent producers, it was argued, conducted most of the high-risk exploration for new oil and were less well capitalized than the major companies. They needed the incentive of higher profits, therefore, to keep them actively drilling for new oil. The amendment carried on a 53-41 vote; a number of traditional foes of the oil industry—many of whom were concerned with reelection prospects in 1980—provided the unexpected but necessary support for it.

The second major amendment delayed the phase-out of the tax and, therefore, increased its total revenue yield. This revision, proposed by Daniel Patrick Moynihan, D-N.Y., moved the revenue figure closer to that contained in the House bill. But it did not make the tax permanent, as President Carter had proposed originally (he later asked for a 1990 phase-out date) and as some liberal Democrats still favored. Moynihan's amendment gained backing as a needed offset to other provisions in the Senate bill that reduced its revenue intake. In addition to the Bentsen amendment just discussed, the bill contained the tax credit provisions that had been tacked on in the Finance Committee. The amendment was adopted easily, 68-26, with opposition coming almost entirely from oil-state senators and from a few of the most conservative Republicans.

The third and most controversial amendment concerned the issue that was most crucial to the Carter administration: Should a windfall profits tax be imposed on newly discovered oil? Obviously, newly discovered oil (oil found after 1978) would constitute an increasing proportion of total production in the future. If it were exempted from the tax or taxed at a relatively low rate, future tax revenues would decline and future windfall profits to producers would increase. Although not wanting to discourage exploration for new oil, Carter was insistent that the tax effectively cover profits from the sale of newly discovered oil.

To produce an acceptable position on this issue from the conference committee, the administration had first to alter on the Senate floor the Finance Committee's exemption of newly discovered oil from the tax. Majority Leader Robert Byrd and two Finance Committee Democrats, Abraham Ribicoff of Connecticut and Bill Bradley of New Jersey, led the administration's fight. They proposed an amendment taxing windfall profits on newly discovered and certain other categories of oil at 20 percent. Long moved to table (and thus kill) their amendment, but his motion was defeated, 44-53; the President and the Democratic Senate leadership held the support of 47 of their party's members.

The battle, however, was not over. Long and other production advocates started to filibuster. After three cloture votes to end the filibuster failed narrowly, both sides agreed to a compromise on December 17, 1979. The tax rate on newly discovered oil was set at 10 percent, and the windfall profits subject to the tax were fixed as the amount in excess of a base price of $20 per barrel instead of $17. The amended Finance Committee bill passed the Senate overwhelmingly, 74-24.

The Issue Is Resolved

Given the complexity of the windfall profits tax bill, the conference committee completed its work with unexpected ease. The conferees agreed to a total revenue figure of $227 billion to be raised by 1990, which split the difference midway between the House and Senate figures, $277 and $178 billion, respectively. A decision on how best to reach the $227 billion was deferred until the start of the second session.

The conflict that remained was a heated one, but it no longer pitted those seeking production solutions to the energy crisis against those seeking conservation-consumer solutions. Instead, various producer interest groups quarreled over which segment of the oil industry should bear what part of the windfall tax burden. In the end the conferees accepted the 30 percent tax rate on newly discovered oil that the House had adopted and some of the benefits the Senate had given to independent producers. Thus, the burden for achieving the compromise revenue figure fell disproportionately on the major producers. Many of the tax credit provisions added by the Senate remained in the conference report. But most of the tax receipts went into general revenues, not into a trust fund for energy projects as Carter had advocated. The conferees, however, did suggest ways in which the monies might be spent if Congress chose to set up such a fund in other legislation.

Production-oriented opponents made last-minute attempts to unglue the compromise bill by moving to recommit it and to add the full 1,000-barrel-per-day exemption given to independent producers in the Senate bill. These efforts, which were easily turned back, probably are best understood as symbolic actions to satisfy producer related constituencies. The key players were aware that a derailing of the windfall profits tax bill at this point might lead President Carter to retaliate by altering his decontrol timetable, and neither side wanted to risk starting over yet again to resolve the energy policy controversy from scratch.

Postscript: An Earlier End to Oil Price Controls (1981)

Under President Carter's oil decontrol schedule, all price controls were due to expire September 30, 1981. With Carter's defeat for reelection in November 1980, his successor, Ronald Reagan, had the option of altering the timetable. During the campaign Reagan had opposed the windfall profits tax and supported decontrol of oil prices, deregulation of natural gas prices, and elimination of the Department of Energy. Making good on his decontrol promise, President Reagan lifted the remaining price controls on oil in late January 1981. By that time, however, less than one-quarter of domestic oil production was still under controls, and the change was not expected to have any significant impact on oil production. Ironically, the main rationale for Reagan's decision appears to have been that "early" decontrol would bring in $3 billion to $4 billion in additional revenues from the windfall profits tax, a benefit of value to an administration that was pledged, at that time, to balance the federal budget by 1984.

SOME QUESTIONS TO EXPLORE

In the face of an energy crisis once described by President Carter as "the moral equivalent of war," why did it take eight years to resolve the oil pricing controversy, the key ingredient in a national energy policy?

Was the oil pricing issue itself unusually controversial? Who would pay the costs and who would receive the benefits from decontrol? How evenly divided were the opposing sides, and did each side's belief that it could win polarize the issue?

Did the organization of Congress contribute to the delay in resolving the oil pricing issue? Why did the House need an ad hoc energy committee in 1977 to manage President Carter's energy package? What was the effect of the divided jurisdiction over energy matters on efforts to reach a compromise? Were some members recognized for their expertise on energy questions, or did every member think of himself or herself as an energy expert? How did the pressure of upcoming elections affect Congress's ability to resolve the oil pricing problem?

Was presidential leadership on energy issues weak or strong? How did Watergate affect Nixon's response to the 1973 Arab oil embargo? And how did Watergate affect Congress's response to Nixon's energy initiatives? Was the embargo an opportunity for effective presidential leadership? What political disadvantages faced President Ford? How did Ford's concern with the 1976 election affect his leadership ability? Could President Carter have capitalized on his political power in Congress to resolve the energy pricing issue sooner? Why, despite substantial Democratic majorities in both houses, did the Crude Oil Equalization Tax (COET) fail? Should Carter have been more willing to compromise with the Senate, and especially with Russell Long, in 1978 rather than fight to the end on COET?

What were the costs of not resolving the oil pricing issue sooner? The linking of oil price decontrol and a windfall profits tax could have been adopted as early as 1975, and the proposal at that time was not very different from the one finally agreed to in 1980. Would significant oil conservation have started sooner if Americans had begun paying world prices earlier? If decontrol had started in 1975, what would have been the effect on American consumers, businesses, and automobile manufacturers? Would an earlier resolution of the issue have influenced the development of alternative energy sources—solar, oil from shale, coal liquification? In examining the effects of not resolving the issue sooner, consider what the costs of oil price decontrol and a windfall profits tax have been. One could make the case that America actually *benefited* from its failure to resolve the issue.

Is the oil pricing case generally reflective of the problems of domestic policymaking? Look at a range of other current issues, such as financing Social Security, welfare reform, agriculture price supports, national health care, or clean air policy. Are they plagued by the same difficulties that attended the oil pricing controversy? Are today's issues increasingly seen in terms of redistributive policy—taking resources from one group of citizens and giving them to another?

Are political moderates under these circumstances less able to build compromises among competing sides or to maintain a middle position at all? Ponder, in this regard, the searching comments of Otis Pike, D-N.Y., a political "moderate," in announcing his retirement from the House in 1979:

> ... I have often wished that I could see issues as clear and simple and one-sided as either doctrinaire liberals or doctrinaire conservatives do. Two-thirds of Congress is completely predictable. It is more difficult being a moderate, being able to see some validity on both sides of an argument, and then having to either try to work out some suitable compromise or vote for one side or the other. The compromise will be unacceptable to both sides. The vote will be troublesome because you're never all that sure you're right and half the people will be absolutely certain you're wrong.

This case study highlights the weaknesses of our political institutions in development of public policies. Compared with the reactions of other western democracies to the energy crisis, the American response was relatively ineffective in the formulation and enactment of policies. The decisionmaking processes of the national government are becoming ever more decentralized and subject to an increasing number of internal checks and vetoes. And this is a time when greater centralization of policymaking authority—not the reverse—may be sorely needed.

SOURCES AND READINGS

Primary sources of this case study include committee hearings (especially those of the Ways and Means and the Energy and Commerce Committees in the House and the Finance and the Energy and Natural Resources Committees in the Senate), the *Congressional Record*, and interviews with participants. Among the secondary sources that offer excellent summary coverage of the energy policy struggle, and especially of the oil pricing issue, see the Congressional Quarterly *Weekly Report* and the *Wall Street Journal* for the appropriate time periods between 1973 and 1981.

For substantive information, Craufurd D. Goodwin, ed., *Energy Policy in Perspective* (Washington, D.C.: The Brookings Institution, 1981) presents a useful account of the post-World War II history of

American energy policy. A more detailed examination of recent energy policy can be found in Sam H. Schurr et al., *Energy in America's Future: A Study Prepared for Resources for the Future* (Baltimore: Johns Hopkins University Press, 1979). *Energy Future: Report of the Energy Project at the Harvard Business School* (New York: Random House, 1979), edited by Robert Stobaugh and Daniel Yergin, provides a more prescriptive analysis. These three works are based largely on economics or economic history.

For energy policy politics, see *Energy Policy*, 2d ed. (Washington, D.C.: Congressional Quarterly, 1981), which provides a detailed account of energy legislation in the 1973-1980 period, organized both chronologically and by subject matter. Walter A. Rosenbaum, *Energy, Politics and Public Policy* (Washington, D.C.: CQ Press, 1981) broadly analyzes energy policy decisionmaking and its context and facilitates its comparison with other public policy issues. David Howard Davis, *Energy Politics*, 2d ed. (New York: St. Martin's Press, 1978) provides an excellent overview of energy policy politics and carefully distinguishes the differences in the politics that apply to each energy source area, such as coal, oil, natural gas, and nuclear power.

In addition, two of the author's related articles on energy policy politics have contributed to this case study: "Congress and the New Obstructionism: Developing an Energy Program," in Lawrence C. Dodd and Bruce I. Oppenheimer, eds., *Congress Reconsidered*, 2d ed. (Washington, D.C.: CQ Press, 1981), pp. 275-295, and "Policy Effects of U.S. House Reform: Decentralization and the Capacity to Resolve Energy Issues," in *Legislative Studies Quarterly* (February 1980): 5-30. Those pursuing research on energy politics can find an extensive review of the available literature in Charles O. Jones, "American Politics and the Organization of Energy Decision Making," in *Annual Review Energy* (1979), pp. 99-121.

7

Defense Policy

Arms Development and Arms Control: The Strange Case of the MX Missile

Paul N. Stockton

"That's the craziest idea I've ever heard of." With these words, President Jimmy Carter dismissed a plan for housing the MX* missile that would have made Rube Goldberg proud. Yet, by the time Carter left office, he was fighting tooth and nail for an even more convoluted plan. This case study examines the causes of Carter's turnaround and other twists in the history of the MX and its relationship to arms control.

The MX would be well worth analyzing for its own sake. When completed, the MX will be an immensely powerful intercontinental ballistic missile (ICBM), armed with 10 nuclear weapons far more powerful than the ones that destroyed Hiroshima and Nagasaki. This missile system will also eat up at least a $20 billion chunk of our national budget and may require a sizable amount of land for basing as well. Finally, the construction of the MX could wreak havoc on future arms control efforts.

Yet the MX may be essential. The system was developed to satisfy certain military requirements that many officials, from President

---

* "MX" is the Defense Department's term, the "M" denoting missile, and the "X" for experimental or not yet designated. Weapons usually are identified by similar letter-numeral codes, such as the B-1 bomber.

Reagan on down, believe are increasingly urgent. Neither is the MX necessarily incompatible with arms control. As long as our military requirements are met with such weapons, the U.S. government may become more willing to take a chance on arms control negotiations, because we can then "bargain from a position of strength." Such agreements in turn can help us develop weapons that meet our military requirements. By permitting more reliable predictions to be made about future enemy force levels and characteristics, arms control treaties can provide a useful background for deciding what capabilities our own weapons should have.

However, there is no all-powerful, all-knowing government official who can tell us exactly which military requirements and arms control objectives must be pursued. Neither is there any such official who can unerringly determine how a particular weapon must be designed to meet both sets of goals. Instead, a variety of officials and legislators struggle over these decisions, none of whom has the power or the wisdom to dictate what must be done.

The process by which such decisions were made for the MX is the focus of this study. The history of the MX also will be used as a tool for examining larger questions about policymaking in American government. These questions include the way different objectives are pursued by the armed services, the White House, and Congress, and the manner in which bargaining between these governmental actors shapes U.S. policies. The study also explores the implications that our policymaking process may have for future arms developments and arms control efforts.

THE AIR FORCE CREATES A WEAPON

U.S. arms developments almost always originate within the armed services and the private companies they employ to construct the weaponry. The Air Force's MX is no exception. Well before the secretary of defense, the White House, or Congress could influence the MX's development, the Air Force already had settled on a basic design for the weapon. The factors that shaped the emergence of the MX missile and its basic system are discussed in this section.

Developing the Missile

Although Missile X is still years away from full production, it is hardly a "new kid on the block." Its roots go back to the late 1960s and the Air Force's Advanced ICBM Technology Program, under which research was begun that provided the basis for developing a new missile. This was years before the service decided a new ICBM was necessary. However, because developing and producing a major weapon system takes at least a decade, the Air Force did not want to postpone research on advanced ICBM technology until such a need became urgent. As Air Force Lieutenant General William Evans (Deputy Chief of Staff for Research and Development) put it: "We just don't want to get caught with our technological pants down."

The absence of a pressing need for a new ICBM did not deprive this research of a focus. Since the laboratories working on advanced ICBM technology already had helped develop earlier missiles, they simply concentrated on surpassing the "effectiveness" of their previous designs. Effectiveness in missile guidance systems is generally equated with precision in directing a missile to its target. Therefore, laboratory engineers tried to develop systems that would make a new ICBM far more accurate than existing ones. Similar efforts were made to improve missile propulsion. A crucial measure of effectiveness in propulsion systems is the amount of missile "payload" they can launch (which, in the case of an ICBM, consists of the nuclear weapons-carrying reentry vehicles on the missile's tip). By working on more efficient fuels, better engine designs, and related developments, engineers tried to increase the payload-lifting potential that a new ICBM might have.

As progress in these areas made it possible to develop an accurate, heavy-payload missile, the Air Force gradually decided that just such a weapon was necessary. The service had long believed that it needed the ability to attack strategic forces in the Soviet Union. But by the early 1970s, the U.S.S.R. had built a large number of new ICBMs, which were being housed in underground silos that would protect them from all but fairly close-by nuclear explosions. As Air Force General Alton Slay noted: "We are getting to the point where we are incapable of putting Soviet silos at perhaps the risk we would want to." According to Slay, the United States was "in a difficult position" relative to the U.S.S.R. in terms of ICBM reentry vehicles, since the newer Soviet missiles carried far more reentry vehicles than our own.

Early efforts were made to develop the MX around precisely these concerns. By November 1971, the Air Force's Strategic Air Command already had outlined some basic characteristics. First, the new missile needed to carry far more reentry vehicles than existing U.S. ICBMs. In turn, this required that it have a heavier payload and great accuracy, so that even strengthened Soviet missile silos could be attacked. Finally, the new ICBM was supposed to be housed in a way that would solve an increasingly urgent problem: the danger that existing U.S. missiles could be destroyed in their silos by Soviet ICBMs.

Basing the Missile

Since the mid-1950s, the Air Force has maintained that to discourage the Soviets from starting a nuclear war, U.S. strategic weapons must be able to survive a surprise attack well enough to inflict tremendous damage on the U.S.S.R. in return. Concern grew in the late 1960s that our ICBMs might lose this ability. As the Soviets improved their own ICBM force, the U.S. Department of Defense became worried that Russia would soon be capable of destroying our ICBMs in a "first strike." Nixon's Secretary of Defense Melvin Laird underscored these concerns in 1969 when he stated that the Soviets were "going for a first strike capability. There is no question about it."

However, for the Soviets to escape a crushing U.S. retaliatory attack, they would have to do more than destroy our ICBMs. They also would need to eliminate the other two forces in our strategic "triad": strategic bombers and the Navy's ballistic missile-carrying submarines. Although bombers cannot reach their targets as quickly as ICBMs, they provide insurance against a surprise attack, since a number of them are kept in the air at all times. Similarly, while submarine-launched missiles in the past have been less accurate than ICBMs, the submarines themselves would be very difficult for the Soviets to locate and destroy.

In spite of the insurance provided by this triad, concerns about ICBM vulnerability intensified. Department of Defense officials were troubled by what might occur if the Soviets were able to destroy our land-based missiles. One official described the following grim scenario:

> First, the Soviets would use a portion of their large ICBM force to destroy our own ICBMs. American cities would be left intact as hostages to Soviet SLBMs [submarine-launched ballistic missiles] and their remaining ICBMs. We would still have our own SLBMs and bombers for retaliation. However, assuming that our bombers would then be destroyed on the ground, or shot down by Soviet air defenses, and that our SLBMs would be too inaccurate to attack anything but Soviet cities, the president would face a terrible dilemma: either destroy those cities, which would provoke the U.S.S.R. into annihilating our own, or capitulate to whatever demands the Kremlin made.

Many Air Force officers had serious doubts about the accuracy of this "suicide or surrender" scenario. To destroy our ICBMs in their silos, the Soviets would need not only great missile accuracy but tight attack coordination to prevent some of our ICBMs from escaping. Many thought the U.S.S.R. incapable of meeting these requirements in the foreseeable future. As late as 1977, for example, General David Jones promised that the Soviets would be unable to destroy our silo-based missiles "for a long time" to come.

Even if the Soviets decided to risk such a strike, "it makes no sense for them to attack only one leg of the triad," General Slay pointed out. If our SLBMs were left intact, we still would be able to impose tremendous destruction on the U.S.S.R. The Kremlin would be taking an enormous gamble if it assumed the president would not order such a massive retaliation response—particularly since many U.S. civilians already would have been killed in the attack on our ICBMs.

Nevertheless, the last thing the Air Force wanted to emphasize was that the Navy's SLBMs could take up the slack if ICBMs became vulnerable. The Navy was pursuing a number of improvements in its SLBM force, including greater missile accuracy and more reliable submarine communication links. In contrast to ICBMs, the ability of SLBM forces to survive attack was widely regarded as superb. Since Congress ultimately decides which weapons to support with development funds, the Air Force was worried that the MX might be dropped in favor of a heavier investment in SLBMs. Such a move would have shattered the Air Force budget and morale.

Many officers had built their careers around ICBMs, and there was a strong belief within the service that these missiles offered indispensable military capabilities. Although progress was being made in SLBM accuracy and submarine communications, Air Force personnel were convinced that ICBMs would never be matched in terms of their ability to carry out stringently controlled, precisely targeted attacks. These officers were equally convinced that the president would need the option of carrying out such strikes during a nuclear war.

However, if our ICBMs did become vulnerable to attack, they would escape destruction only if they were launched as soon as Soviet missiles were detected in flight. Although Air Force officials were not worried that this situation would arise in the near future, they recognized that Soviet missile accuracy was improving steadily. Even though problems of coordinating an actual anti-ICBM attack would persist for the Russians, the service wanted to make sure that future ICBMs would be able to survive Soviet missiles for use in subsequent, carefully controlled retaliatory strikes. Without that assurance, there was a real danger that Congress might conclude that new ICBMs were too vulnerable to support.

Strengthening the silos in which ICBMs were protected would not provide a long-term solution to missile vulnerability. By 1970, the Air Force already had abandoned the development of "superhard" silos, since it became evident that missiles with sufficient accuracy could destroy even the strongest missile shelter. Fears spread within the service that silo-based ICBMs "were likely to go the way of cavalry," as writer John Newhouse put it.

The alternative was to base ICBMs in a mobile system to thwart Soviet efforts to locate and attack them. This might be done on the ground, by carrying ICBMs on trucks or other vehicles. It also might be done by carrying them on aircraft, which would either launch the missiles in flight or land them at a variety of launching sites. In any case, the Air Force decided in 1971 that the next ICBM—Missile X—

should be adapted for basing in some type of mobile system. Work soon proceeded on both land and aircraft mobility schemes.

By 1974 (the year the Air Force officially notified the secretary of defense it wanted a new ICBM), the service already had gone far toward developing a missile that met its own perception of what was militarily necessary. The MX's mobile basing also promised to help meet the political demands of selling the weapon to Congress. However, while the Air Force expected its friends on Capitol Hill to be supportive, it also knew that the MX would face an uphill battle unless championed by the president and his secretary of defense.

THE FORD ADMINISTRATION APPROVES

Every year the president recommends to Congress the weapons he believes should receive funding. Although many presidential appointees help shape these recommendations, usually the most influential is the secretary of defense. He manages the Defense Department and serves as the president's chief spokesman before Congress on military affairs.

An Ally in the E-Ring

The secretary of defense, whose huge office is in the outermost ring of the Pentagon building, is not just an errand boy for the armed services. His position as a presidential appointee gives him a unique perspective on weapons development issues. Within the budgetary constraints set by the president and his staff, and within the military requirements he helps formulate within the administration, the secretary must decide which weapons are genuinely necessary. In doing so, he must try to integrate his development decisions with the arms control objectives he participates in shaping. Finally, he must remain mindful of the political implications these policy choices may have for the president, both at home and abroad.

Military Requirements. By the time the MX came up for review in 1974, the Defense Department's sense of urgency about ICBM vulnerability had diminished. Professorial, pipe-smoking James Schlesinger, the secretary of defense, agreed with his analysts that Soviet missile accuracy was not improving at a rate that posed immediate problems. As a result, Schlesinger suggested that the MX might initially be placed in silos. But because he also believed that the Soviets eventually would become capable of destroying a silo-based force, he supported the development of a mobile basing system as well.

As the Secretary saw it, the U.S. had a far more immediate need for the MX's ability to carry out limited, precisely targeted attacks against Soviet military targets. If the Soviets attempted a preemptive attack against us, Schlesinger felt it would be "suicidal" to respond by destroying Soviet cities. Instead, we needed "forces to execute a wide range of options in response to potential actions by the enemy, including a capability for precise attacks on both hard [that is, protected] and soft targets, while at the same time minimizing unintended collateral damage."

The MX was perfectly suited for meeting this requirement. For that reason, Schlesinger's successor, Donald Rumsfeld, also supported the MX during the remainder of the Ford administration. Acknowledging that existing U.S. ICBMs were accurate enough to destroy many protected military targets, Rumsfeld noted in 1976 that those silo-based ICBMs eventually would become vulnerable to attack. Since the MX would be a "highly accurate . . . ICBM in a survivable basing mode," he argued that the missile was needed to enable America to retaliate against Soviet forces.

Schlesinger and Rumsfeld also believed that the MX was required for the U.S. to maintain "essential equivalence" with the U.S.S.R. If we fell behind the Soviet Union in an important component of strategic power, such as in the total number of ICBM warheads each side possessed, Schlesinger feared that the Soviets might try to use that advantage to intimidate—or even blackmail—the U.S. and its allies. Claiming in 1974 that U.S. force developments had to ensure that "no apparently favorable asymmetries could . . . be exploited for political advantage," Schlesinger urged that the MX be developed to match Soviet ICBM improvements. Similarly, Rumsfeld noted that these Soviet improvements might lead to a "dangerous asymmetry" if the United States did not keep pace.

(**Arms Control.**) Schlesinger and Rumsfeld also had to decide whether the MX was compatible with the arms control objectives they wanted the U.S. to pursue. Although other officials contribute to the formation of an administration's arms control policies, including the secretary of state and members of the Arms Control and Disarmament Agency, the secretary of defense generally has a special voice—particularly because his opinion that an arms agreement bolsters our security is important for winning its ratification by the Senate.

While the MX was still largely hidden within the bowels of the Air Force, the Nixon administration tried to ban land-mobile ICBMs under the 1972 Strategic Arms Limitation Treaty (SALT) I Agreement. U.S. negotiators feared that if Soviet missiles were not restricted to fixed silos, our spy satellites would have difficulty verifying their number. The Soviets refused to accept the proposed ban, perhaps because they were much further along than the U.S. in developing a land-mobile ICBM (the SS-X-16). Nevertheless, the U.S. declared in a Unilateral Statement to the SALT I pact that it would consider the deployment of such missiles "inconsistent with the objectives of the agreement."

When Schlesinger later began reviewing the MX, this preexisting arms control objective did not prevent him from supporting development work on mobile basing. He shared the Air Force's desire to have in place a capacity to build a mobile-based ICBM system rapidly, should that system suddenly be needed. More importantly, to the extent that Schlesinger viewed mobile Soviet ICBMs as a potential threat to arms control, he believed that the MX should be developed as rapidly as possible. Only if we had a mobile missile to bargain away would the Soviets be willing to give up on their own. Air Force General William Evans admitted that one reason the Department of Defense supported ICBM mobility work was to get "a bargaining chip for SALT II," which could be cashed in for a total ban on land-mobile missiles. Moreover, according to this bargaining-chip logic, the closer a weapon is to being produced, the greater the concessions that can be won by trading it away. This encouraged the development of the MX to continue.

However, after Rumsfeld became secretary of defense, he soon concluded that the MX mobility was too important militarily to give up. Soviet ICBM improvements were bringing the day close when U.S. silo-based missiles would be vulnerable. Therefore, Rumsfeld urged the Ford administration to change America's SALT II negotiating stand to accommodate the MX, rather than the other way around.

As long as the mobile MX and other new strategic weapons could be built, however, Rumsfeld was willing to tolerate pressure by other members of the administration (including Secretary of State Henry Kissinger) for SALT II limits on the number of U.S. and Soviet ICBM launchers. Numerical limits would not prevent the U.S. from replacing earlier ICBMs with the MX, which carried far more numerous and more accurate warheads. In fact, among some Air Force and Defense Department officials the MX was seen as a useful means of compensating for the restrictions SALT II might impose.

Persuading the President

Executive officials other than the secretary of defense can play an important role in weapons decisions, including members of the National Security Council, the White House Science Advisory Board, and the president's personal staff. Moreover, representatives of these offices are likely to have differing perspectives on what is militarily, fiscally, or politically the wisest development policy. But the president has a great deal of discretion in deciding whose recommendations to follow. In the Ford administration, the secretary of defense had a crucial role in shaping development policy, and Rumsfeld's contention that the MX was militarily essential met little opposition.

Altering the administration's SALT negotiating objectives to accommodate MX mobility received similar support. For a short time,

Secretary of State Henry Kissinger attempted to block the development of the MX as a mobile system because he feared the missile would complicate efforts at reaching a SALT II agreement. However, by 1975, the Ford administration no longer sought a complete ban on mobile basing. Instead, Russia was informed that mobile ICBMs would be acceptable to America if they were deployed on trucks, railroads or other systems visible to U.S. spy satellites. The Air Force already was examining these systems as possible mobile bases for the MX.

Finally, neither domestic political concerns nor fiscal constraints jeopardized the building of the weapon. According to Ford's presidential reelection campaign strategies, a "big boost" in spending on weapons would help hold off Ronald Reagan's challenge for the Republican nomination. President Ford recommended in 1976 that the MX be put into engineering development, the last stage before full production of the missile could begin.

The progress of the MX through the Pentagon and the White House to this point may be summarized as follows: The different positions from which the Ford administration and Air Force viewed the MX did not prevent them from agreeing that the missile was necessary; although the Air Force already had shaped the basic characteristics of Missile X by the time Ford was inaugurated, his defense secretaries soon decided that the weapon met their own conceptions of what was militarily essential. Furthermore, while the MX's mobile basing originally conflicted with the U.S. arms control objective of banning mobile ICBMs, that conflict rapidly disappeared—first by developing the MX as a bargaining chip, and then by reversing our SALT negotiating stance when the chip became too valuable to cash in. No countervailing pressures existed within the Ford administration to undermine this support for the weapon.

CARTER TAKES ANOTHER LOOK

When Jimmy Carter assumed office in early 1977, he felt in no way bound to continue Ford's support of the MX. In fact, he and many of his appointees initially were skeptical of the need for the MX, and feared that it would undermine their critical arms control objectives.

Renewing the Defense Department's Support

Carter's cerebral secretary of defense, Harold Brown, came to his new job with a strong background of weapons development experience. As the director of Defense Research and Engineering in the mid-1960s, Brown had overseen a number of strategic development programs, including work on improvements in missile accuracy. He had also served as the secretary of the Air Force—the top civilian job in the service. However, far from wedding him to the Air Force's particular point of view, Brown's background gave him the confidence he needed in his new role to reexamine whether the MX was necessary militarily.

Do We Really Need It? Brown began his tenure by questioning whether it was in the interest of the U.S. to develop a new missile which might make the Soviets fear that their ICBM force could be destroyed in a surprise attack. As soon as the Russians decided (rightly or wrongly) such a surprise attack was imminent, they might choose to "beat us to the punch" by quickly launching a preemptive strike of their own. In that sense, Brown pointed out, the MX could give the Soviets an "advantage in firing first." Since a catastrophic mistake might be made by the U.S.S.R. in predicting whether the U.S. was about to attack, one of Brown's spokesmen emphasized that "a Soviet force that was vulnerable to American attack ... would be dangerous."

In a seeming paradox, the exact reverse situation—the vulnerability of American missiles to a Soviet surprise attack—also was seen as tempting the Soviets to attack first. Since Brown believed that Russia's military strength did pose such a threat to our own missiles, he concluded it would be no less dangerous for the Soviets to possess such a capability alone. This reasoning led him to call for the adoption of a "countervailing strategy," under which the U.S. would be able to respond in kind to any type of attack (including anti-ICBM strikes) so that the enemy "would have no illusion of making any gain without offsetting losses." The MX, Brown concluded, would contribute significantly to meeting this strategic objective.

From yet another perspective, Brown gradually came to the decision that the MX was needed to maintain "essential equivalency" with Soviet forces. Initially, Brown felt that "none of the land-based missile options" looked as promising as cruise missiles "as a way of retaining our retaliatory capability at parity with the Soviets through the 1980s." Continuing improvements in the submarine-launched ballistic missile force also led him to view the MX as less than essential. However, as Brown listened to the Air Force, he became persuaded that dangerous international political repercussions might ensue if the U.S. did not match Soviet ICBM improvements with our own:

> ... [A] decision not to modernize the ICBM force would be perceived by the Soviets, and perhaps by others, as demonstrating U.S. willingness to accept inferiority, or at least as evidence that we were not competitive in a major (indeed, what the Soviets have chosen as *the* major) area of strategic power.

Beyond this political rationale, Brown also became convinced that it was militarily prudent to maintain the ICBM leg of our strategic "triad," along with the bomber and SLBM legs. He argued:

the idea behind the triad is that if one leg gets weak, you concentrate on building it up while the other two are strong. But if you let one leg go to hell, you are telling the Soviets fine, you can now concentrate on the other two legs.

Arms Control Revisited. Brown's initial attempts at integrating his arms control objectives with the MX's development were bound up in President Carter's desire to ban mobile ICBMs. In his first press conference as president, Carter suggested that the mobile MX would make an excellent bargaining chip:

> if the Soviets would agree, for instance, to a cessation of the use or deployment of the mobile type missile . . . that would be very important for us to join them in a mutual agreement . . . but if the Soviets should move toward the development of an intercontinental-type missile that can be moved from one place to another undetected and its location cannot be pinpointed, then that would put a great pressure on us to develop a mobile missile of our own.

Shortly thereafter, the Soviets did propose a ban on deploying solid-fuel ICBMs in a mobile mode. Evidently, they had come to the conclusion that sacrificing the SS-X-16 was not too high a price to pay for blocking the mobile MX. However, the Soviets also rejected a U.S. call for "deep cuts" in the ICBM forces of both countries. Secretary Brown decided that without such mutual reductions our existing ICBM force would become dangerously vulnerable to attack, and that the MX would have to be built as a mobile missile to remedy this situation. Subsequently Brown not only discouraged the Carter administration from making any further mention of using MX mobility as a bargaining chip, but suggested that the U.S. would refuse to sign any agreement that did not allow the MX to be based in a mobile mode.

Paradoxically, Brown raised the possibility that the MX missile itself (and not mobile basing) might be useful as a bargaining chip after SALT II was ratified. Looking ahead to the possibility of SALT III negotiations for further nuclear weapons restrictions, Brown argued that improving the U.S. strategic arsenal would "provide the Soviets with an incentive for mutual reductions through negotiations in which we, too, will have to forego something." But Brown did not suggest that the U.S. stop developing the MX to encourage similar restraint by the U.S.S.R. This would have run counter to the traditional logic of bargaining chips, which assumes that the closer a weapon is to being produced, the greater the concessions that can be won by trading it away.

At bottom, Brown was deeply skeptical about the possibility of ever limiting the gradual technical improvement of weapons such as the MX. To enforce a mutual ban on improvements in missile guidance and in other areas, close scrutiny would have to be maintained over the day-to-day work of Soviet laboratory engineers. The difficulty of doing so would be prohibitive. Furthermore, even if the U.S. simply tried to limit its own progress in ICBM guidance, Brown argued that "It is naive to think it can be controlled—you are only talking about software and small component parts."

Brown's skepticism about limiting the performance of future ICBMs did not stop him from working to limit their total numbers. He actively supported the Carter administration's pursuit of numerical force restrictions in negotiations for SALT II. However, Brown argued that the MX would have to be built if our security was to be preserved under the proposed agreement: "We must start to modernize our strategic forces with specific goals in increasing our survivable strategic payload, while limiting the Soviet planner's ability to target our systems."

Political Considerations. It was Secretary Brown's job to get the rest of the military "on board" in support of the President's proposals. The Joint Chiefs of Staff (JCS), which is composed of the leaders of each armed service and a chairman selected from one of them, can have considerable influence on Capitol Hill. Many senators and representatives place enormous credence in the testimony given by service and JCS officers on the president's defense policies. These officers are widely seen as military "professionals," in contrast to the political appointees of the administration (including the secretary of defense). As such, they are often urged by members of Congress to give their honest, independent opinions on administration proposals. It falls to the secretary of defense to make sure that their testimony does not undermine what the president proposes for adoption by the Congress.

Early in the Carter administration, Harold Brown got a stark lesson in the power of the services on Capitol Hill. He and the President decided that the B-1 bomber, which the Air Force enthusiastically wanted as a replacement for existing aircraft, was too costly and uncertain in military effectiveness to build. Brown therefore requested that Congress halt funding for the bomber. However, the Air Force then waged a none-too-subtle campaign on Capitol Hill to reverse the administration's decision. Even with all-out administration opposition, the B-1 came within a very few votes of being funded.

Brown's reluctance to face a similar battle over the MX helped reinforce his conclusion that the missile should be built. Moreover, to antagonize the Air Force and JCS by opposing the MX would threaten the support he needed from them to gain Senate ratification of SALT II. This was no idle fear since the chairman of the Joint Chiefs of Staff had pointedly announced that he would have "deep reservations" about supporting the SALT agreement unless the MX was built. Without unified service backing, Senate confirmation of SALT was unlikely.

Larger political considerations on arms control thus further reinforced Brown's decision to support the missile.

A Turnaround by the President

No member of the Carter administration had greater influence over the President's defense decisions than Harold Brown. But Carter had his own sense of which military and arms control requirements should be pursued, and—in contrast to Gerald Ford—he looked far beyond the Pentagon for advice on the MX. Many of these advisers shared Carter's early doubts about the missile.

Military Requirements. Soon after entering office, Carter appointed a special White House Task Group of independent scientists and defense analysts, which he instructed to examine whether the MX should be developed. These analysts concluded that the Soviets would have difficulty attacking our ICBMs and therefore the MX was not essential. Secretary of State Cyrus Vance and other officials maintained that even if our ICBMs did become vulnerable, the Soviets would never risk attacking them as long as we could retaliate with bombers and SLBMs. Vice President Walter Mondale also argued that existing U.S. forces were adequate, and he shared the Arms Control and Disarmament Agency's concern that MX mobility would complicate the SALT negotiations.

However, other Carter officials eventually joined Harold Brown in arguing that the MX was militarily essential. National Security Advisor Zbigniew Brzezinski, concerned with the suicide-or-surrender scenario, argued that the U.S. would be in a politically dangerous position unless it could respond in kind to threats of anti-ICBM attacks. Brzezinski's case was bolstered by the emergence of new data on Soviet missile accuracy, which indicated that their ICBM guidance was improving at a faster rate than many analysts had predicted.

By mid-1979, Brown and Brzezinski had helped persuade Carter that the MX was necessary. The President agreed that an "acknowledged inferiority" in our ICBM force would be "destabilizing," and that when we "deploy new types of missiles to stay current and to keep our equivalency with the Soviets, that ... contributes to peace." In June 1979, Carter announced that the MX had his full support. However, this decision was prompted by far more than concern over our military requirements.

Arms Control: Bargaining at Home and Abroad. Winning a new SALT agreement was one of Jimmy Carter's paramount goals. He came into office with a vision of "abolishing" nuclear weapons, and put the reversal of the arms race at the top of his foreign policy agenda. However, he soon found that to achieve a new arms limitation treaty, a weapon would have to be built that threatened to undermine the very foundations of arms control.

The Joint Chiefs of Staff had made their support for the SALT II treaty contingent on Carter's approval of the MX, and the President became convinced that their support was essential for Senate ratification. As Paul Warnke, director of the Arms Control and Disarmament Agency, bluntly put it: "We had to have the Chiefs on board. Forget the other arguments. Politically, there was no choice." Even Carter staffers who doubted a military need for the MX urged that the missile be approved as a bargaining chip, not for use with the Soviets, but for winning Senate support for SALT. Carter aide Joel McCleary, when asked in June 1979 whether the President used the MX to win the backing of Senate conservatives for SALT II, answered, "Yes. You could say to a certain extent we are wasting billions of dollars to placate that particular group in Congress."

On the other hand, even if the MX succeeded as a domestic bargaining chip, the problem still remained of devising a missile basing system that could satisfy the requirements of both arms control and military security. The Air Force decided late in the Ford administration that the MX should be hidden in buried trenches, from which they could be moved about to prevent the Soviets from locating and attacking them. However, Harold Brown was informed by outside scientists that a single nuclear explosion might destroy such trenches by creating a shock wave that would travel down their entire length. Working feverishly to devise something better, the Air Force ultimately chose a "shell game" system, in which each missile would be shifted deceptively among a number of silos so the Soviets would never know where it was. Air Force General Lew Allen asserted that this "multiple aim point (MAP) ICBM system appears to be the best of the options for redressing the vulnerability concern."

But only days later, President Carter said MAP had "some very serious defects." The most important of the President's concerns was that MAP might be incompatible with the verification requirements of SALT. According to SALT I, which the U.S. and U.S.S.R. ratified in 1972, neither country could interfere with the ability of the other to monitor its compliance with the agreement through "national technical means," that is, satellites. If MAP prevented the Soviets from knowing in which silos the U.S. had hidden its MX missiles, they might claim that the U.S. was violating a similar noninterference clause slated for inclusion in SALT II. Indeed, the Soviets did object to MAP basing as "a deceptive mode inconsistent with SALT II."

The Air Force argued that MAP could be adapted to meet the requirements of verification. General Allen suggested that the lids might be drawn back on all silos in a given field while a Soviet satellite passed overhead, in order to prove to them that only a few of the silos actually contained missiles. However, some Pentagon analysts had been arguing that to prevent the Soviets from discovering the location of U.S. missiles on their own, all silos would have to be filled with decoys which the Soviets could not distinguish from actual missiles. The presence of such decoys would undercut, in effect, SALT verification requirements.

Moreover, if the Soviets chose to match the U.S. deployment of a MAP system with one of their own, Soviet compliance with an arms agreement would then become difficult to verify. Fear of possible Soviet cheating might jeopardize any chance of congressional approval of future SALT agreements. Given Carter's commitment to making progress in strategic arms control, MAP was rejected.

Another alternative was then proposed: The MX would be carried around on aircraft, which would either fire the missiles in flight or land at one of a large number of airstrips for launching on the ground. Either approach was well suited for arms control verification, since the aircraft could be made easily recognizable and therefore possible for satellites to count. However, the Air Force thought the aircraft would be tremendously expensive to build and operate, and it also feared that missiles launched in flight would not be sufficiently accurate.

After considering yet another version of the buried trench system (one which would have had removable roofs to aid in SALT verification), the Carter administration settled on the "racetrack" system. This option envisioned an oval roadway with spurs leading off to a number of horizontal shelters where missiles would be hidden. A mammoth vehicle would move these missiles at random between the shelters in such a way that the Soviets could not tell where the vehicle had actually dropped off a missile. For arms verification, each missile would be assembled in an open area, and transported to their individual roadways over railroad tracks that would then be destroyed.

Although this ludicrously complicated system was soon modified to array the MX shelters along a straight road, each missile was still supposed to be shifted among twenty-three "Multiple Protective Shelters." The MPS system would require 4,600 shelters for the 200 missiles to be built. Yet even then some defense analysts worried that the Soviets could build enough missiles, with multiple warheads, to be able to destroy all these shelters.

Here, SALT II came to the rescue. By placing a limit on the number of missiles the Soviets could deploy, and on the number of warheads each missile could carry, the proposed SALT II Agreement would have made it impossible for the Soviets to destroy the MPS system and still have a significant ICBM force left over. This brought the relationship of the MX and arms control to one of complete interdependence. The MX had to be approved if Congress was to ratify SALT II, and SALT II had to be ratified if the MX's basing system was to survive against Soviet threats.

In sum, the Carter administration's initial doubts about the MX became buried in a shower of SALT. Although Secretary of Defense Brown worried that the MX might back the Soviets into a dangerous corner, he concluded that Soviet ICBM improvements had to be matched, particularly since a failure to do so would undercut our military's support for SALT. The need to win SALT ratification led even the most reluctant administration officials to support the MX. However, to make the MX compatible with arms control verification requirements and still provide survivability against Soviet attack, increasingly bizarre basing proposals were considered. Carter was finally left with a system that needed SALT to ensure its effectiveness, just as SALT needed the MX to ensure its ratification. Whether Congress would fund such a system remained to be seen.

CONFLICTS ON CAPITOL HILL

Control of the nation's purse gives Congress potentially enormous power to decide how military requirements should be met. The requirement that a two-thirds majority of the Senate approve ratification of arms control agreements gives that body power over weapons limitations as well. However, in attempting to exercise these powers, Congress can be strongly influenced by presidential guidance and by local political demands and considerations.

The Larger Issues

Long before Congress became concerned with local implications of the MX, such as where the missile would be based, some influential senators and representatives led a battle to reshape the weapon to meet their own sense of what was militarily necessary. This battle revolved around both the missile and its basing system.

Mobile Basing. When the Air Force and secretary of defense first tried to convince Congress in 1974 that our silo-based ICBMs were becoming vulnerable, they met with some skepticism. A high-ranking staff member of the Senate Armed Services Committee noted that it was "rather difficult" to understand why this problem was appearing since Congress had just spent millions to strengthen ICBM sites. Nevertheless, Senator Thomas McIntyre, D-N.H., chair of the Armed Services Subcommittee on Research and Development, indicated that he and his colleagues were willing to support "even questionable" proposals for eliminating strategic force vulnerability.

Congress soon became far more convinced of the need for ICBM mobility than were the Air Force and Department of Defense. By 1975, the department reversed its position of the previous year, and concluded that silos would be able to survive Soviet attack for some time to come. Hence it joined with the Air Force in 1975 and 1976 in proposing to keep the MX in silos until the more expensive mobile basing system proved necessary. Congress balked at this turnaround. The House-Senate conference committee for the fiscal year 1977 budget made a substantial cut in the MX funding request and laid down the following instructions:

> The rationale behind the development of a new missile system (MX) is to provide a land-based survivable strategic force. The development of an alternate basing mode as opposed to a fixed or silo-based mode is the key element in insuring this survivable force. The conferees are in agreement that providing a survivable system should be the only purpose of this effort, that the design of this system should not be constrained for silo basing; that none of this program's funds shall be expended in fixed or silo basing for MX; and that none of the program reduction shall reduce the department's proposed investigations of mobile deployment.

The Department of Defense capitulated to these congressional directives. The next year, Secretary Rumsfeld declared himself in agreement with the objections that had been raised against even temporary silo basing, and the Air Force began concentrating on developing the buried trench system for the MX. Similarly, Secretary Brown's flirtation with silo basing in the first year of the Carter administration was abandoned in the face of congressional pressure.

Although Congress clearly succeeded in shaping the MX's basing to meet its own conception of what was strategically necessary, its success hinged in part on the absence of opposition from the Air Force and the secretary of defense. In that sense Congress only accelerated the adoption of what the Defense Department thought would become essential anyway. However, when Senator McIntyre and some of his colleagues attacked the rationale for the design of the missile itself, the opposition of the department became much more powerful—and wily.

Missile Design. The Air Force had developed the MX in order to increase our nation's ability to attack the Soviet ICBM silos and other protected military targets. Not everyone agreed, however, that this was a wise thing to do. Harold Brown, you will recall, initially doubted whether such an increase was prudent. Some members of Congress similarly believed that we would endanger ourselves to threaten Soviet missiles with destruction. The risk that the Soviets would put their ICBMs on a "hair trigger" alert because of the MX led McIntyre to call the missile's design "a disastrous mistake that could trigger nuclear war."

The suicide-or-surrender scenario had led some Carter officials reluctantly to accept the need for matching Soviet ICBM-killing capabilities, but others were not persuaded by that reasoning. Representative Thomas J. Downey, D-N.Y., noted that if the U.S. attacked the Soviet ICBMs that were held in reserve after a Soviet surprise attack, the Soviets would almost certainly fire those ICBMs after the U.S. missiles were detected in flight. The U.S. missiles would find nothing, then, but "empty holes." Even Air Force General Slay admitted that "if you attack [the Soviets' residual ICBMs], that will force him to shoot at your countervalue"—that is, at U.S. population and industry.

Not all members of Congress, of course, doubted the wisdom of building an ICBM that would threaten Soviet missiles. Nevertheless, the Air Force and Department of Defense were well aware that Congress had voted down funding requests in 1971 and 1972 for work on ICBM accuracy improvements. The possibility that Congress might reject the MX missile was highlighted when Senator Mark O. Hatfield, R-Ore., and others argued for developing a mobile version of an existing U.S. ICBM, the Minuteman. Paul Nitze, a highly respected former Pentagon official, originally suggested basing Minuteman missiles in a "shell game" system until the MX could be completed. However, Hatfield wanted to build such a system as a replacement for the MX, since Minuteman missiles were less accurate and therefore "far less strategically destabilizing."

Tactics Against Congress. The Department of Defense took a number of steps to secure congressional approval of the MX in the face of this opposition. At first, it tried to mollify congressional concerns that American missile developments might be seen as threatening Soviet ICBMs. A Department of Defense spokesman promised in 1971 that

> It is the position of the United States *not* to develop a weapons system whose deployment could reasonably be construed by the Soviets as having a first-strike capability. Such a deployment might provide an incentive for the Soviets to strike first.

Later, as the Air Force's Advanced Technology Program provided an increasingly firm foundation for the MX, Air Force and Defense Department spokesmen told Congress that no request was yet being made to develop such a missile. General William Evans told the Senate in 1973 that the program was merely designed "to put us in a position that if, in time downstream, it is necessary to start development on an MX, we will be in a better position to do so."

McIntyre and other senators later decried this incrementalism as a "back door" attempt to gain funding for counterforce improvements without proper congressional scrutiny. Incrementalism, however, is a time-honored way of doing business on Capitol Hill. By making decisions in a slow, orderly, and manageable fashion, Congress can deal more efficiently with complex problems such as the development of the MX. Equally important, by postponing as long as possible the need for giving final approval to a weapon, members of Congress can avoid sticking their necks out unnecessarily on issues as controversial as the MX's construction. Supporters of the MX, pointing to the Defense Department's repeated contention that they were not yet being asked to build the missile, reassuringly insisted that "the development of the MX is not a commitment to the deployment of the MX."

The Ford administration also promoted congressional incrementalism by selling the MX as a SALT bargaining chip. Air Force and Defense Department spokesmen argued that, far from seeking a commitment to complete the MX, they merely wanted to strengthen our negotiating hand by developing the missile. Echoing this rationale, the Senate Armed Services Committee noted in 1974 that it was "extremely sensitive to the importance of negotiating from a position of strength."

Another Air Force and Defense Department tactic was to prevent Congress from considering funds for mobile basing apart from support for the MX missile. By presenting Congress with a "package" development program that simultaneously provided survivability (which was popular on the Hill) and counterforce potential (which was less so), the Defense Department hoped to coalesce broad-based support for what was, in fact, a counterforce weapon. General Slay told the House Armed Services Committee that he would want the MX as a counterforce missile even if the Minuteman had remained invulnerable; however, if the need had not emerged for a mobile, survivable replacement for Minuteman, he admitted that he "probably would not be able to convince the committee or the Congress that they should be putting $35 billion into the [MX] program."

MX opponents in Congress attempted to split the structure of the program so that funding for counterforce-related work, such as guidance hardware development, could be voted on separately from funding intended to support mobile basing. Senator McIntyre, who favored the development of a mobile ICBM but opposed the design of the MX as a counterforce weapon, claimed that the Defense Department had "stubbornly resisted" such a program split for years. Under continuing congressional pressure, Secretary of Defense Brown finally agreed in 1979 to separate the funding of the missile and its basing mode.

By that time, however, the Air Force and Defense Department had succeeded in their determined effort to educate Congress about the MX's strategic justifications. The department discovered early on that it could win congressional support for strategic force improvements by lauding the benefits of the strategic triad, and pointing out that "a stool can't stand on only two legs." By 1978, John Ford, staff director for the

House Armed Services Committee, could state without fear of contradiction that "everyone treats the Triad like the Holy Trinity. Everybody says it is sacred, including the secretary of defense. . . ." The MX was inevitably justified on the grounds that it would help maintain this icon.

In addition, Defense Department witnesses at congressional hearings tried to familiarize senators and representatives with the intricacies of deterrence theory. Figure 7-1 presents two slides shown to the House Armed Services Committee by the Department of Defense in 1978. Through the use of such materials, and the frequent repetition of the suicide-or-surrender scenario, the witnesses soon had many influential members—including Robert W. Daniel, R-Va., and Samuel S. Stratton, D-N.Y.—arguing that the deployment of a counterforce-capable MX was essential to avert national disaster.

Many other members of Congress, however, required no intricate theoretical arguments to sway support for the MX. The fear that the U.S. was simply "falling behind" the Soviet Union in military strength was enough to persuade some that any Air Force weapons request should be supported. Uncritical enthusiasm for Air Force strategic programs was not lacking in the Senate either, thanks to such defense stalwarts as Barry Goldwater, R-Ariz., who argued that the MX had to be deployed to prevent emergence of a "vulnerability gap" between U.S. and Soviet ICBMs. (This predisposition to support whatever the Air Force wants reflects many legislators' belief that the professionals of the armed services are the best judges of U.S. weapon requirements. Lacking military expertise of their own, many members of Congress are prone to rely on the recommendations of the Pentagon.)

Thus, while some opposition arose to the MX on military grounds, many of representatives and senators were persuaded by the Defense Department's reasoning—or by the simple fact that the Air Force wanted a new missile—to support the MX. The much stronger opposition that emerged was based on a different, more traditional concern, namely, the impact the missile's construction would have on particular congressional constituencies.

The Local Issues

Ordinarily, representatives aggressively compete with each other to determine whose district gets a military base. These bases produce a significant number of jobs and generally enrich the local economy, which in turn can boost a member's reelection prospects. In sharp contrast to this standard behavior of legislators, local elected officials were reluctant from the start to allow the MX to be based in their areas.

Figure 7-1 Slides shown by the Department of Defense to the House Armed Services Committee in March 1978.

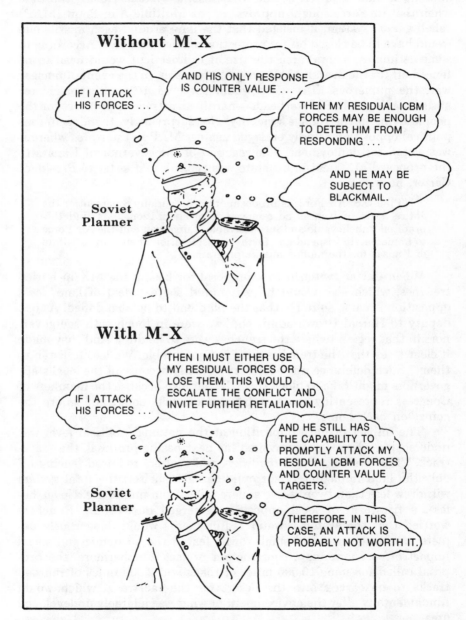

SOURCE: U.S. Congress, House, Armed Services Committee, Hearings on Military Posture and H.R. 10929, authorizing appropriations for fiscal year 1979; part 3, book 2, 95th Congress, 2d Session (Washington: USGPO, 1978) pp. 870-871.

Their reluctance stemmed in large part from the tremendous amount of land required by the MX's basing system. During the time when the Air Force sought approval of the Multiple Aim Point (MAP) "shell game" system, it insisted that the land around each missile silo would have to be closed off for protection against sabotage. According to some estimates, a total area the size of Connecticut would need to be fenced off for the overall MAP system. Moreover, in the event of nuclear war, the numerous MAP silos would serve as a "great sponge" for absorbing Soviet ICBM warheads—hardly an attractive prospect for the people living in the sponge's vicinity! Not surprisingly, then, vociferous political opposition rapidly emerged against MAP in the states where it was slated for deployment. The reaction of the governor of Kansas to the proposed MX field in his state was typical; in a letter to President Carter, he wrote:

> ... [T]he U.S. Air Force is proposing that potentially 8 percent of the entire State of Kansas be removed from civilization.... I find this proposal unbelievable and inconceivable. I urge you and the Air Force to immediately suspend any further consideration of sites in the State of Kansas for the mobile missile program....

When Carter switched to a proposal for basing the MX in buried trenches, which also would have required a great deal of land, local opposition became so fierce that the plan had to be abandoned. As one deputy to Harold Brown admitted, "we were in touch with the governors in that region [where the trenches were to be dug]. And they made it clear to us that the trenches were not acceptable. We had to listen to them." Such deference was necessary not only because of the local steps governors might take to block the MX, but also because the members of Congress representing those states and districts could not ignore the goings-on back home.

The impact of local opposition at the national political level was underscored when Carter unveiled his next basing proposal, the "racetrack." This system of oval roadways and shelters required fencing off only the land immediately surrounding each shelter; the total system withdrew less than twenty-five square miles from public use. Nevertheless, a firestorm of local opposition emerged once again. Ranchers worried that the system's water requirements would dangerously deplete area resources, and small towns feared the economic and social impact of so enormous a construction project. Furthermore, the proposal called for some 10,000 miles of roads and 2,000 miles of railroad tracks to be carved into the desert for the racetrack, which would fundamentally alter the environment of what was a largely undeveloped area.

Carter's subsequent elaborations on the shell-game theme proved no more popular. In the face of mounting public opposition, the governors of Utah and Nevada called on Congress to reject the MX's mobile basing system. Governor Scott M. Matheson, D-Utah, told House members that "Governor List [of Nevada] and I are here today to state that we do not accept the President's plan for the MX. I personally do not believe that the MX can or should be deployed as suggested."

National legislators from Nevada and Utah soon moved to change sites for the MX's basing system. Senator Howard Cannon of Nevada proposed that the Defense Department be prevented from placing more than half of the MX shelters in the Utah-Nevada region. Somewhat reluctantly, the Air Force responded by examining the possibility of basing some missiles in Texas and New Mexico. The reaction from those areas was predictable. "I endorse the MX program 100 percent," said Texas Governor Bill Clements. "But there are better locations than New Mexico and Texas." Similarly, New Mexico Governor Bruce King stated, "I just don't want to see [the shelters] put in New Mexico."

Integrating SALT with the MX

One Carter administration aide bragged that "we put on quite a dog and pony show" to win ratification of the SALT II treaty by the Senate. Members of the armed services, the Joint Chiefs of Staff, and the secretary of defense's office dutifully trooped around Capitol Hill, assuring skeptical senators that they honestly believed SALT II (along with the MX) would promote U.S. security. These officials also emphasized that SALT II was necessary to ensure the survivability of the MX's shell-game basing, since the treaty would limit the total number of warheads the Soviets deployed. This last point was not lost on Congress. As Democratic Representative Thomas Downey of New York told his Senate counterparts, "Listen carefully, all you Air Force hardware freaks out there: if you want the MX, you had better see that SALT is ratified."

Some members were uneasy about the joint packaging of the MX and SALT II. Senator Sam Nunn, D-Ga., complained that the U.S. seemed to agree on arms limits first, and then make strategic weapons decisions "almost as an afterthought." Carter had to reassure Congress that his MX basing proposal was "dictated largely by military considerations; other factors—such as verifiability—have influenced the design only in matters of detail." (This statement was less than candid in light of the convoluted attempts made by the Carter administration to find a verifiable basing mode.)

Other members were taken aback by Carter's use of the MX to win support for SALT. Senator John Tower, R-Texas, noting that Carter's MX approval appeared to have been timed to coincide with the signing of the SALT accord, accused Carter of engaging in "transparent salesmanship" to "buy" ratification of the treaty. Some liberal MX critics, such as Ted Kennedy, D-Mass., and George McGovern, D-S.D., warned that they might have to reexamine their support for SALT II if the treaty were tied to endorsement of the missile. On the other hand, most senators appeared to share the sentiments of John Culver, D-Iowa, who argued that Carter's MX decision "should strengthen support for SALT." Indeed, Robert Byrd, D-W.Va., the Senate majority leader whose support was vital for SALT's passage, maintained that if the "MX had been scrapped, I think the treaty would have been scrapped."

However, many senators did not judge the SALT agreement solely in terms of strategic weapons concerns. Some influential members felt that SALT should be linked to our global relationship with the U.S.S.R., and that if the Soviets behaved "recklessly" abroad, we should punish them by withholding our cooperation in arms control. Support for ratification of SALT II waned during the summer of 1979 when the existence of a Soviet troop brigade in Cuba received heavy publicity. The Russian invasion of Afghanistan in December of that year sealed the treaty's fate. President Carter, faced with insurmountable opposition to SALT II on Capitol Hill, requested on January 3, 1980, that the Senate postpone "indefinitely" further consideration of the agreement. The Senate agreed, and SALT II lost any chance for ratification.

Once the SALT agreement no longer seemed likely to pass, doubts about the survivability of the shell-game basing mode emerged. Without SALT II's limitations, the Soviets would be free to build enough warheads to attack every missile shelter in the MX system. The Air Force sought to provide reassurance by arguing that the U.S. could build new shelters faster and more cheaply than the Soviets could add warheads. But many members of Congress were unconvinced, and they hardly welcomed the prospect that the MX might require an ever expanding number of shelters and acres of land.

The role of Congress in the MX story may be summarized as follows. Acting on its own view of what was militarily required, Congress managed to quash the Defense Department's proposal for temporary silo basing of the MX. However, the opposition of some members to the design of the missile as a counterforce weapon was effectively dealt with by the Ford and Carter administrations. By selling the weapon as a set of incremental development proposals, a bargaining chip, and a package combining the basing system and the missile, both administrations were able to persuade Congress that the MX was necessary. The willingness of many legislators to defer to the judgments of the "professionals" of the military contributed to that persuasion process. However, once Congress became convinced that the mobile MX was necessary, concerns about the weapon's local impact aroused powerful opposition. This opposition was hardly reduced by the close relationship between shell-game basing and SALT II, particularly after SALT II fell by the wayside.

BACK TO THE BEGINNING:
THE REAGAN ADMINISTRATION'S FIRST YEAR

In the face of a strong electoral challenge by Ronald Reagan, who accused Carter of being "soft" on defense, President Carter continued to push for the MX even after SALT II collapsed. But opposition to the missile from areas where it might be based remained as firm as ever. Indeed, after Reagan took office, criticism of the MX soon emerged from new and unexpected quarters—including the politically conservative Mormon church. Reagan had no desire to antagonize the western states that made up his political base, and many of his closest Republican allies (including Senator Paul Laxalt of Nevada) were dead set against shell-game basing. Arms control considerations reinforced these pressures on Reagan to dump the system. He opposed the revival of Carter's SALT II agreement, and in its absence, nothing would prevent the Soviets from deploying enough ICBM warheads to overcome shell-game basing.

On October 2, 1981, Reagan and Secretary of Defense Caspar Weinberger announced that Carter's basing proposal was being abandoned. In its place, they proposed that the first group of completed MX missiles be housed temporarily in existing (but specially strengthened) ICBM silos, while the search continued for a permanent basing system. This neatly sidestepped the political dangers of pressing forward with some new shell-game alternative. Furthermore, while Reagan admitted that the strengthened silos would eventually become vulnerable, he argued that, without SALT, the shell-game system was also vulnerable. "No matter how many shelters we built," Reagan maintained, "the Soviets can build more missiles, more quickly and just as cheaply."

Secretary Weinberger tried to persuade a skeptical press and defense community that "these decisions, and I'm sure no one will believe this, were absolutely based on the best kinds of professional advice and examination of the objectives." Yet the Air Force was taken completely by surprise, which meant that the Reagan proposal to harden existing silos was created without support from the service that deployed the MX. That service remained convinced that some form of shell-game basing was essential. The Joint Chiefs of Staff were equally disappointed. Their chairman, Air Force General David Jones, noted that he still preferred a shell-game system, and that he "remained to be convinced that hardened silos would give survivability."

Some members of Congress argued even more forcefully against the Reagan proposal. Senator John Tower, chair of the Armed Services Committee, said that he was enormously skeptical to the point of feeling that "this plan . . . leaves us with a highly vulnerable land-based system." Tower was not alone. In late 1981, the Senate directed that all but $20 million of the $354 million in MX basing development funds be used to come up with a permanent, survivable basing system by July 1, 1983.

Yet it remained clear that no legislator was rushing forward with a plea that the MX be deployed in his or her state. The split between what Congress thinks is militarily necessary and what local political concerns will allow thus remains as wide as ever. Reagan may be able to bridge that gap with a basing proposal that requires little land. One proposal currently in favor is that of housing the MX in silos, and defending those silos against Soviet ICBMs with antiballistic missiles. However, building antiballistic missile systems would require the U.S. to abandon or to renegotiate our SALT I limitations on them. Since doing so would open a whole new range of military concerns, the integration of arms development decisions with arms control will become more important than ever before.

SOME QUESTIONS TO EXPLORE

The MX's history is one of pulling and hauling between different participants in governmental decisionmaking. The Air Force, the presidency, and Congress all have their own perspectives on weapons development issues, and each pursues a different set of interests. The Air Force seeks to continue providing an essential element of our nation's security. The presidency strives to balance its own conception of what is militarily necessary against other policy goals, including arms control, with an eye toward what is politically possible. So does Congress, which has the additional concern of balancing local interests against the demands of national security.

Even where the interests of these different governmental actors coincide, the tremendous ambiguity of arms development issues fosters conflict. It is fortunate that this study did not set out to determine whether the MX should be built. Does the suicide-or-surrender scenario justify building a major weapons system? How much environmental damage is acceptable for what level of potential ICBM survivability? Even on technical issues, which do not involve questions of deterrence technology or competing political goals, the best informed experts are often at odds. Who really knows whether temporary silo basing will be excessively vulnerable?

While differences of substance and perspective create divisions between elements of government, policymakers are also forced to join together in a bargaining process to reach their desired goals. The Air Force needed congressional approval for the MX; it already had learned with the B-1 bomber controversy that getting such approval would be extremely difficult without presidential support. The Carter administration likewise needed the support of both the armed services and Congress to reach its arms control and military goals. Finally, Congress depended on the presidency and the Air Force for much of its guidance and needed to bargain with them over the local impact the MX might have.

Some important questions remain about the consequences of this bargaining process for future arms development and arms control efforts. The need to win Pentagon support for arms control proposals will persist, as will the Pentagon's ability to trade that support for the weapons developments it desires. Therefore, the president may need to continue using potential weapons as internal bargaining chips if he hopes to achieve his arms control objectives. But arms control proposals are vulnerable to other pressures in the Senate (including Soviet "misbehavior"). When these pressures defeat an arms agreement, as they did in SALT II, we are still left with the weapons used to win support for arms control. The MX is still going strong, for example, even though SALT is now dead. Are internal bargaining chips so likely to produce one-sided results that presidents should abandon their use? If so, how else can the president persuade the Pentagon to support arms control agreements on Capitol Hill?

An attempt might be made to wean Congress away from reliance on the Pentagon's opinions in arms control and thereby eliminate the need for internal bargaining chips. However, the history of the MX has illustrated the scope and strength of the armed services' influence on Capitol Hill and the effectiveness with which that influence can be manipulated to win the services' goals. Will growth in members' expertise in military matters reduce this dependency? If so, will Congress be better able to judge arms control and development issues according to security considerations, or will greater congressional independence make it all the more vulnerable to local concerns?

The same questions might be asked of using weapons as "external" bargaining chips with the Soviet Union. Both the Ford and Carter administrations initially supported the MX as something to trade away, in hopes of winning a total ban on mobile ICBMs. Both continued to push for weapons development since the logic of bargaining chips holds that the closer a weapon is to completion, the more that can be won by giving it up. Yet both ended up concluding that MX mobility was too valuable to cash in. Is this result inevitable? Or, in the case of the Carter administration, did the inescapable need for an internal bargaining chip require the continued development of the MX as an external one?

Ultimately, the most important question is whether arms control and arms development can be integrated successfully so that both military requirements and SALT objectives can be met in a complementary manner. The MX might have achieved this goal. By limiting the total number of Soviet ICBM warheads, SALT would have helped the MX satisfy our requirement for survivability. And designing the MX to allow for SALT verification would have promoted our goal of limiting strategic force levels.

However, the MX missile encountered two stumbling blocks that may bode ill for future integration attempts. First, local political pressures arose against the type of basing systems needed to meet both military and arms control requirements. Such opposition was encouraged by the ridiculously complicated basing designs that appeared necessary. Future weapons systems may escape this fate, particularly if they are not based on U.S. territory. More difficult to escape will be the political vulnerability of SALT. As long as we link our willingness to pursue arms control with the foreign policies of the U.S.S.R., and the U.S.S.R. disputes or disregards this linkage, attempts at integrating arms developments with arms control will be hamstrung. Is it time to narrow the goals we expect arms control to serve? If so, are there alternatives to the use of internal and external bargaining chips in pursuing these goals?

SOURCES AND READINGS

This study was written on the basis of congressional hearing transcripts, newspaper and magazine articles, and interviews with government and Air Force officials. The most important Senate hearings for the MX have been held since 1974 by the Committee on Armed Services on the subject of authorizations for appropriations for the Department of Defense. Some Appropriations Committee hearings also dealt with the MX. Similarly, House Armed Services Committee hearings provide an excellent source of material on the MX, with some Appropriations hearings also of interest. These hearings are useful not only for the insights they provide into the thinking of the members of Congress (and, often as important, their staffs), but also for their role in providing a permanent record of witnesses' testimony. Representatives of the Air Force, the Defense Department, and other organizations often offer good expositions of their respective views, and they sometimes respond to congressional proddings for criticism of each other's stands.

The *Washington Post*, *New York Times*, and *Baltimore Sun* provide the best newspaper information on the MX. Among magazines, there are far more sources to pursue. *Aviation Week and Space Technology* can be counted on to describe in numbing detail the latest technical developments on the MX. For political issues and critiques of the missile, the *Bulletin of the Atomic Scientists, Scientific American, The New Republic, Science,* and a number of other magazines are helpful. *Newsday* published a series of articles on the Carter administration's MX decisionmaking that were of use in writing this study. Finally, *Congressional Quarterly* and other periodicals devoted to Capitol Hill are useful for following the political maneuvers surrounding the MX.

The only book published thus far on the MX is Herbert Scoville, Jr., *MX: Prescription for Disaster* (Cambridge, Mass.: MIT Press, 1981). It offers a strong case against the military rationale for the missile and suggests some alternative weapon designs.

Studies of other weapons may facilitate useful comparisons with the MX; a particularly informative one is Ted Greenwood, *Making the MIRV: A Study of Defense Decision Making* (Cambridge, Mass.: Ballinger Publishing Co., 1975). It offers a rich history of the factors that shaped this strategic development program. For a general analysis of nuclear issues, Michael Mandelbaum, *The Nuclear Question* (Cambridge, Mass.: Harvard University Press, 1980) is excellent. Herbert York's *Race to Oblivion: A Participant's View of the Arms Race* (New York: Simon & Schuster, 1970) gives a close look at the pressures within the government that drive weapons development and make it difficult to control.

The Contributors

BRUCE I. OPPENHEIMER is an associate professor of political science at the University of Houston. In 1974 and 1975, he served in Washington, D. C., as a Congressional Fellow of the American Political Science Association. His published studies have dealt with energy politics and policy and the reform of congressional procedures.

GERALD M. POMPER is a political science professor at Rutgers University and the Eagleton Institute of Politics. He has written widely about political parties, presidential nominations and elections, and public opinion. RODNEY FORTH was a research associate at the Eagleton Institute at Rutgers and is currently on the political science faculty at the University of Missouri-St. Louis. MAUREEN W. MOAKLEY is a political science instructor at Rutgers and a coeditor and contributor to a forthcoming book on American state politics.

ROBERT REINHOLD joined the *New York Times* in 1965 after receiving a master's degree in journalism at Columbia. His reporting assignments have included science, higher education, and urban affairs. In recent years, he has been in Washington covering national government, with special emphasis on the regulatory activity of federal agencies.

AUSTIN SARAT has taught at Johns Hopkins and Yale and is now an associate professor of political science at Amherst. He has a particular interest in constitutional law and has written about American court systems, the workings of the Department of Justice, and federal crime policy.

ALLAN P. SINDLER is a professor and dean at the Graduate School of Public Policy at the University of California, Berkeley, and has taught at Duke, Yale, and Cornell. His writings have treated national and state politics, political reforms, equal opportunity and affirmative action. He has also edited and contributed to three earlier volumes of case studies in American policy and politics.

STEVEN S. SMITH is an assistant professor of political science at George Washington University. During 1980 and 1981 he worked with the House Democratic Steering and Policy Committee as a Congressional Fellow of the American Political Science Association. In that capacity, he was a close observer of the events covered in his case study.

PAUL N. STOCKTON is completing his Ph.D. in government at Harvard; his dissertation analyzes the MX missile and the weapons development process. He is a graduate of Dartmouth College and has served as a consultant to the Department of Defense.

DATE DUE

12. 15. '83	
MAY 0 4 1993	

BRODART, INC.   Cat. No. 23-221